MW00651370

Prentice Hall *LITERATURE*

PENGUIN EDITION

Unit Three
Resources

Grade Ten

PEARSON

Upper Saddle River, New Jersey
Boston, Massachusetts
Chandler, Arizona
Glenview, Illinois

BQ Tunes Credits
Keith London, Defined Mind, Inc., Executive Producer
Mike Pandolfo, Wonderful, Producer
All songs mixed and mastered by Mike Pandolfo, Wonderful
Vlad Gutkovich, Wonderful, Assistant Engineer
Recorded November 2007 – February 2008 in SoHo, New York City, at
Wonderful, 594 Broadway

ISBN-13: 978-0-13-366460-7
ISBN-10:   0-13-366460-0

3 4 5 6 7 8 9 10 V011 13 12 11 10

CONTENTS
UNIT 3

For information about the Unit Resources, assessing fluency, and teaching with BQ Tunes, see the opening pages of your Unit 1 Resources.

"Everest" *from* Touch the Top of the World by Erik Weihenmayer

"The Spider and the Wasp" by Alexander Petrunkevitch

from Longitude by Dava Sobel

"A Toast to the Oldest Inhabitant—The Weather of New England"
by Mark Twain

"The Dog That Bit People" by James Thurber

"Keep Memory Alive" by Elie Wiesel

from Nobel Lecture by Alexander Solzhenitsyn

from **Desert Exile: The Uprooting of a Japanese-American Family**
by Yoshiko Uchida

from **The Way to Rainy Mountain** by N. Scott Momaday

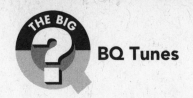 **BQ Tunes**

Palm of Our Hands, performed by Polina Goudieva

I'm waiting for the day I get out of this grind
A way to **adapt**, and to change, something to open my mind
Awareness of unfairness / I see
Makes me wanna cry sometimes

So many problems, we're facing it's crazy and nobody knows how to solve
I figure it's either I move to the moon or we all gotta learn to adapt and **evolve**
How we're spinning around (it's a mystery)
If we're **ignorant** of **history**

Looking for some peace and **understanding**
Asking all these **question**s without end
Looking for some love and **empathy**
Do you feel what I feel

Looking for some peace and **understanding**
Asking all these **questions** without end
Looking for the mind that knows it all
Enlightenment it's in the palm of my hands

I'm growing and not just in height
The truth about **growth** is it only comes from **insight**
Reflecting, thinking about what
Is wrong and what is right

The **influence** of science is in us—even the food's **modified**
Genetics and ethics are changing, we expect it all to be **revised**
How we're spinning around (it's a mystery)
If we're **ignorant** of **history**

Looking for some peace and **understanding**
Asking all these **question**s without end
Looking for some love and **empathy**
Do you feel what I feel

Continued

Looking for some peace and **understanding**

Asking all these **questions** without end

Looking for the mind that knows it all

Enlightenment it's in the palm of my hands

Palm of my hands, palm of my hands, palm of my hands,

It's in the palm of my hands, palm of my hands, palm of my hands,

palm of my hands

So many problems, we're facing it's crazy and nobody knows how to solve

I figure it's either I move to the moon or we all gotta learn to adapt and **evolve**

How we're spinning around (it's a mystery)

If we're **ignorant** of **history**

Song Title: **Palm of Our Hands**
Artist / Performed by Polina Goudieva
Lyrics by Polina Goudieva
Music composed and produced by Polina Goudieva and Dimitiri Ehrlich
Post production: Mike Pandolfo, Wonderful
Executive Producer: Keith London, Defined Mind

Unit 3: Types of Nonfiction
Big Question Vocabulary—1

The Big Question: What kind of knowledge changes our lives?

In your textbook, you learned words that are useful for talking about information and how it changes our understanding of ourselves and the world around us.

DIRECTIONS: *Review the following definitions of words you can use when talking about information and change.*

adapt: to adjust or modify to suit new conditions

awareness: the state of having knowledge of or alertness to a situation

empathy: the ability to imagine how another person feels or thinks

enlighten: to make someone aware or to impart knowledge to others

evolve: to grow, change, or develop in some way

On the lines provided, write an answer to each question. Refer to the meanings of the underlined vocabulary words in your responses.

1. How might a person <u>adapt</u> after moving to a new town and a new school?

   _____

   _____

2. How does the audience at a sporting event show its <u>awareness</u> of what is going on in the game?

   _____

   _____

3. What is an example from your life in which you or someone you know displayed <u>empathy</u> toward another person?

   _____

   _____

4. What is one method that a teacher might use to <u>enlighten</u> her students about a literary selection they are reading?

   _____

   _____

5. How might learning new information about an issue cause a person's opinion on that issue to <u>evolve</u>?

   _____

   _____

Name _____ Date _____

Unit 3: Types of Nonfiction
Big Question Vocabulary—2

The Big Question: What kind of knowledge changes our lives?

DIRECTIONS: *Review the following definitions of words you can use when talking about information and change.*

growth: a gradual development or increase

history: a record of past events

ignorance: the state of being uneducated or of lacking knowledge

influence: to change the actions, behavior, or opinions of others

insight: an understanding of the true nature or underlying truth of a thing

Create two different sentences for each of the following words. Try to use the word to explain something entirely different in your second sentence.

1. **growth**
   _____
   _____

2. **history**
   _____
   _____

3. **ignorance**
   _____
   _____

4. **influence**
   _____
   _____

5. **insight**
   _____
   _____

Name _____ Date _____

Unit 3: Types of Nonfiction
Big Question Vocabulary—3

The Big Question: What kind of knowledge changes our lives?

DIRECTIONS: *Review the following definitions of words you can use when talking about information and change.*

modified: changed somewhat or partially altered

question: *n.* a matter or problem of some uncertainty; *v.* to challenge or dispute a conclusion

reflect: to think deeply about something

revise: to modify or change something, especially to improve it

understanding: comprehension; knowing

On the lines below, write a paragraph about how learning new information about a situation has changed how you felt or behaved. Use at least three of the Big Question vocabulary words.

_____

_____

_____

_____

_____

_____

_____

_____

_____

_____

_____

_____

_____

_____

_____

_____

3

Name _____ Date _____

Unit 3: Types of Nonfiction
Applying the Big Question

The Big Question: What kind of knowledge changes our lives?

DIRECTIONS: *Complete the chart below to apply what you have learned about how knowledge can change your life One row has been completed for you.*

Example	Type of knowledge	What was learned?	Who acquired knowledge	Lives changed? Who?	What I learned
From Literature	Knowledge learned from experience in "Keep Memory Alive"	Silence about brutality to others harms everyone.	Elie Wiesel	Yes, Wiesel's life was changed, and his story changed others.	One person's knowledge can affect the world.
From Literature					
From Science					
From Social Studies					
From Real Life					

4

Unit 3: Types of Nonfiction Skills Concept Map—1
What kind of knowledge changes our lives?

Literary Analysis:
Nonfiction

Essays

can be

expository

or

reflective

(demonstrated in this selection)
Selection name:

(demonstrated in this selection)
Selection name:

Reading Skills and Strategies:
Main Ideas and Supporting Detail

You can analyze main ideas and supporting details

by

summarizing

and by

asking questions

(demonstrated in this selection)
Selection name:

Informational Text:
User's Guide

Looking at a technical document's structure and format will help you

follow and critique technical directions

Words you can use to discuss the Big Question

Basic Elements of Essays and Speeches
- Style
- Tone
- Perspective
- Purpose

Types of Essays
- Narrative
- Descriptive
- Expository
- Persuasive
- Reflective

Types of Speeches
- Address
- Talk
- Oration
- Lecture

Comparing Literary Works:
Humorous Writing

can be created by using

understatement

hyperbole

(demonstrated in these selections)
Selection names:
1.
2.

Student Log

Complete this chart to track your assignments.

Writing	Extend Your Learning	Writing Workshop	Other Assignments

Vocabulary Warm-up Word Lists

Study these words from "Everest." Then, complete the activities.

Word List A

accomplished [uh KAHM plisht] *v.* succeeded in doing; did
  I accomplished my goal of getting a straight-A report card.

barriers [BA ree erz] *n.* anything that keeps things apart
  The bull charged toward the barriers between the arena and the spectators.

confirmed [kuhn FERMD] *v.* proved to be true
  The evidence confirmed the detective's guess.

descent [di SENT] *n.* the way down; going down
  The roller coaster's rapid descent was thrilling.

despite [di SPYT] *prep.* in spite of; regardless of
  The track team kept on running despite the rain.

destiny [DES ti nee] *n.* fate; predetermined events
  Her mastery of the violin at an early age foretold her destiny as a musician.

horrendous [hawr EN duhs] *adj.* horrible; frightful
  A horrendous car wreck brought the movie to its grim conclusion.

spectacular [spek TAK yuh luhr] *adj.* very striking; unusually impressive
  The Grand Canyon is truly a place of spectacular natural beauty.

Word List B

benefiting [BEN uh fit ing] *v.* doing good for; aiding
  The funds raised at our car wash are benefiting a local hospital.

implemented [IM pluh men ted] *v.* put into use or effect
  Accidents were reduced as soon as the new speed limit was implemented.

inevitable [in EV i tuh buhl] *adj.* not avoidable; certain to happen
  She knew it was inevitable that she would outgrow her favorite shoes.

negative [NEG uh tiv] *adj.* having an unfavorable attitude; not positive
  The director was disappointed by the negative reviews of his new film.

periodic [peer ee AH dik] *adj.* appearing from time to time
  The comet made its periodic appearance in our skies last year.

sponsorship [SPAHN ser ship] *n.* official, often financial, support
  Our uniforms were purchased thanks to the sponsorship of Central Bank.

stereotypes [STER ee oh typs] *n.* fixed ideas about groups of people
  Forming opinions based on stereotypes ignores people's uniqueness.

unprecedented [un PRES i den tid] *adj.* unheard of; groundbreaking
  The auction brought in an unprecedented amount of money.

Name _____ Date _____

"Everest" *from* Touch the Top of the World by Erik Weihenmayer
Vocabulary Warm-up Exercises

Exercise A *Fill in each blank in the paragraph with an appropriate word from Word List A. Use each word only once.*

Delta Daniels felt that it was her [1] _____ to be the greatest actress on the planet. Her high opinion of her own talent was happily [2] _____ when she got the leading role in her school play. Unfortunately, instead of being the [3] _____ success she expected, her opening-night performance was a [4] _____ disaster. She not only forgot every line, but she also ignored the invisible [5] _____ between actor and audience by chatting with her friends in the front row. [6] _____ her awful mistakes, she thought that she was a great success. Of course, it was true that she [7] _____ a great deal that night. Unfortunately, she did not realize that she had only succeeded in speeding up her [8] _____ from merely bad to truly awful.

Exercise B *Write a sentence of your own for each word on Word List B.*

Example: negative
   I wish you would not be so negative about our chances of winning.

1. benefiting
   _____

   inevitable
   _____

3. sponsorship
   _____

4. stereotypes
   _____

5. periodic
   _____

6. unprecedented
   _____

7. implemented
   _____

8

Name _____   Date _____

Read the following passage. Pay special attention to the underlined words. Then, read it again, and complete the activities. Use a separate sheet of paper for your written answers.

Many people remember that Sir Edmund Hillary was the first man to reach the top of Mount Everest. Fewer remember that Tenzing Norgay was right there with him, sharing each step of the treacherous journey to reach the spectacular view from the top of the world.

Tenzing Norgay was born into the Sherpa culture high in the mountains of Nepal. Living at high altitudes has helped Sherpas develop powerful climbing abilities. For many Sherpas, climbing is a way to make a living. For Norgay, however, Mount Everest was one of the final barriers he was determined to overcome; climbing Everest was part of his destiny. "For in my heart," he explained, "I needed to go. . . . The pull of Everest was stronger for me than any force on Earth."

Norgay first tackled Everest at the age of 19, when he joined Eric Shipton's climbing team. This team did not reach its goal, but Norgay proved his dedication and strength. He became a trusted member of many other climbing teams. However, it was not until 1953 that he accomplished his ultimate goal when he and Sir Edmund Hillary reached the highest point on Earth.

Climbing Mount Everest requires great endurance and strength. As one climbs higher, the conditions become more horrendous. The icy winds shift unpredictably. The air becomes thinner, holding less and less essential oxygen. Hillary and Norgay reached the summit despite these terrible hardships. Any mountaineer knows that climbing up the mountain is only half the journey. The descent is an equally dangerous adventure.

After Hillary and Norgay completed their mission, they became world-famous. Their fame was confirmed once again when they were included on *Time* magazine's list of the "most important people of the century." The magazine praised both men not only for their climb, but for using their fame to improve life for the Sherpas.

1. Underline the words that tell what was spectacular. Then, describe something *spectacular* you have seen.

2. Circle the words that name one of the barriers Norgay hoped to overcome. Then, tell what *barriers* means in this passage.

3. Underline the words that explain why Norgay felt that climbing Everest was part of his destiny. Then, tell what *destiny* means.

4. Circle the words that name the goal that Norgay accomplished. Then, tell about something you *accomplished* last year.

5. Underline the sentences that describe the horrendous conditions. Then, describe a *horrendous* trip.

6. Circle the words that tell what the two men did despite the hardships. Tell something that you would like to do *despite* the fact that it is very difficult.

7. Circle the words that mean the opposite of descent. Then, tell what a *descent* is.

8. Underline the words that tell what event confirmed Hillary and Norgay's fame. Then, describe something that *confirmed* one of your opinions.

"Everest" *from* **Touch the Top of the World** by Erik Weihenmayer
Reading Warm-up B

Read the following passage. Pay special attention to the underlined words. Then, read it again, and complete the activities. Use a separate sheet of paper for your written answers.

The National Federation of the Blind was established in 1940 with two aims: to support blind people as they achieve self-confidence and to promote understanding of the blind. The federation's growth has been <u>unprecedented</u>. Today, it is the largest organization for the blind in the United States.

The National Federation of the Blind operates programs that are <u>benefiting</u> many of the 1.1 million blind people living in the United States today. It publishes magazines, an Internet site, and books. It also creates <u>periodic</u> bulletins and brochures whenever new research is available. The organization also helps people receive and use blindness aids, such as specially designed kitchen equipment, clocks, and rulers.

The federation also provides education about blindness. It hopes to replace <u>negative</u>, inaccurate ideas about the blind with positive, accurate information. Some sighted people think that blind people need constant assistance and cannot lead independent lives. The Federation of the Blind's outreach programs help to shatter these unfortunate <u>stereotypes</u>. As its mission statement explains, "The real problem of blindness is not the loss of eyesight, but the misunderstanding and lack of information which exist."

Recently, the federation opened the Jernigan Institute in Baltimore, Maryland. This facility is dedicated to research and development of technology for the blind. Researchers want to ensure that the latest findings are <u>implemented</u> in the development of new tools and practical strategies.

A century ago, blind people had few options. Their activities were limited. Today, these limits are no longer <u>inevitable</u> due to a wealth of information and technology. For example, in September 2004, a group of twelve blind high school students worked with NASA scientists to build and launch a rocket. The students used sound signals to monitor the rocket's ascent to 4,901 feet. Through the Foundation of the Blind's <u>sponsorship</u> of this program, these students achieved goals that might once have seemed impossible.

1. Underline the sentence that tells why the growth of the federation has been <u>unprecedented</u>. Then, tell what *unprecedented* means.

2. Underline the words that tell who the federation is <u>benefiting</u>. Then, tell about something that is *benefiting* your school.

3. Underline the words that explain when the <u>periodic</u> bulletins are published. Then, tell what *periodic* means.

4. Circle the antonym for <u>negative</u>. Then, describe how someone with a *negative* point of view sees things.

5. Underline the sentence that describes <u>stereotypes</u> of the blind. Then, tell what *stereotypes* are.

6. Circle the words that tell what researchers want <u>implemented</u>. Then, describe a rule or program that has been *implemented* in your school this year.

7. Tell something that you think is *inevitable* and will happen tomorrow.

8. Explain why a school science club might seek the *sponsorship* of a national business.

Erik Weihenmayer
Listening and Viewing

Segment 1: Meet Erik Weihenmayer
- According to Weihenmayer, why is writing more challenging than mountain climbing? Does his point of view surprise you? Why or why not?

_____

_____

_____

_____

Segment 2: The Essay
- According to Weihenmayer, why is honesty important in writing? Why is honesty important when you are conveying your ideas in an essay?

_____

_____

_____

_____

Segment 3: The Writing Process
- How does Weihenmayer prepare to write? How do you prepare to write?

_____

_____

_____

_____

_____

Segment 4: The Rewards of Writing
- Does Weihenmayer's attitude toward writing make you think differently about the importance of literature? Why or why not?

_____

_____

_____

_____

Learning About Nonfiction

Essays and speeches are short works of nonfiction. An **essay** is a written work in which the author examines a topic and often presents his or her views. A **speech** is delivered orally to an audience. Both essays and speeches include these elements:

- **Style:** the distinctive way in which an author uses language
- **Tone:** the author's attitude toward his or her subject and audience
- **Perspective:** the viewpoint or opinion that the author expresses
- **Purpose:** the author's reason for writing or speaking

This list presents different kinds of essays and speeches:

- **Narrative essay:** the presentation of real events or personal experiences
- **Descriptive essay:** an impression about a person, an object, or an experience
- **Expository essay:** the presentation of information or the explanation of a process
- **Persuasive essay:** an attempt to persuade readers to act or think in a certain way
- **Reflective essay:** a writer's thoughts about an experience or an idea
- **Address:** a formal, prepared speech that is usually delivered by an important person
- **Talk:** an informal speech that is delivered in a conversational tone
- **Oration:** an eloquent speech that is delivered on a formal occasion
- **Lecture:** a prepared speech with which the speaker instructs or informs his or her audience

A. DIRECTIONS: *Read the description of each work. Then, identify it. Choose from the terms in boldface type in the preceding list.*

1. a short, written work that tells readers why they should buy a small car
   _____

2. a short, written work that tells about the writer's encounter with a shark
   _____

3. a short, formal work delivered orally by the winner of the Nobel peace prize at the awards ceremony _____

4. a short, written work that tells what Costa Rica's rain forest looks like _____

5. a short, written work that tells how to make pizza _____

6. a short work about Renaissance art delivered orally by a professor to his or her students
   _____

B. DIRECTIONS: *The following paragraph opens a speech or an essay. Identify the kind of work it begins. Explain your answer.*

   Hi. I am glad you could come today. I just wanted to say a few words about the literary magazine and what we are trying to do. And I want to encourage you to speak out if you have ideas about how to make it better.

_____

_____

"Everest" *from* Touch the Top of the World by Erik Weihenmayer
Model Selection: Nonfiction

"Everest" is a **narrative essay,** an essay that tells about an experience that the writer, Erik Weihenmayer, has had. Like all essays, it expresses the writer's style, tone, and perspective. **Style** may be defined as the way in which the writer uses language. It involves level of formality; the use of figurative language, word choice, and sentence patterns; and methods of organization. **Tone** is the writer's attitude toward his or her subject and audience. **Perspective** is the writer's point of view or opinion.

A. DIRECTIONS: *On the chart, write details from "Everest" that reveal Weihenmayer's style, tone, and perspective.*

Style:
Tone:
Perspective:

B. DIRECTIONS: *Although "Everest" is a narrative essay, it includes elements of other types of essays. Briefly explain the ways in which "Everest" is characteristic of each of the following types of essay.*

1. **Expository:** _____

_____

2. **Reflective:** _____

_____

3. **Descriptive:** _____

_____

4. **Persuasive:** _____

_____

Name _____ Date _____

Short Answer *Write your responses to the questions in this section on the lines provided.*

1. If a writer wanted to convey what it was like to play piano publicly for the first time, which type of essay would be most suitable? Should she write a persuasive essay, an expository essay, or a narrative essay? Explain your answer briefly.

   _____

   _____

2. What is the main goal of someone who is giving a lecture?

   _____

   _____

3. Tone is the author's attitude toward both his subject and the audience. Use the diagram to provide four examples of tones that a writer of a speech or essay might use. Then, on the line below, identify which tone best suits an expository essay.

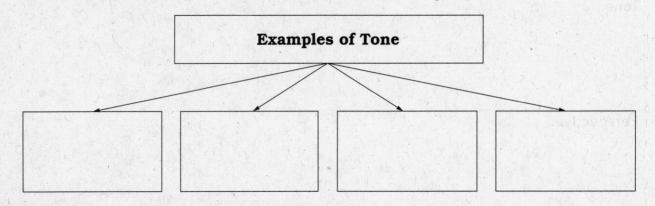

   _____

4. If an essay contained a lot of figurative language—metaphors, similes, hyperbole, and so on—what kind of essay would it most likely be? What would be the author's goal in writing the essay?

   _____

   _____

   _____

5. What type of essay is "Everest"? Explain your answer briefly.

   _____

   _____

   _____

6. In "Everest," what are the main obstacles that the climbers face in trying to make it to the top of Mt. Everest? Are the obstacles mostly internal, external, or both? Explain your answer.

_____

_____

_____

_____

7. Considering what happens earlier in the story, what is surprising about Jeff's appearance at the summit toward the end of "Everest"?

_____

_____

_____

8. Near the end of "Everest," Weihenmayer addresses some criticism that people aimed at him after his Everest climb. How does he view this criticism?

_____

_____

_____

9. What is the main emotion that emerges in the last paragraph of "Everest" as Weihenmayer reflects on his climb?

_____

_____

_____

10. Which activity would you more likely feel *apprehension* about—relaxing on a lounge chair on a beach or taking your first bungee jump? Explain your answer, based on the meaning of *apprehension* in "Everest."

_____

_____

_____

Essay

Write an extended response to the question of your choice or to the question or questions your teacher assigns you.

11. "Everest" is an essay with many elements—rich description, adventure, and strong emotions. Which part of "Everest" did you find to be the most interesting, moving, or exciting? Answer this question in an essay. Support your response with details and examples from "Everest."

12. In "Everest," Weihenmayer says that being blind makes his climb harder in some ways and easier in others. In an essay, explain the role that his blindness plays in the climb. Do you think being blind made his task easier or harder overall? Support your response with specific examples from the essay.

13. Every essay contains a tone, which is the author's attitude toward both the subject and the audience. How would you characterize Weihenmayer's tone in "Everest"? Choose a single word to define his tone. Then, in a brief essay, explain why you chose that word. Support your response with specific examples from "Everest."

14. **Thinking About the Big Question: What kind of knowledge changes our lives?** In an essay about "Everest," explain how the knowledge that the climbers gained about the weather affected their chances of making it to the top of the mountain. What techniques did they use to gain this knowledge? How did it change their attitude toward their task and their chances of achieving their goal? Support your response with examples from "Everest."

Oral Response

15. Go back to question 2, 6, or 7 or to the question your teacher assigns you. Take a few minutes to expand your answer and prepare an oral response. Find additional details in "Everest" that support your points. If necessary, make notes to guide your oral response.

Name _____ Date _____

"Everest" *from* Touch the Top of the World by Erik Weihenmayer
Selection Test A

Critical Thinking *Identify the letter of the choice that best answers the question.*

____ 1. Which item best describes essays and speeches?
A. nonfiction works spoken to an audience
B. short works of fiction set in the past
C. short works of nonfiction
D. works of nonfiction that try to persuade

____ 2. Which type of essay would most likely tell the story of a writer's personal experiences?
A. descriptive
B. expository
C. persuasive
D. narrative

____ 3. Which type of essay would most likely express a writer's thoughts about a frightening event?
A. reflective
B. persuasive
C. expository
D. descriptive

____ 4. What is the main purpose of a lecture?
A. to inform or instruct
B. to persuade
C. to amuse or entertain
D. to praise a person

____ 5. What kind of speech would be delivered in eloquent language on a formal occasion to honor a hero?
A. an address
B. a talk
C. an oration
D. a lecture

Critical Reading

____ 6. What kind of essay is "Everest"?
   A. persuasive
   B. narrative
   C. descriptive
   D. expository

____ 7. According to "Everest," in what way does Weihenmayer's blindness make the ascent of Mt. Everest easy for him?
   A. He cannot see how far up he is and get afraid.
   B. He does not have to worry about snow blindness.
   C. He does not have to worry about frostbite.
   D. He cannot see how far he is from getting help.

____ 8. In "Everest," why does PV turn back?
   A. He is suffering from the cold.
   B. He does not want his family to worry about him.
   C. He is afraid of climbing in the dark.
   D. He is exhausted and cannot catch his breath.

____ 9. According to "Everest," why does Weihenmayer want Jeff to continue to the summit?
   A. He knows that this is Jeff's last chance to reach the summit.
   B. He and Jeff have climbed together since he started climbing.
   C. He feels a strong attachment to Jeff because they are both blind.
   D. He has promised Jeff's family he would get him to the summit.

____ 10. According to "Everest," what factor makes the South Summit of Mt. Everest extremely dangerous?
   A. There are steep drops on either side.
   B. The wind is especially fierce.
   C. It is the coldest spot on the mountain.
   D. There are deep, hidden crevices.

____ 11. Which of these statements from "Everest" shows that Weihenmayer uses figurative language?
   A. "I'd scan my pole until it dropped into a boot mark, then cautiously lower my foot."
   B. "My heavy sluggish muscles felt as if they were pushing through wet cement."
   C. "A team could be turned back for so many reasons at any time."
   D. "One of the greatest joys of my summit was that Jeff hadn't turned back at all."

___ 12. According to "Everest," why does the team have to start back down the mountain right away?

    A. They are dangerously exhausted.

    B. They are low on fuel and water.

    C. The weather has begun to change.

    D. The ice shelf is beginning to melt.

___ 13. According to "Everest," what does Weihenmayer hope his success will accomplish?

    A. It will allow him to make enough money to support himself.

    B. It will help to destroy negative stereotypes about what is possible.

    C. It will help him raise money to help other blind people.

    D. It will encourage other blind people to climb Mt. Everest.

___ 14. According to "Everest," why does Weihenmayer climb mountains?

    A. because it brings him great joy

    B. to prove that blind people can do it

    C. because it allows him to earn a living

    D. to stay in good physical shape

___ 15. Which words best describe Erik Wiehenmayer, the author of "Everest"?

    A. humorous and easy-going   C. determined and self-assured

    B. timid and hesitant   D. forceful and dictatorial

Essay

16. What moment in "Everest" did you find the most moving or the most exciting? In an essay, tell why that moment affected you more than any other. Cite two details from the selection to support your opinion.

17. In "Everest," Erik Weihenmayer presents his own and some other people's perspective on his ascent of Mt. Everest. In an essay, describe those viewpoints. First, describe Weinhenmayer's perspective. That is, tell why he climbs mountains and what he hopes his achievements will accomplish. Then, tell what some of his critics have said about his achievements. Finally, tell whether any of those critics' opinions reveal a bias. Explain your answer.

18. **Thinking About the Big Question: What kind of knowledge changes our lives?** In "Everest," the climbers consult a weather report as they climb the mountain. In an essay, describe how the climbers' knowledge about the weather helped them make it to the top of Everest. As you write, think about the following questions: How did the weather report change the climbers' attitude toward their task? Support your response with details from the selection.

Name _____ Date _____

"Everest" *from* Touch the Top of the World by Erik Weihenmayer
Selection Test B

Critical Thinking *Identify the letter of the choice that best completes the statement or answers the question.*

____ 1. Which item describes an element of an author's style?
   A. his or her attitude toward the audience
   B. his or her use of figurative language
   C. his or her viewpoint
   D. his or her reason for writing

____ 2. Which statement reveals bias?
   A. Dogs need a place in which to run freely.
   B. People who complain about dogs hate animals.
   C. Many people complain about unleashed dogs in city parks.
   D. Dogs who are given regular exercise are usually in good physical condition.

____ 3. Which items are modes of composition that can be used for an essay?
   I.   expository
   II. narrative
   III. persuasive
   IV. science fiction
   A. I, II, III   B. I, II, IV   C. I, III, IV   D. II, III, IV

____ 4. Which items describe functions of reflective writing?
   I.   to convey thoughts
   II. to convey feelings
   III. to persuade others
   IV. to discuss an idea
   A. I, II, III   B. I, II, IV   C. I, III, IV   D. II, III, IV

____ 5. Which items characterize an address?
   I.   It is formal in tone.
   II. It is conversational in style.
   III. It is usually delivered by an important person.
   IV. It is composed off the cuff as it is being delivered.
   A. I and II   B. I and III   C. II and III   D. II and IV

____ 6. Which item best describes an oration?
   A. It is a speech given to instruct.
   B. It is a written work that explores ideas.
   C. It is a speech given on a formal occasion.
   D. It is a written work that conveys feelings.

Critical Reading

____ 7. According to "Everest," which items explain why blindness is an advantage for Weihenmayer while he is climbing?

    I.   He is not hampered by darkness.

    II. He is not susceptible to snow blindness.

    III. He is not bothered by the sound of the wind.

    IV. He does not worry about his goggles freezing.

    A. I, II, III   **B.** I, II, IV   **C.** I, III, IV   **D.** II, III, IV

____ 8. In "Everest," how does PV make it back to camp?

    A. He sees the lights from the tents.

    B. He stumbles onto the camp by accident.

    C. He is brought back by someone who goes to meet him.

    D. He shouts until someone hears him and guides him back by the sound of his voice.

____ 9. In "Everest," why do the climbers decide not to turn back?

    A. Reports from below indicate that the weather is improving.

    B. They know that the storm is weaker higher up the mountain.

    C. They are afraid they will never get another chance to summit.

    D. The author persuades the other members of the team to go on.

____ 10. According to "Everest," Jeff feels faint and dizzy because

    A. his oxygen regulator has malfunctioned.

    B. he has gone too long without eating.

    C. he is suffering from frostbite.

    D. he is sick from a virus.

____ 11. According to "Everest," why is it advantageous that the ridge of the South Summit is drier than it has been?

    A. The weather is likely to be warm and sunny.

    B. The ridge will be less snowy and less steep.

    C. The ridge will be less likely to collapse.

    D. The climbers will be able to think clearly.

____ 12. According to "Everest," with what sense does Weihenmayer appreciate the summit?

    A. sight

    B. smell

    C. hearing

    D. taste

____ 13. According to "Everest," what do people say about Weihenmayer's climb?

    A. He was able to achieve it only with the assistance of others.

    B. He should not have undertaken such a costly adventure.

    C. He should be considered a national hero.

    D. He should be ashamed of himself.

____ 14. According to "Everest," what negative consequence of Weihenmayer's achievement does one critic describe?
   A. Other climbers will boast about their accomplishments.
   B. Inexperienced climbers will be encouraged to climb Everest.
   C. Climbers will become depressed if they do not reach the summit of Everest.
   D. Climbers will think that they have reached the summit before they actually have.

____ 15. What attitude toward his critics does Weihenmayer express in "Everest"?
   A. They are ignorant and pitiable.
   B. They are narrow-minded and cynical.
   C. They should not be blamed for doubting his achievement.
   D. They should be disregarded unless they have also climbed Everest.

____ 16. What tone does Weihenmayer reveal in this passage from "Everest"?

   My teammates constantly come to my rescue with carefully crafted comebacks like "Before you start spouting a bunch of lies over a public forum, get your facts straight, dude!"

   A. angry   C. hopeful
   B. ironic   D. careless

____ 17. In "Everest," what is Weihenmayer's perspective on his climb?
   A. He is unsurprised that he made it to the summit.
   B. He is proud of what he has achieved.
   C. He is ashamed that he needed help.
   D. He is angry that the climb was so difficult.

Essay

18. In "Everest," Weihenmayer describes the ways in which his blindness makes his climb both easier and more difficult. In an essay, describe how his blindness affects his climb. Do you think that on the whole it makes the ascent easier or harder? Explain your answer.

19. How would you define Weihenmayer's tone in "Everest"? In an essay, define the tone in a single word, and then explain why you chose that word. Cite details from the selection to support your conclusion.

20. In response to those who speak ill of his accomplishment, Weihenmayer says,

   I'd be lying if I didn't admit my secret satisfaction in facing those cynics and blowing through their doubts, destroying their negative stereotypes, taking their very narrow parameters of what's possible and what's not, and shattering them into a million pieces.

   In an essay, comment on this passage. Answer these questions: To what doubts and stereo-types does Weihenmayer refer? In what way does he "blow through" and "destroy" them? Why does doing that give him satisfaction?

21. **Thinking About the Big Question: What kind of knowledge changes our lives?** In an essay about "Everest," explain how the knowledge that the climbers gained about the weather affected their chances of making it to the top of the mountain. What techniques did they use to gain this knowledge? How did it change their attitude toward their task and their chances of achieving their goal? Support your response with examples from "Everest."

Vocabulary Warm-up Word Lists

Study these words from "The Spider and the Wasp." Then, complete the activities.

Word List A

aggressive [uh GRES iv] *adj.* behaving in an angry or violent way
  The <u>aggressive</u> toddler knocked his playmate over.

efficient [e FISH uhnt] *adj.* working well, without wasting time
  The <u>efficient</u> mail carrier did her entire route in just five hours.

hostile [HAHS tuhl] *adj.* very unfriendly
  The lumber company had a <u>hostile</u> response to the environmental activists.

instinctive [in STINGK tuhv] *adj.* based on instinct, or natural tendency
  Bears have an <u>instinctive</u> need to hibernate through the winter.

maneuvering [muh NOO ver ing] *v.* skillfully moving
  The children had fun <u>maneuvering</u> their bikes through the obstacle course.

persistent [per SIS tuhnt] *adj.* continuing; sticking with something
  Lynn's <u>persistent</u> efforts to get a summer job paid off.

solitude [SAHL i tood] *n.* the state of being alone
  Greg read in <u>solitude</u> while the others went to town.

tarantula [tuh RAN chuh luh] *n.* a large, hairy spider
  Cindy shrieked when she found a <u>tarantula</u> hidden under a leaf.

Word List B

adequately [AD i kwit lee] *adv.* done well enough
  Alan was not superb at tennis, but he played <u>adequately</u>.

dimensions [di MEN shuhnz] *n.* measurements of something in length, height, and width
  We need to determine the <u>dimensions</u> of the room to see if the sofa will fit.

ghastly [GAST lee] *adj.* extremely bad; shocking or upsetting
  I could not get the <u>ghastly</u> images of the burn victims out of my mind.

inflict [in FLIKT] *v.* to make someone suffer something bad
  Teachers are no longer allowed to <u>inflict</u> corporal punishment.

initiative [i NISH ee uh tiv] *n.* the ability to make decisions and take action
  As the play fell apart, Ben took the <u>initiative</u> and ran the ball in to score.

insufficient [in suh FISH uhnt] *adj.* not enough
  Our funds were <u>insufficient</u> to buy both the TV and the DVD player.

ruthless [ROOTH lis] *adj.* not caring if you do harm to get what you want
  The <u>ruthless</u> executive fired half the staff to fund his annual bonus.

vigorously [VIG er uhs lee] *adv.* with a lot of energy and strength
  Tammy began to sweat as she shoveled the snow <u>vigorously</u>.

"The Spider and the Wasp" by Alexander Petrunkevitch
Vocabulary Warm-up Exercises

Exercise A *Fill in each blank in the paragraph with an appropriate word from Word List A. Use each word only once.*

Nico was the school's star basketball player. His long, spindly legs and speedy style quickly earned him the nickname [1] "_____," after the fast-running spider. As a team player, Nico was an expert at [2] _____ between players and passing the ball. He seemed to have an [3] _____ sense of which teammate could make the best play. Opponents thought his style was a bit [4] _____ as he moved forcefully to the basket, yet he was seldom [5] _____ and rarely committed any offensive fouls. Nico never gave up; he was [6] _____ in his efforts to score. Even in the [7] _____ of the free-throw line, Nico always came through for his team. Never was a player more [8] _____ at racking up points on the court!

Exercise B *Write a complete sentence to answer each question. For each item, use a word from Word List B to replace each underlined word or group of words without changing the meaning.*

Example: What is something you do <u>strenuously</u>?
I rollerblade <u>vigorously</u>.

1. What meal can you make <u>satisfactorily</u>?

   _____

2. When have you had <u>a lack of</u> funds to get something you wanted?

   _____

3. Would you allow a toddler to watch a <u>horrifying</u> movie?

   _____

4. How might you unintentionally <u>cause</u> harm?

   _____

5. When have you shown <u>energy</u> by improving something?

   _____

6. How can you determine what the <u>measurements</u> of your room are?

   _____

7. Why is it <u>uncaring</u> to cheat in order to get ahead in life?

   _____

Name _____ Date _____

"The Spider and the Wasp" by Alexander Petrunkevitch
Reading Warm-up A

Read the following passage. Pay special attention to the underlined words. Then, read it again, and complete the activities. Use a separate sheet of paper for your written answers.

Are you interested in a pet that is unique and fun to watch? Consider the <u>tarantula</u>. Though this spider is not harmful, it may make your friends scream. A tarantula can hurt small mammals, but it does not have a <u>hostile</u> reaction to human beings. Even if it does become <u>aggressive</u>, its bite will not do us much harm. In fact, the tarantula actually helps us by feeding on cockroaches and scorpions.

When you buy a tarantula, try to get a female. Male tarantulas do not live as long as females, and they spend all of their time <u>maneuvering</u> to find a female, even if there are none for miles around. They are amazingly <u>persistent</u> at this effort.

Female tarantulas can live for many years. They do not seem to mind <u>solitude</u> as much as the males, and they can make fine pets.

Know what kind of tarantula you are getting. Some species of tarantula require a lot of moisture. These need more care than species of tarantula from drier regions. If you do not give a tropical tarantula enough water, you can kill it. Likewise, you can kill a desert tarantula if you give it too much water.

While it might seem like fun to catch insects for your tarantula's dinner, it is probably easier and more <u>efficient</u> to buy crickets at a pet store. Furthermore, outdoor insects may be exposed to pesticides.

A terrarium makes a good home for a tarantula—just make sure that your pet cannot escape. Cover the bottom with topsoil; use more for species that like to burrow. Invert a small clay pot, or plastic container, and place it in the pet house so that the tarantula can use it as a hideaway. It has an <u>instinctive</u> need to retreat.

If you treat your tarantula well, you can enjoy your pet for years.

1. Circle the word that tells what type of animal a <u>tarantula</u> is. Then, write a sentence using the word *tarantula*.

2. Circle the words that name a <u>hostile</u> reaction tarantulas have to certain species. Then, explain what *hostile* means.

3. Underline the phrase that tells what happens if a tarantula becomes <u>aggressive</u> toward humans. Tell what *aggressive* means.

4. Circle the word that tells what male tarantulas spend their time <u>maneuvering</u> to find. Explain what *maneuvering* means.

5. Use your own words to rewrite the sentence in which the word <u>persistent</u> appears.

6. Circle the creature that does not seem to mind <u>solitude</u>. Tell whether or not you enjoy *solitude* and why.

7. Circle the words that tell what might be more <u>efficient</u> than hunting insects. Explain why.

8. Circle the words that identify one of the tarantula's <u>instinctive</u> needs. Give two other examples of animals' *instinctive* needs.

"The Spider and the Wasp" by Alexander Petrunkevitch
Reading Warm-up B

Read the following passage. Pay special attention to the underlined words. Then, read it again, and complete the activities. Use a separate sheet of paper for your written answers.

The world's most famous spider may be Charlotte, the well-spoken heroine of *Charlotte's Web* by E. B. White. This beloved story of many generations is also the best-selling paperback book for children. What makes this book remain so popular? It is hard to <u>adequately</u> describe the book's appeal.

E. B. White was a masterful author who wrote noted essays for adults. After living in New York City for years, he and his wife fell in love with a farm in Maine. They bought it on impulse. There, he spent a lot of time observing the animals. They inspired his children's books. He hated to <u>inflict</u> harm on his animals.

The close observation and compassion for his characters are obvious in the rich world he creates in his books. Fern, the little girl, Wilbur the pig, and Charlotte the spider are fully described in all their <u>dimensions</u>. Fern loves Wilbur, and when she realizes he may be killed, she is frustrated that her persuasive powers are <u>insufficient</u> to save him. When it looks like Wilbur will certainly be slaughtered, Charlotte <u>vigorously</u> and forcefully takes the <u>initiative</u> to prevent this outcome. She ends up saving Wilbur from his <u>ghastly</u> fate by weaving words about him into her web. Wilbur becomes a celebrity when Charlotte writes that he is "some pig."

Perhaps White's book is so successful because he knew how to balance the noble with the mundane. While Charlotte is a wonderful friend to Wilbur, she is <u>ruthless</u> when dealing with the flies she snares. Wilbur is first and foremost a pig, and he enjoys the mud as much as any pig. The characters are not sugarcoated, as characters in children's stories so often are. No doubt this has helped the book achieve its exceptional status. *Charlotte's Web* can also teach all readers a great deal about sacrifice, grieving, and, most of all, friendship.

1. Underline the phrase that tells what is hard to <u>adequately</u> describe. Then, explain what *adequately* means.

2. Underline the phrase that tells what E. B. White hated to <u>inflict</u>. Then, tell what *inflict* means.

3. Explain why a character with multiple <u>dimensions</u> might be more interesting to read about than a one-dimensional figure.

4. Write about a time when your own persuasive powers were <u>insufficient</u> to change someone's mind.

5. Circle the word that is a synonym for <u>vigorously</u>. Then, use *vigorously* in a sentence.

6. Underline the phrase that tells what Charlotte took the <u>initiative</u> to do. Then, explain what *initiative* means.

7. Explain why the word <u>ghastly</u> is suited to describe Wilbur's possible fate.

8. Write about an example of <u>ruthless</u> behavior.

Name _____ Date _____

"The Spider and the Wasp" by Alexander Petrunkevitch
Writing About the Big Question

What kind of knowledge changes our lives?

Big Question Vocabulary

adapt	awareness	empathy	enlighten	evolve
growth	history	ignorance	influence	insight
modified	question	reflect	revise	understanding

A. *Use one or more words from the list above to complete each sentence.*

1. Animals must _____ , changing in the face of insurmountable odds, to survive.

2. The spider usually has a delicate sense of touch, so its _____ of the wasp's presence is striking.

3. The wasp has no _____ for the spider and is focused only on a home for her egg.

4. The _____ of the wasp larva toward adulthood means the death of the spider.

B. *Follow the directions in responding to each of the items below.*

1. List two pieces of knowledge about current events you acquired this week.

_____

_____

2. Choose one piece of knowledge you listed and explain whether it changed your life. Use at least two of the Big Question vocabulary words.

_____

_____

C. *Complete the sentence below. Then, write a short paragraph in which you connect this experience to the big question.*

Concrete information can be overruled by a gut reaction when _____

_____

_____

_____

Name _____ Date _____

"The Spider and the Wasp" by Alexander Petrunkevitch
Literary Analysis: Inductive and Deductive Reasoning in an Expository Essay

An **expository essay** is a brief nonfiction work that informs, defines, explains, or discusses a particular topic. Often, an expository essay includes a conclusion the writer reaches through reasoning. The writer's reasoning may be inductive or deductive. In "The Spider and the Wasp," Alexander Petrunkevitch uses both inductive and deductive reasoning.

With **inductive reasoning,** the writer reviews a number of cases and then makes a generalization from them.

In **deductive reasoning,** the writer proves that a conclusion is true by applying a general principle to a specific case.

DIRECTIONS: *Fill in the chart below to show how Petrunkevitch uses inductive and deductive reasoning to draw conclusions about whether tarantulas and wasps act instinctively or intelligently.*

	Spider	**Wasp**
Rule or Evidence	The spider will react defensively if approached from above.	Wasps will not attack the wrong species of tarantula.
Rule or Evidence		
Rule or Evidence		
Rule or Evidence		
Conclusion: Intelligent or Instinctive? (Circle One)	Intelligent Instinctive	Intelligent Instinctive

Name _____ Date _____

"The Spider and the Wasp" by Alexander Petrunkevitch
Reading: Analyze Main Ideas and Supporting Details by Summarizing

To fully understand an essay, **analyze main ideas and supporting details.** In other words, recognize each main point the writer makes and identify its relation to the ideas or facts that explain or illustrate it. To help you organize your thoughts and remember the relationships you identify, pause occasionally to summarize. To **summarize,** restate main ideas in your own words. Begin by stating the main idea and then tell the most important facts or examples that support this idea.

A. DIRECTIONS: *Use the graphic organizer below to identify the main idea and a few important supporting details in "The Spider and the Wasp."*

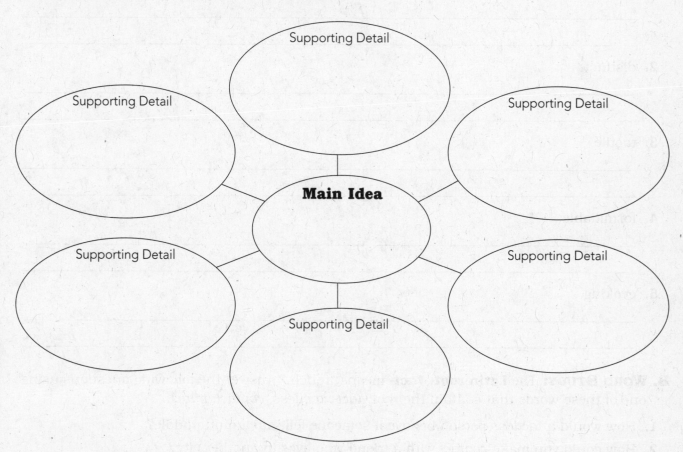

B. DIRECTIONS: *Use your completed graphic organizer to help you summarize "The Spider and the Wasp" on the lines below.*

_____

_____

_____

_____

"The Spider and the Wasp" by Alexander Petrunkevitch
Vocabulary Builder

Word List

customarily   distinct   evoking   formidable   instinct   tactile

A. DIRECTIONS: *Create two different sentences for each of the following words. You may use a different form of the word in your second sentence if you wish.*

    Example: Wasps use <u>instinct</u> to release a strong odor when they feel threatened.

              If approached from above, the spider <u>instinctively</u> reacts with a threatening posture.

1. customarily

_____

_____

2. distinct

_____

_____

3. tactile

_____

_____

4. formidable

_____

_____

5. evoking

_____

_____

B. WORD STUDY: The **Latin root -tact-** means "touch." Answer the following questions using one of these words that contain the root -tact-: *tactless, contact, intact.*

1. How would a *tactless* person behave if someone fell into a mud puddle?
2. How could you make *contact* with a friend who lives in another city?
3. Why would you be happy if you dropped a glass and it remained *intact*?

"The Spider and the Wasp" by Alexander Petrunkevitch
Enrichment: Planning a Nature Documentary

Documentaries are films or television programs that give factual information about a topic. Work with a group of your classmates to plan a nature documentary about tarantulas and digger wasps. Base your documentary plan on Alexander Petrunkevitch's essay "The Spider and the Wasp." You may use other resources as well. To plan your documentary, complete the following steps.

- If possible, watch a nature documentary.
- Write down the main idea you would like to convey with your documentary.
- Write a summary of the narrator's script. List the main points the narrator must make in order to convey the documentary's main idea.
- List specific scenes you would like to capture on film, such as a wasp inspecting a spider to determine its species.
- Visually sketch out the most important shots of your documentary in the order you would like to present them.

Each person in your group should take on a specific job—summarizing a script, listing scenes, or sketching shots—to help plan the group's documentary. Before you begin the assignment, list each group member's job and responsibilities on the lines below.

_____

_____

_____

_____

_____

_____

_____

_____

_____

_____

_____

_____

_____

_____

_____

_____

_____

_____

"The Spider and the Wasp" by Alexander Petrunkevitch
Open-Book Test

Short Answer *Write your responses to the questions in this section on the lines provided.*

1. An expository essay is a brief nonfiction work in which an author informs readers about something or explains something. What key difference between spiders and wasps does Alexander Petrunkevitch seek to explain in "The Spider and the Wasp"?

   _____

   _____

   _____

2. In "The Spider and the Wasp," Petrunkevitch states, "Tarantulas customarily live in deep cylindrical burrows." Based on your knowledge of the word *customarily,* how often would you be likely to find tarantulas living in shallow triangular holes?

   _____

   _____

3. In "The Spider and the Wasp," Petrunkevitch discusses the spider's "three tactile responses." Would the sight of an enemy cause a *tactile* response? Base your answer on the meaning of the word *tactile.*

   _____

   _____

4. In "The Spider and the Wasp," Petrunkevitch describes several ways in which a tarantula reacts to touch. Then, he states that these protective reactions do not happen when a digger wasp attacks. Write three of the tarantula's responses to touch in the web. Then, on the lines below, answer the following question: What logical conclusion does the tarantula's failure to respond to the digger wasp suggest about the digger wasp's attack?

Tarantula's responses to touch

   _____

   _____

5. In "The Spider and the Wasp," Petrunkevitch states that a tarantula will react defensively if approached from above. Since a tarantula does not react defensively to a digger wasp, what conclusion can the reader draw?

_____

_____

6. In "The Spider and the Wasp," Petrunkevitch points out that tarantulas are protected as a species even though they are such easy prey for wasps. What key detail supports this main idea?

_____

_____

7. In "The Spider and the Wasp," Petrunkevitch assumes that a creature's ability to change its behavior is a form of intelligence. He provides this example: If the digger wasp finds a tarantula of the wrong species, the wasp will not attack the tarantula. What conclusion does Petrunkevitch draw based on this evidence?

_____

_____

8. In "The Spider and the Wasp," the tarantula finally mounts a last-minute defense after allowing the wasp to crawl all over it for a long time. What does this behavior show about the spider's awareness of its situation?

_____

_____

9. In "The Spider and the Wasp," Petrunkevitch gives a detailed explanation of what happens when the spider and the wasp meet. What is the main idea of this part of the essay?

_____

_____

10. In "The Spider and the Wasp," Petrunkevitch suggests that the spider operates mainly through instinct rather than intelligence. What detail concerning the spider's web-building technique supports this idea?

_____

_____

_____

Essay

Write an extended response to the question of your choice or to the question or questions your teacher assigns you.

11. Write an essay in which you summarize one of the main ideas of "The Spider and the Wasp." For the main idea you discuss, provide the key supporting details. At the end of your essay, state the importance of the main idea.

12. In "The Spider and the Wasp," Petrunkevitch discusses the difference between instinctive behavior and intelligent behavior. In an essay, explain how the author defines *instinct* and *intelligence*. Then, explain how tarantulas and digger wasps illustrate these definitions. Give examples from the essay to support your response.

13. In "The Spider and the Wasp," Petrunkevitch cannot explain why tarantulas fail to protect themselves while the digger wasps are inspecting them. In an essay, give your opinion about why this situation occurs. Support your opinion through inductive or deductive reasoning based on details from the essay. You can use one of Petrunkevitch's theories or offer one of your own.

14. **Thinking About the Big Question: What kind of knowledge changes our lives?** Think about the different ways in which the spider and the wasp respond to new information, or potential knowledge. Do they change equally effectively when confronted with new situations? Provide details from "The Spider and the Wasp" to support your response.

Oral Response

15. Go back to question 6, 9, or 10 or to the question your teacher assigns you. Take a few mintues to expand your answer and prepare an oral response. Find additional details in "The Spider and the Wasp" that support your points. If necessary, make notes to guide your oral response.

Name _____ Date _____

"The Spider and the Wasp" by Alexander Petrunkevitch
Selection Test A

Critical Reading *Identify the letter of the choice that best answers the question.*

____ 1. Why is "The Spider and the Wasp" an expository essay?
  A. It informs readers about the behavior of tarantulas and wasps.
  B. It tries to persuade readers to consider tarantulas as good pets.
  C. It contains the author's memory of a meaningful time in his life.
  D. It entertains readers with amusing fictional stories about insects.

____ 2. According to "The Spider and the Wasp," which of a tarantula's senses is the most developed?
  A. sight
  B. touch
  C. hearing
  D. smell

____ 3. Petrunkevitch describes three ways a tarantula reacts to touch. Then he states that these protective reactions fail the spider against a digger wasp. What logical conclusion can you draw from this information?
  A. The spider ignores its instincts because it likes the wasp.
  B. The wasp gives off some sort of chemical that calms the spider.
  C. The wasp knows how to avoid triggering the spider's defenses.
  D. The spider's instincts are simply not as strong as the wasp's instincts.

____ 4. Petrunkevitch states that a tarantula will react defensively if approached from above. Since a tarantula does not react defensively to a digger wasp, the reader can conclude that the wasp does not approach the spider from above. What kind of reasoning is this?
  A. inductive
  B. deductive
  C. instinctive
  D. illogical

____ 5. When does the wasp sting the tarantula?
  A. as soon as she finds it
  B. as soon as she determines its species
  C. right after she digs its grave
  D. right after she lays her egg

_____ 6. How are tarantulas as a species protected from extinction?

    A. Wasps only kill old and sick tarantulas.

    B. Tarantulas are learning how to kill wasps.

    C. Scientists work to protect and save tarantulas.

    D. Tarantulas have many more young than wasps do.

_____ 7. Petrunkevitch uses deductive reasoning to draw a conclusion about a mother digger wasp's behavior. He begins by assuming that the ability of a creature to change its behavior is a form of intelligence. He provides an example of the digger wasp changing her behavior: If she finds that a tarantula is of the wrong species, she will not attack it. What conclusion does he draw?

    A. that the wasp behaves entirely on instinct

    B. that the wasp behaves in an intelligent way

    C. that the wasp cannot change her behavior in any other ways

    D. that the wasp feels sorry for tarantulas and does not want to kill them

_____ 8. Which is the best statement of the main idea of "The Spider and the Wasp"?

    A. Digger wasps seem to use intelligent behavior to take advantage of tarantulas' blind instincts.

    B. A tarantula's three instinctive responses to touch help it to avoid most annoyances and dangers.

    C. Digger wasps need to find adult tarantulas of the correct species on which to lay their eggs.

    D. A newly hatched digger wasp feeds on a paralyzed tarantula until it is ready to live on its own.

_____ 9. Which most directly supports the main idea of "The Spider and the Wasp"?

    A. Digger wasps are usually a beautiful deep shiny blue in color.

    B. Tarantulas live in the tropics and in the southern United States.

    C. A mother digger wasp will not attack a tarantula of the wrong species.

    D. A female tarantula lays 200 to 400 eggs at a time and has mating capability for several years.

Vocabulary and Grammar

_____ 10. One of a tarantula's *tactile* responses is to move away when something prods it. Which of the following is an example of a typical human tactile response?

    A. spitting out something bitter

    B. laughing when being tickled

    C. blinking when a light is turned on

    D. jumping slightly at a sudden noise

____ **11.** In which of the following sentences is the word *customarily* used correctly?

A. The principal customarily gives out achievement awards at the end of each school year.

B. Though it is very unusual, we sometimes customarily get to stay out late on a school night.

C. The new store opened early, and the salespeople waited for the customarily to arrive.

D. I always do my homework as soon as I get home, but customarily I did not do it last night.

____ **12.** What is the direct object in the following sentence?

The wasp stings the tarantula in its soft spot.

A. wasp

B. stings

C. tarantula

D. spot

____ **13.** What is the indirect object in the following sentence?

The mother wasp digs the tarantula a grave.

A. wasp

B. digs

C. tarantula

D. grave

Essay

14. In an essay, summarize the main ideas and most important supporting details of "The Spider and the Wasp." Begin by stating the main idea. Then, tell the most important facts or examples that support this idea.

15. In "The Spider and the Wasp," Petrunkevitch discusses instinctive behaviors and behaviors that seem intelligent. In an essay, explain how Petrunkevitch defines instinct and intelligence. Then, tell how he classifies tarantulas and digger wasps. Does he consider tarantulas to be instinctive or intelligent? What about wasps? Give examples from the essay to support Petrunkevitch's classifications.

16. Thinking About the Big Question: What kind of knowledge changes our lives?
In an essay, explain how the spider and the wasp respond to new information differently. In your final paragraph, explain your answer to the following question: Do the spider and the wasp change equally well when faced with new situations? Provide details from "The Spider and the Wasp" to support your response.

"The Spider and the Wasp" by Alexander Petrunkevitch
Selection Test B

Critical Reading *Identify the letter of the choice that best completes the statement or answers the question.*

____ 1. Why is "The Spider and the Wasp" an expository essay?
  A. It explains a natural phenomenon to readers.
  B. It persuades readers to try to save tarantulas.
  C. It contains the author's memory of a meaningful time in his life.
  D. It entertains readers with fascinating fictional stories about insects.

____ 2. In "The Spider and the Wasp," Petrunkevitch describes how tarantulas react to three types of touch. Which type of touch is NOT discussed in the essay?
  A. stroking of the body hair
  B. poking of the eyes
  C. flexing of the trichobothria
  D. pressure against the body wall

____ 3. Petrunkevitch provides evidence that protective reactions fail the spider when it encounters a digger wasp. Based on this evidence, he makes the following inductive conclusion:
  A. The spider is ignoring its instincts because it likes the wasp.
  B. The wasp is excreting some sort of drug that calms the spider.
  C. The wasp knows how to avoid triggering the spider's defenses.
  D. The spider reacts instantly and aggressively to the wasp's touch.

____ 4. Which of the following sentences is the best statement of the main idea of "The Spider and the Wasp"?
  A. In the feeding and safeguarding of their progeny, insects and spiders exhibit some interesting analogies to reasoning and some crass examples of blind instinct.
  B. The trichobothria, very fine hairs growing from disclike membranes on the legs, are sensitive only to air movement.
  C. Perhaps in this case, the spider follows its usual pattern of trying to escape, instead of seizing and killing the wasp, because it is not aware of its danger.
  D. In any case, the survival of the tarantula species as a whole is protected by the fact that the spider is much more fertile than the wasp.

____ 5. Which of the following is a detail that does NOT directly support the main idea of "The Spider and the Wasp"?
  A. A mother digger wasp examines a tarantula to make sure it is the right species.
  B. A wasp's behavior seems intelligent because she can modify it to fit a situation.
  C. A tarantula has three instinctive responses to touch that enable it to avoid danger.
  D. A female tarantula lays from 200 to 400 eggs at a time and has mating capability for several years.

____ 6. After allowing the wasp to crawl all over it for quite some time, the tarantula finally attacks the wasp. What triggers the tarantula's defenses at last?
  A. The wasp corners the tarantula and grasps its leg in her jaws.
  B. The wasp digs a grave, causing the spider to realize its danger.
  C. The wasp lays her egg on its abdomen, which annoys the tarantula.
  D. The wasp accidentally brushes against the tarantula's trichobothria.

___ 7. Where does the wasp sting the tarantula?
   A. where the spider's legs join its body
   B. just behind the spider's head
   C. on the side of the spider's abdomen
   D. between the spider's fangs

___ 8. According to Petrunkevitch, what does the wasp do in the dark once the tarantula is trapped in the bottom of the grave?
   A. She determines the spider's species.
   B. She thrusts her sting into the spider.
   C. She releases an odorless secretion.
   D. It is not known what the wasp does.

___ 9. Which of the following is an example of how Petrunkevitch uses deductive reasoning to draw a conclusion about a tarantula's behavior? Begin with the assumption that an instinctive behavior is one an animal cannot change.
   A. The tarantula is behaving in an intelligent way by allowing itself to be inspected thoroughly by the mother wasp.
   B. Since the tarantula does not react to the wasp's investigation, it must realize that the wasp is not large enough to kill it.
   C. The tarantula is behaving in an instinctive way by jumping violently and baring its fangs when the wasp touches its body hairs.
   D. Since the tarantula does not seem to realize that it is in danger until it is too late, it must be reacting to the wasp entirely on instinct.

___ 10. Petrunkevitch uses deductive reasoning to draw a conclusion about a mother digger wasp's behavior. He begins with the principle that the ability of a creature to adapt its behavior to suit the needs of a given situation is a form of intelligence. He draws the conclusion that the wasp behaves in an intelligent way. What is one example he uses to deductively prove this conclusion?
   A. The wasp lays her egg on the tarantula and buries it.
   B. The wasp flies away, leaving her young to begin life on its own.
   C. The wasp knows that it is time to find a tarantula when an egg ripens in her ovary.
   D. The wasp inspects each tarantula she finds and does not attack one of the wrong species.

___ 11. "The Spider and the Wasp" could be divided into four main sections: a description of tarantulas, a description of wasps, an explanation of what happens when these two creatures meet, and a discussion of instinct versus intelligence. What is the main idea of the third section?
   A. Tarantulas' instinctive reactions usually protect them from most dangers.
   B. The wasp ruthlessly takes advantage of the tarantula's apparent confusion.
   C. After paralyzing the tarantula, the mother wasp attaches her egg to its abdomen.
   D. Digger wasps are beautiful and solitary creatures that grow as large as four inches.

Vocabulary and Grammar

___ 12. All spiders have an extremely delicate *tactile* sense, which allows them to
   A. hear the chirping of insects.
   B. distinguish various types of touch.
   C. identify the change in intensity of light.
   D. see moving objects with keen eyesight.

___ 13. Which of the following is the best example of things that are *distinct*?
   A. the overlapping edges of two clouds
   B. the sound of individual voices in a crowd
   C. the physical appearance of identical twins
   D. the opinions of opposing political candidates

___ 14. What is the direct object in the following sentence?
   The tarantula shows an amazing tolerance to the mother wasp's inspection.
   A. tarantula
   B. shows
   C. tolerance
   D. inspection

___ 15. Which of the following sentences contains an indirect object?
   A. The wasp finds a tarantula of the correct species.
   B. The mother wasp digs the tarantula a grave.
   C. She paralyzes the spider with a well-placed sting.
   D. Wasps give off a pungent odor when they feel threatened.

Essay

16. In an essay, explain how Petrunkevitch defines instinct and intelligence in "The Spider and the Wasp." Then, describe how he classifies tarantulas and digger wasps in these two categories. Give examples from the essay to support Petrunkevitch's classifications. Finally, state whether you agree or disagree with these classifications and explain why.

17. In an essay, summarize the main ideas and most important supporting details of "The Spider and the Wasp." Then, refer to your summary to make a generalization about instinct versus intelligence. Based on the example of tarantulas and digger wasps, decide whether a creature that displays intelligent behavior will generally succeed in a conflict with one that acts on instinct alone.

18. Petrunkevitch is unable to provide a definite explanation for why tarantulas fail to react defensively while being inspected by digger wasps. In an essay, speculate about why a tarantula does not defend itself when a wasp inspects it. Support your explanation inductively or deductively, using information from the essay. You may use one of the theories stated by Petrunkevitch or come up with your own.

19. **Thinking About the Big Question: What kind of knowledge changes our lives?** Think about the different ways in which the spider and the wasp respond to new information, or potential knowledge. Do they change equally effectively when confronted with new situations? Provide details from "The Spider and the Wasp" to support your response.

Vocabulary Warm-up Word Lists

Study these words from Longitude. *Then, apply your knowledge to the activities that follow.*

Word List A

accuracy [AK yuh ruh see] *n.* quality of being exact or precise
    Have you checked the <u>accuracy</u> of your multiplication?

astronomer [uh STRAHN uh mer] *n.* one who studies the stars, planets, and space
    The <u>astronomer</u> took advantage of the clear night to view Mars.

devised [di VYZD] *v.* worked out by thinking
    We <u>devised</u> a way to use duct tape to fix our broken lawn mower.

era [EER uh] *n.* a period of time with a significant focus
    Henry Ford lived in an <u>era</u> of rapid change and progress.

fervor [FER ver] *n.* great enthusiasm, emotion, or belief
    The <u>fervor</u> in the commander's speech brought cheers from the troops.

triumphed [TRY uhmft] *v.* was successful or victorious
    Our field hockey team <u>triumphed</u> over our opponents.

virtually [VER choo uh lee] *adv.* for all practical purposes; almost entirely
    Due to erosion, there is <u>virtually</u> no earth left on the hillside.

whereabouts [HWER uh bowts] *n.* place where a person or thing is
    A reward was offered for information on the <u>whereabouts</u> of the lost dog.

Word List B

arbitrarily [ar bi TRER uh lee] *adv.* randomly
    It did not make any sense for the coach to choose the pitcher <u>arbitrarily</u>.

crisscrossing [KRIS kraws ing] *v.* making a pattern of crossed lines
    Snowboarders were <u>crisscrossing</u> the snow-covered slopes.

deformity [di FAWR mi tee] *n.* state of having a changed or bad form
    A hunchback is a <u>deformity</u> that is rarely seen now.

modifications [mahd i fi KAY shuhnz] *n.* slight changes
    Changing to solar energy required some <u>modifications</u> to our roof design.

notable [NOH tuh buhl] *adj.* worthy of notice; remarkable
    Her success was <u>notable</u> because she achieved it at such a young age.

orb [awrb] *n.* sphere; globe
    The sun was a golden <u>orb</u> as it sank below the horizon.

ultimately [UL tuh mit lee] *adv.* finally; at last
    We had our doubts, but we <u>ultimately</u> realized the change was for the best.

variations [vair ee AY shunz] *n.* things that are a bit different from others of the same kind
    The new T-shirts are slight <u>variations</u> on last year's design.

Name _____   Date _____

from **Longitude** by Dava Sobel
Vocabulary Warm-up Exercises

Exercise A *Fill in each blank in the paragraph with an appropriate word from Word List A. Use each word only once.*

Galileo Galilei was the first [1] _____ to use a telescope to view the sky. Although he did not invent this tool, he [2] _____ many new ways to use it. His [3] _____ for exploring science led him to make many discoveries. For example, he located the [4] _____ of Jupiter's four largest moons. The [5] _____ of his measurements and calculations is amazing even when compared with today's electronic computations. He was interested in [6] _____ every scientific topic. Through dedication and hard work, he [7] _____ over ignorance and helped launch a new [8] _____ of rapid scientific progress.

Exercise B *Decide whether each statement is true or false. Circle T or F. Then, explain your answer.*

1. You can use a <u>notable</u> fact to support an opinion.
   T / F _____

2. A <u>crisscrossing</u> path is usually the shortest route between two points.
   T / F _____

3. You should always make an important decision <u>arbitrarily</u>.
   T / F _____

4. You can see the shape of an <u>orb</u> in a baseball, an orange, or a pea.
   T / F _____

5. <u>Variations</u> usually share some features with the original.
   T / F _____

6. A <u>deformity</u> probably improves the quality and value of a diamond.
   T / F _____

7. You would be unrecognizable after making <u>modifications</u> to your hairstyle.
   T / F _____

8. If you <u>ultimately</u> achieve your goal, you accomplish nothing.
   T / F _____

Name _____ Date _____

from **Longitude** by Dava Sobel
Reading Warm-up A

Read the following passage. Pay special attention to the underlined words. Then, read it again, and complete the activities. Use a separate sheet of paper for your written answers.

20 January, 1762

Our ship, the *Deptford*, arrived in Jamaica yesterday. Though I had planned to write an entry daily, there has been so much to do that I have fallen behind. This note-book remains <u>virtually</u> blank. Today, I am determined to record some details of our trip.

Master Harrison has <u>devised</u> an amazing timepiece. If it works, he will finally win the Longitude Prize. For more than thirty years, he has worked to create a clock that will keep good time on board a ship. The purpose of our journey was to test the <u>accuracy</u> of his fourth design. As his apprentice, I have sat at Master Harrison's side for nearly three years, watching every day from dusk until past sunset as he worked with an intense <u>fervor</u> on this remarkable watch. Unlike the first three versions, this one is small enough to hold in one hand.

Though I am glad to be on this voyage, I am an uneasy sailor. In the thick morning fog, I often felt lost. Luckily, our ship's navigator always knew our exact <u>whereabouts</u>.

I am Master Harrison's secretary. I have discovered that he is an enthusiastic <u>astronomer</u> as well as a watch-maker. Each night, we stand on deck and gaze at the stars. I record his observations and then read them aloud during our midday meal.

When we arrived, we learned that our mission has been more than a success. We have <u>triumphed</u>! After sixty-three days, the watch was only 5.1 seconds behind the actual time. This result is even more than we hoped for. It is surely worthy of the prize, although Master Harrison suspects that the Board of Longitude may not be convinced. Their attitude toward his work has been unfair.

Nonetheless, I am certain that Master Harrison has met his goal. I feel lucky to be living in an <u>era</u> when such great things are being done.

1. Underline the words that tell why the notebook is <u>virtually</u> blank. Then, tell something that you think is *virtually* impossible.

2. Circle the words that tell what Harrison <u>devised</u>. Then, tell what *devised* means.

3. Circle the words that name what had its <u>accuracy</u> tested on the journey. Then, name another tool that measures with great *accuracy*.

4. Underline the phrases that show that Harrison worked with intense <u>fervor</u>. Then, tell what *fervor* means.

5. Underline the sentence that describes the opposite of knowing one's <u>whereabouts</u>. Then, tell what *whereabouts* means.

6. Underline the sentence that tells what this <u>astronomer</u> does. Then, tell one quality you think every *astronomer* needs.

7. Circle the words that tell what the men <u>triumphed</u> over. Describe a situation in which you *triumphed* over something difficult.

8. Underline the words the writer uses to describe his <u>era</u>. Then, describe your own *era*.

Name _____ Date _____

from **Longitude** by Dava Sobel
Reading Warm-up B

Read the following passage. Pay special attention to the underlined words. Then, read it again, and complete the activities. Use a separate sheet of paper for your written answers.

The Earth is a sphere. This simple fact creates great challenges for mapmakers. A globe can show the relative shapes and sizes exactly as they are on Earth's giant <u>orb</u>. However, a flat map always creates some distortion, a bending or twisting of the true shape or size. For centuries, mapmakers have tried to reduce this <u>deformity</u> as much as possible.

Flemish mapmaker Gerardus Mercator (1512–1594) was one of the first people to create a projection of Earth. A projection is a two-dimensional (flat) map of a three-dimensional (curved) surface. In his world map of 1569, Mercator used longitude and latitude lines. This grid of imaginary lines <u>crisscrossing</u> the map provided a way to locate places.

The Mercator projection became the standard for maps of Earth for centuries. Though it is a clear and easy-to-read map, it has some <u>notable</u> problems. The size of land near the equator is very accurate, but sizes become more distorted the farther they are from the equator. Mapmakers call this the "Greenland Problem": On a Mercator projection, Greenland and Africa appear to be about the same size, while in reality, Africa is nearly *thirteen times* larger than Greenland.

Dr. Arthur Robinson (1915–2004) tried to solve the "Greenland Problem." He made several important <u>modifications</u> in the way land was mapped onto a flat surface. Instead of using the equator as the place where size is most accurate, he selected 38 degrees south and 38 degrees north as the standard parallels. He did not make this choice <u>arbitrarily</u>. It was based on many calculations and observations. The zones between these parallels contain most of Earth's land and people.

However, the Robinson projection is not perfect. Land near the poles is still unrealistic. <u>Ultimately</u>, no map of Earth can be totally accurate. Nonetheless, mapmakers are likely to produce new <u>variations</u> that will yield more and more truthful views of the world.

1. Circle two synonyms for <u>orb</u>. Then, describe two common objects that have the shape of an *orb*.

2. Underline the words that describe the <u>deformity</u> of Earth's shape as shown on a map. Then, explain what *deformity* means.

3. Underline the words that tell what were <u>crisscrossing</u> Mercator's map. Then, tell what *crisscrossing* means.

4. Write a sentence about a *notable* problem in your community.

5. Underline the sentence that details one of the <u>modifications</u> Robinson made. Then, tell what *modifications* means.

6. Underline the words that mean the opposite of <u>arbitrarily</u>. Then, describe a decision you often make *arbitrarily*.

7. Describe how you think a current problem will *ultimately* be solved.

8. Underline the words that tell why mapmakers will create new <u>variations</u> of world maps. Then, tell why these *variations* will not be completely different from earlier maps.

Unit 3 Resources: Types of Nonfiction

from **Longitude** by Dava Sobel
Writing About the Big Question

What kind of information changes our lives?

Big Question Vocabulary

adapt	awareness	empathy	enlighten	evolve
growth	history	ignorance	influence	insight
modified	question	reflect	revise	understanding

A. *Use one or more words from the list above to complete each sentence.*

1. The _____ of longitude is filled with jealousy, deception, and perseverance.

2. Construction of clocks had to _____ from pendulum clocks to portable time pieces.

3. Our _____ for Harrison is great, because we, too, would want recognition for a great achievement.

4. The _____ of how to compute longitude was asked by many scientists.

B. *Follow the directions in responding to each of the items below.*

1. List an area of study that has the potential to change our lives.

   _____

   _____

2. Write two sentences explaining how knowledge gained in that area of study can be life-changing. Use at least two Big Question vocabulary words.

   _____

   _____

C. *Complete the sentence below. Then, write a short paragraph in which you connect this experience to the big question.*

Information that changes the world often deals with _____

_____

_____

_____

Name _____   Date _____

from **Longitude** by Dava Sobel

Literary Analysis: Inductive and Deductive Reasoning in an Expository Essay

An **expository essay** is a brief nonfiction work that informs, defines, explains, or discusses a particular topic. Often, an expository essay includes a conclusion the writer reaches through reasoning. The writer's reasoning may be inductive or deductive. In this excerpt from *Longitude*, Dava Sobel uses both inductive and deductive reasoning.

With **inductive reasoning,** the writer reviews a number of cases and then makes a generalization from them. ·

In **deductive reasoning,** the writer proves that a conclusion is true by applying a general principle to a specific case.

DIRECTIONS: *Fill in the chart below to show how Sobel uses inductive and deductive reasoning to draw conclusions about the importance of clocks in measuring longitude.*

	Importance of Accurate Clocks in Navigation	**How Harrison's Clock Solved the Longitude Problem**
Rule or Evidence	Distances in longitude are proportionate to hours in the day.	Design modifications enabled the clock to be mass produced.
Rule or Evidence		
Rule or Evidence		
Rule or Evidence		
Conclusion		

Name _____ Date _____

from **Longitude** by Dava Sobel
Reading: Analyze Main Ideas and Supporting Details by Summarizing

To fully understand an essay, **analyze main ideas and supporting details.** In other words, recognize each main point the writer makes and identify its relation to the ideas or facts that explain or illustrate it. To help you organize your thoughts and remember the relationships you identify, pause occasionally to summarize. To **summarize,** restate main ideas in your own words. Begin by stating the main idea and then tell the most important facts or examples that support this idea.

A. DIRECTIONS: *Use the graphic organizer below to identify the main idea and a few important supporting details in Sobel's essay from* Longitude.

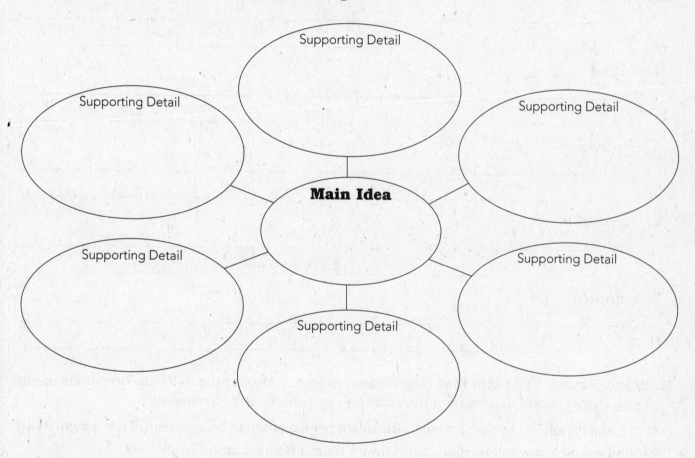

Supporting Detail

Supporting Detail

Supporting Detail

Main Idea

Supporting Detail

Supporting Detail

Supporting Detail

B. DIRECTIONS: *Use your completed graphic organizer to help you summarize Sobel's essay from* Longitude *on the lines below.*

_____

_____

_____

_____

_____

Name _____   Date _____

from **Longitude** by Dava Sobel
Vocabulary Builder

Word List

contested   configuration   converge   derived   haphazardly   impervious

A. DIRECTIONS: *Create two different sentences for each of the following words. You may use a different form of the word in your second sentence.*

   Examples: Early sea captains wandered <u>haphazardly</u> across the oceans.

   This <u>haphazard</u> method of exploration nevertheless resulted in many great discoveries.

1. configuration

   _____

   _____

2. derived

   _____

   _____

3. impervious

   _____

   _____

4. converge

   _____

   _____

5. contested

   _____

   _____

B. WORD STUDY: The **Latin root -fig-** means "to form." Answer the following questions using one of these words that contain the root *-fig-: figment, figurine, reconfigure.*

1. If a child is caught breaking a rule, why might her explanation be a *figment* of her imagination?

2. Why would a rag doll be more appropriate than a *figurine* for a baby's toy?

3. Why might a teacher need to *reconfigure* his classroom before parents come to visit?

Name _____ Date _____

from **Longitude** by Dava Sobel
Enrichment: Planning a Documentary

Documentaries are films or television programs that give factual information about a topic. Dava Sobel's *Longitude* has been made into a documentary. Work with a group of your classmates to plan a documentary about a topic related to geography, navigation, or the history of navigation. Use Sobel's essay from *Longitude* to help you select a topic. You may use other resources as well. To plan your documentary, complete the following steps.

- If possible, watch a documentary.
- Write down the main idea you would like to convey with your documentary.
- Write a summary of the narrator's script. List the main points the narrator must make in order to convey the documentary's main idea.
- List specific scenes you would like to capture on film, such as a re-enactment of a famous explorer trying to plot his course across the ocean using the tools available during the Age of Exploration.
- Visually sketch out the most important shots of your documentary in the order you would like to present them.

Each person in your group should take on a specific job—summarizing a script, listing scenes, or sketching shots—to help plan the group's documentary. Before you begin the assignment, list each group member's job and responsibilities on the following lines.

_____

_____

_____

_____

_____

_____

_____

_____

_____

_____

_____

_____

_____

_____

_____

_____

"**The Spider and the Wasp**" by Alexander Petrunkevitch
from **Longitude** by Dava Sobel
Integrated Language Skills: Grammar

Direct and Indirect Objects

A **direct object** is a noun or pronoun that receives the action of an action verb. You can determine whether a word is a direct object by asking *Whom?* or *What?* after an action verb.

An **indirect object** is used with a direct object and names the person/thing that something is given to or done for. You can tell whether a word is an indirect object by finding the direct object and asking *To or for whom?* or *To or for what?* after the action verb.

Examples: Latonya wore her new <u>dress</u>. (*Dress* is the direct object because it receives the action of the verb *wore*.)

Tami gave <u>Latonya</u> a <u>compliment</u>. (*Latonya* is the indirect object and *compliment* is the direct object.)

A. PRACTICE: *The following sentences are based on "The Spider and the Wasp" or the excerpt from* Longitude. *Circle each indirect object and underline each direct object. One sentence has more than one direct object.*

1. The mother wasp examines a tarantula closely.
2. She paralyzes the spider with venom.
3. The wasp then digs the spider a grave and buries it with her young.
4. Any sailor can determine latitude by looking at the position of the sun.
5. Longitude gave early sailors a much more difficult problem, though.
6. One must know the time in two places at once to determine longitude.

B. Writing Application: *On the lines below, write a paragraph about either "The Spider and the Wasp" or the excerpt from* Longitude. *Be sure to include at least four direct objects and three indirect objects. Circle each indirect object and underline each direct object.*

_____

_____

_____

_____

_____

_____

_____

_____

_____

_____

Name _____ Date _____

from **Longitude** by Dava Sobel
"The Spider and the Wasp" by Alexander Petrunkevitch

Integrated Language Skills: Support for Writing a Business Letter

To help you write your business letter asking King George III for recognition for Harrison's invention, use the following chart to organize your thoughts. Make a list of points and examples to answer the question in each column.

What makes your (Harrison's) clock different from previous clocks?	How does your (Harrison's) clock solve the problem of determining longitude?	What problems have you (Harrison) had trying to get recognition for your invention?

Now, use your notes to write a business letter from Harrison's point of view asking King George III for recognition for solving the problem of determining longitude.

To help you write your business letter requesting funds to do more research on tarantulas and wasps, use the following chart to organize your thoughts. Make a list of points and examples to answer the question in each column.

Why is the topic of scientific interest?	What do we currently know about the topic?	What mysteries could be solved with more research?

Now, use your notes to write your business letter requesting funds to do additional research on tarantulas and wasps.

Name _____ Date _____

"The Spider and the Wasp" by Alexander Petrunkevitch
from **Longitude** by Dava Sobel

Integrated Language Skills: Support for Extend Your Learning

Listening and Speaking: "The Spider and the Wasp"

Fill in the chart below to help you prepare for your humorous persuasive speech encouraging your classmates to view wasps and tarantulas as great potential pets.

Qualities of a Good Pet	Humorous Ways in Which Tarantulas and Wasps Fulfill These Qualities

Listening and Speaking: *from* Longitude

Fill in the chart below to help you prepare for your humorous persuasive speech proposing to move the prime meridian to your hometown.

Description of the Prime Meridian	Humorous Ways in Which Your Hometown Would be a Good Location for the Prime Meridian

from **Longitude** by Dava Sobel
Open-Book Test

Short Answer *Write your responses to the questions in this section on the lines provided.*

1. An expository essay is a brief nonfiction work in which an author informs readers about something or explains something. In *Longitude*, Dava Sobel explains the difference between two ways of measuring distances on the globe. What are these two ways?

   _____

   _____

2. If someone created a map *haphazardly*, would the map be reliable or not? Explain your answer, based on the meaning of *haphazardly* in *Longitude*.

   _____

   _____

3. In *Longitude*, Sobel states that "Ptolemy himself had only an armchair appreciation of the wider world." What does Sobel mean by "an armchair appreciation"? From what piece of information can you deduce the meaning of this term?

   _____

   _____

   _____

   _____

4. What key details from *Longitude* support the idea that "the placement of the prime meridian is a purely political decision"? Consider the history of the prime meridian's location.

   _____

   _____

   _____

5. In *Longitude*, Sobel explains that an exact knowledge of the time in two places at once is necessary to navigate accurately on the high seas. Based on what key fact does she deduce that captains in the Age of Exploration were often lost at sea?

   _____

   _____

   _____

   _____

6. In *Longitude*, Sobel explains that "each hour's time difference between the ship and the starting point marks a progress of fifteen degrees of longitude to the east and west." Without any accurate clocks, how did navigators gauge their position by observing the sun?

_____

_____

_____

7. In *Longitude*, Sobel states that the main problem for navigators before the eighteenth century was that clocks were inaccurate. Use the diagram to provide three details that explain why the clocks were inaccurate. Then, on the line below, identify one change that would have made clocks more accurate.

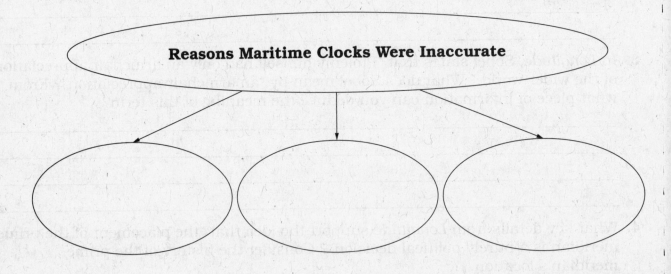

Reasons Maritime Clocks Were Inaccurate

_____

8. According to *Longitude*, why were some people against John Harrison's claiming the prize for creating an accurate maritime clock?

_____

_____

9. According to *Longitude*, why did the governments of great seafaring nations offer large rewards for a workable solution to the problem of longitude?

_____

_____

_____

10. If you remarked that someone was *impervious* to reason, would you be complimenting or insulting him? Explain your answer, based on the meaning of *impervious* in *Longitude*.

_____

_____

_____

Essay

Write an extended response to the question of your choice or to the question or questions your teacher assigns you.

11. In an essay, summarize the key ideas and facts that Sobel provides in *Longitude*. Begin by stating the main idea. Then, identify the most important facts or examples that support this idea.

12. In an essay, discuss the differences between latitude and longitude. Explain why determining longitude is so much more difficult than determining latitude. Use examples from *Longitude* to support your response.

13. How important was the invention of John Harrison's clock? Did it change the course of history, and if so, how? Explain your answer in an essay. Use specific examples from *Longitude* to support your response.

14. **Thinking About the Big Question: What kind of knowledge changes our lives?** In an essay, reflect on the changes brought about by the invention of an accurate maritime clock. What impact did this clock—and the knowledge it provided to sailors—have on the art and science of sailing? How did it change the lives not only of navigators but also of people around the world? Provide examples from *Longitude* to support your points.

Oral Response

15. Go back to question 4, 6, or 9 or to the question your teacher assigns you. Take a few minutes to expand your answer and prepare an oral response. Find additional details in *Longitude* that support your points. If necessary, make notes to guide your oral response.

Name _____ Date _____

from **Longitude** by Dava Sobel
Selection Test A

Critical Reading *Identify the letter of the choice that best answers the question.*

____ 1. Why is this excerpt from *Longitude* an expository essay?
   A. because it informs readers
   B. because it entertains readers
   C. because it contains the author's special memories
   D. because it tries to persuade readers to do something

____ 2. Sobel states that Ptolemy never traveled the world. How, then, did he make his maps?
   A. He relied on travelers' reports.
   B. He copied previous mapmakers' work.
   C. He guessed at how the world looked based on myths and legends.
   D. He frequently had vivid dreams about maps and drew them when he awoke.

____ 3. According to Sobel, what is the prime meridian?
   A. the place where the sun, moon, and planets pass almost directly overhead
   B. the northern boundary of the sun's apparent motion over the course of a year
   C. the southern boundary of the sun's apparent motion over the course of a year
   D. the zero-degree line of longitude and the starting line of reference for longitude

____ 4. How did the great captains of the Age of Exploration find their way?
   A. They used Ptolemy's maps and charts.
   B. They sailed in a straight line along the Equator.
   C. They wandered willy-nilly and got lost all the time.
   D. They used Harrison's clocks to help them determine longitude.

____ 5. Sobel establishes the rule that exact knowledge of the hour in two places at once is necessary to navigate with accuracy. However, due to mechanical problems, it was impossible to know the exact time on board ships up to and including the use of pendulum clocks. Therefore, all captains in the Age of Exploration must have spent a great deal of time lost at sea. What kind of reasoning leads Sobel to reach this conclusion?
   A. inductive
   B. deductive
   C. instinctive
   D. illogical

Name _____ Date _____

6. Sobel lists several facts about Harrison's clock. She states that it was made of materials that did not rust or wear down; its parts were made of different metals that made up for changes in motion and temperature; and it kept accurate time on board ships. She states earlier in the essay that an accurate clock is all that was needed to solve the problem of longitude. Using inductive reasoning, what conclusion is Sobel able to draw?
A. that Harrison's clock solved the problem of measuring longitude
B. that Harrison's clock was still not as accurate as pendulum clocks
C. that Harrison's clock was too expensive for ordinary sailors to afford
D. that Harrison's clock was amazing, but it failed to solve the problem of longitude

7. Why were some people against John Harrison claiming the prize for solving the problem of longitude?
A. Harrison failed to prove how his clock would solve the problem of longitude.
B. They thought his clock would not remain accurate once it was aboard a ship.
C. Someone else claimed that he had invented an accurate clock before Harrison did.
D. They wanted an astronomical solution and did not want the prize to go to a watchmaker.

8. How did the commissioners in charge of awarding the longitude prize try to keep Harrison from getting the prize?
A. They sabotaged Harrison's clock.
B. They spread untrue rumors about him.
C. They changed the rules of the contest.
D. They persuaded the king to withdraw the prize.

9. What is the main idea of this excerpt from *Longitude*?
A. John Harrison invented a clock that could keep accurate time on a ship.
B. Ptolemy was one of the first people to use lines of latitude and longitude.
C. Early navigators struggled with the problem of finding a way to determine longitude.
D. The author remembers owning a small wire ball that reminded her of a globe of Earth.

10. Which detail most directly supports the main idea of this excerpt from *Longitude*?
A. Latitude is easy to determine for any sailor worth his salt.
B. John Harrison was not able to claim his prize for 40 years.
C. Sobel remembers seeing a statue of Atlas holding Earth when she was a child.
D. The world's greatest minds tried for centuries to find a way to determine longitude.

Vocabulary and Grammar

___ 11. Stainless steel is _____ to rust.
   A. configuration
   B. derived
   C. impervious
   D. penetrable

___ 12. Which of the following is the best example of a *configuration*?
   A. the effects of frequent exercise
   B. leaves that have fallen from a tree
   C. desks arranged in rows in a classroom
   D. the grades of a student who studies well

___ 13. What is the direct object in the following sentence from the passage?
   The Equator marked the zero-degree parallel of latitude for Ptolemy.
   A. Equator
   B. marked
   C. parallel
   D. Ptolemy

Essay

14. In an essay, summarize the excerpt from *Longitude.* Begin by stating the main idea. Then, tell the most important facts or examples that support this idea.

15. In an essay, explain why determining longitude is so much more difficult than determining latitude. Then, explain why it was so important during the Age of Exploration to solve the problem of determining longitude at sea. Use details from the *Longitude* excerpt to support your essay.

16. **Thinking About the Big Question: What kind of knowledge changes our lives?**
   In an essay, explain how the invention of an accurate maritime clock changed people's lives. Provide at least three examples from *Longitude* to support your points.

Name _____ Date _____

from **Longitude** by Dava Sobel
Selection Test B

Critical Reading *Identify the letter of the choice that best completes the statement or answers the question.*

____ 1. Why is this excerpt from *Longitude* an expository essay?
   A. because it tries to persuade readers to feel sorry for John Harrison
   B. because it entertains readers with fictional accounts of sea captains
   C. because it informs readers about interesting and important historical events
   D. because it contains the author's memories of a very special time in her life

____ 2. Sobel states that Ptolemy "had only an armchair appreciation of the wider world." What does she mean?
   A. He knew a great deal about furniture styles from around the world.
   B. He feared that he would melt from high heat if he traveled below the Equator.
   C. He never explored the world himself; he relied instead on travelers' reports to make his maps.
   D. He could think clearly about his discoveries only when he was at home, relaxing in his favorite chair.

____ 3. According to Sobel, how did Ptolemy know where to place the Equator, the zero-degree parallel of latitude?
   A. All the lines of longitude come together at the Equator.
   B. The Fortunate Islands were an important trading center.
   C. The location of the Equator had been known since ancient times.
   D. The sun, moon, and planets pass almost directly overhead at the Equator.

____ 4. Sobel states that accurate timekeeping is necessary to determine longitude. She explains that early clocks slowed down, sped up, or stopped on board ships. She goes on to say that sea captains got lost and countless sailors died during the Age of Discovery. Using deductive reasoning, what conclusion can you draw from this information?
   A. The lack of accurate clocks was dangerous to sailors.
   B. The prime meridian must have been placed incorrectly.
   C. There was an astronomical solution to the problem of longitude.
   D. The kings of England and France offered a reward for a solution.

____ 5. According to Sobel, how did the lack of a practical method of determining longitude affect the great captains of the Age of Exploration?
   A. Every one of them became lost at sea, and their discoveries were accidental.
   B. It did not greatly affect them because they had excellent charts and compasses.
   C. They were always late to arrive at their destinations because their clocks were not accurate.
   D. They could only sail in straight lines along the parallels of latitude because they feared getting lost.

_____ 6. Why did the governments of great seafaring nations offer large rewards for a workable solution to the problem of longitude?
   A. They all wanted to have the smartest person in the world in their countries.
   B. It amused the kings of Europe to have a friendly competition over longitude.
   C. They were losing ships, men, and trade due to the lack of ability to navigate accurately.
   D. They were tired of the bickering among scientists and inventors who were working on it.

_____ 7. What was the Reverend Nevil Maskelyne's role in the quest to solve the problem of determining longitude?
   A. He represented the church's opposition to exploring the world.
   B. He opposed John Harrison's claim to the prize money for solving it.
   C. He was the first to find an astronomical method of determining longitude.
   D. He offered a huge monetary reward to anyone who could solve the problem.

_____ 8. Sobel lists several facts about Harrison's clock. She states that it was made of materials that did not rust or create friction; its parts were made of different metals that compensated for changes in motion and temperature; and it kept accurate time on board ships. Since she has already established that an accurate clock was needed to solve the problem of longitude, Sobel is able to draw the conclusion that Harrison did indeed solve the problem. What kind of reasoning did Sobel use to reach this conclusion?
   A. inductive   C. instinctive
   B. deductive   D. illogical

_____ 9. What is the main idea of this excerpt from *Longitude*?
   A. Ptolemy was one of the first cartographers to establish lines of latitude and longitude on his maps.
   B. John Harrison invented an accurate clock, but his accomplishment was not immediately acknowledged.
   C. Early navigators struggled with the problem of finding an accurate way to determine longitude at sea.
   D. The author remembers being carried on her father's shoulders and seeing a statue of Atlas holding the globe.

_____ 10. Which of the following details does NOT directly support the main idea of this excerpt from *Longitude*?
   A. As a child, Sobel had a collapsible wire ball that she thought resembled a tiny globe of Earth.
   B. Latitude is fixed by the laws of nature, but accurate clocks are needed to determine longitude.
   C. Renowned astronomers tried for many years to find a solution to the problem of measuring longitude.
   D. The governments of great maritime nations offered rewards to anyone who could solve the problem of longitude.

_____ 11. Which of the following is the best statement of the main idea of the section about John Harrison's invention in the *Longitude* excerpt?
   A. Harrison's clock was friction-free and did not rust.
   B. King George III took an aging Harrison under his wing.
   C. Harrison was a mechanical genius who devoted his life to the quest for portable precision timekeeping.
   D. Harrison invented an accurate clock, but his accomplishment was not acknowledged for several decades.

Vocabulary and Grammar

_____ 12. In which of the following sentences is the word *impervious* used correctly?
   A. Stainless steel is impervious to rust.
   B. Our new towels are impervious to water.
   C. She smiled warmly at me in an impervious way.
   D. The impervious little boy giggled and scampered away.

_____ 13. Which of the following is the best synonym for the word *derived*?
   A. explored   C. exited
   B. insulted   D. deduced

_____ 14. Which of the following sentences contains an indirect object?
   A. The prime meridian runs through London.
   B. John Harrison invented an accurate clock.
   C. The commissioners eventually gave Harrison the prize.
   D. Ptolemy made 27 maps that showed lines of latitude and longitude.

_____ 15. What is the direct object in the following sentence from the passage?
   Lines of latitude and longitude began crisscrossing our worldview in ancient times, at least three centuries before the birth of Christ.
   A. Lines   C. worldview
   B. crisscrossing   D. times

Essay

16. In an essay, discuss the differences between latitude and longitude. Explain why determining longitude is so much more difficult than determining latitude. Use examples from the *Longitude* excerpt to support your essay.

17. In an essay, summarize the main ideas and most important supporting details of the excerpt from *Longitude.* Then, refer to your summary to state and support your opinion on why this episode in history is important.

18. In an essay, evaluate the importance of John Harrison's clock as an invention that changed the course of history. How important is it compared to other historic inventions, such as the printing press, the sewing machine, or the personal computer? How might the world have been different without Harrison's clock?

19. **Thinking About the Big Question: What kind of knowledge changes our lives?** In an essay, reflect on the changes brought about by the invention of an accurate maritime clock. What impact did this clock—and the knowledge it provided to sailors—have on the art and science of sailing? How did it change the lives not only of navigators, but also of people around the world? Provide examples from *Longitude* to support your points.

Study these words from "The Sun Parlor." Then, apply your knowledge to the activities that follow.

Word List A

appointed [uh POYN tid] *v.* having agreed or settled upon
  On the day <u>appointed</u> for the class trip, I was ill and could not go.

energy [EN er jee] *n.* vitality
  The athletes were filled with vigor and <u>energy</u> on the day of the big game.

mingling [MING guh ling] *v.* mixing with
  The sound of the creek <u>mingling</u> with the bird songs was pretty.

premises [PREM is ez] *n.* a building or a section of a building
  Lab workers need special clearance to enter the secure area of the <u>premises</u>.

referred [ri FERD] *v.* to make reference to; to mention
  After their feud, the father never <u>referred</u> to his son again in public.

sentiments [SEN tuh ments] *n.* thoughts or opinions
  The politician's speech made her <u>sentiments</u> about the proposal very clear.

separation [sep uh RAY shuhn] *n.* being apart
  The child's first <u>separation</u> from his parents came when he went to camp.

smudges [SMUHJ iz] *n.* a dirty mark, blotch, or smear
  After finger painting, the toddler left <u>smudges</u> on the wall.

Word List B

abnormal [ab NAWR muhl] *adj.* unusual or out of the ordinary
  It was <u>abnormal</u> to see frost on the ground on a July morning.

babysitter [bay bee SIT er] *n.* someone who tends to children
  A <u>babysitter</u> watched the children while their parents were at the movies.

cajoling [kuh JOH ling] *v.* trying to persuade someone gently
  She tried <u>cajoling</u> and then begging her mother to buy her some candy.

diligence [DIL i juhns] *n.* hard work and persistent effort
  The student's <u>diligence</u> paid off when he received an A on his test.

pap [pap] *n.* soft, semi-liquid food, usually for babies or sick people
  We tried feeding the baby some <u>pap</u>, but she spit it right up again.

subconscious [sub KAHN shuhs] *n.* a deep, hidden part of the mind
  Her <u>subconscious</u> memory of the incident emerged in her dream that night.

subordinate [suh BAWR din it] *adj.* beneath; secondary
  Basketball must be <u>subordinate</u> to homework in your daily schedule.

uncounted [un KOWN tid] *adj.* countless; too many to name
  Tim's grades slipped as he spent <u>uncounted</u> hours playing video games.

Name _____   Date _____

Vocabulary Warm-up Exercises

Exercise A *Fill in each blank in the paragraph with an appropriate word from Word List A.*
Use each word only once.

The day [1] _____ for the wedding had finally arrived. All the
[2] _____ spent in planning had paid off. The banquet room and the
surrounding [3] _____ were stylish and elegant. The sounds of cocktail
music were heard [4] _____ with the guests' conversations. When the
bride's cousin commented that this was the most beautiful wedding reception she had
ever seen, everyone agreed with her [5] _____. The bride was thrilled
when she [6] _____ to the groom as "my husband" for the first time.
When they kissed after cutting the cake, he got [7] _____ of frosting on
his cheek. From that day forward, they would experience a [8] _____
from their parents, but that loss was worth the gain of starting a new life together.

Exercise B *Write a complete sentence to answer each question. For each item, use a word*
from Word List B to replace each underlined word or group of words without changing its
meaning.

Example: What is something you have spent <u>innumerable</u> hours trying to achieve?
I have spent <u>uncounted</u> hours trying to get high marks in school.

1. When was the last time you tried <u>coaxing</u> someone to get what you wanted?
   _____

2. Do you think dreams come from <u>the subliminal part of your brain</u>?
   _____

3. Can you name a time when you have worked with special <u>attentiveness</u>?
   _____

4. Have you ever had an illness that seemed <u>unusual</u> to you?
   _____

5. Why do you think it is important to feed babies <u>pureed food</u>?
   _____

6. Has anyone ever made you feel <u>secondary</u> to his or her own goals?
   _____

7. Did you ever have a <u>boy or girl hired to watch you</u> whom you really liked?
   _____

Name _____ Date _____

Read the following passage. Pay special attention to the underlined words. Then, read it again, and complete the activities. Use a separate sheet of paper for your written answers.

The Harlem Renaissance was a wonderful period in the American arts. During the 1920s and '30s, many African Americans moved north from southern states, searching for better opportunities. Though the separation from family and friends must have been difficult, it was an exciting time.

Certain sections of northern cities became home to large groups of African Americans. In New York City, Harlem was that section. Harlem became a center of energy and vitality. Some great African American writers got their start during this period, including Langston Hughes, Zora Neale Hurston, W.E.B. Du Bois, and Dorothy West. These writers supported one another's efforts to write credibly about the African American experience. They believed that the arts were important for African Americans, and they acted on those sentiments.

Harlem was not just a home for young writers. Musicians like Duke Ellington were flourishing, their jazzy sounds mingling in the streets with the popular music of the day. Artists like Aaron Douglas and Romare Bearden were also hard at work.

Some who lived through the period did not necessarily realize that it was a "renaissance." They were poor and sometimes had to give "rent parties" to pay their landlords.

On the night appointed for the party, guests would pay to come in. The hosts usually moved furniture and rolled up carpets, but soil and smudges came along with the rent money. There usually was a piano player on the premises: famous musicians like Fats Waller and James P. Johnson played regularly at these affairs.

Some famous writers of the period, like Langston Hughes and Claude McKay, wrote fondly of rent parties. Other intellectuals, like W.E.B. Du Bois, never referred to them in their works. They thought that rent parties, and the dire economic straits that prompted them, reflected poorly on the black community.

1. Underline the phrase that tells from whom some African Americans who moved north experienced separation. Then, explain what *separation* means.

2. Circle the word with a meaning similar to energy. Then, use *energy* in a sentence.

3. Underline the phrase that tells which sentiments the writers of the Harlem Renaissance acted upon. Explain what *sentiments* are.

4. Circle the two sounds that were mingling in the streets. Write about the sounds you hear *mingling* in your home while you get ready for school.

5. Circle the word that tells what the night was appointed for. Then, tell what *appointed* means.

6. Explain why smudges would come with the money at the rent parties.

7. Circle the words that tell who was on the premises to provide music. Then, tell what *premises* are.

8. Underline the sentence that tells why certain African American intellectuals never referred to rent parties in their stories, poems, or essays. Tell what *referred* means.

Name _____ Date _____

"The Sun Parlor" by Dorothy West
Reading Warm-up B

Read the following passage. Pay special attention to the underlined words. Then, read it again, and complete the activities. Use a separate sheet of paper for your written answers.

When my Aunt Miranda became ill, we children were at a loss as to what to do. We tried to carry on as usual, but that became more difficult as time went on. Because it was on the first floor of the house, my mother set up our playroom as a sickroom for her sister. At first, it did not seem at all <u>abnormal</u> or out of the ordinary to grab our toys while we visited with our favorite aunt. As Aunt Miranda became sicker, my mother spent much time <u>cajoling</u> and then pleading with us to play elsewhere.

Because I was only about eight years old at the time, I did not realize the seriousness of the situation. Oh, perhaps in my <u>subconscious</u>, I could sense my mother's fears. Most of the time, however, I was just aware that our favorite place to play was off-limits, and our favorite aunt was out of our reach.

My father spent <u>uncounted</u> hours with us, trying to distract us from Miranda's illness. We appreciated his efforts and the remarkable <u>diligence</u> with which he approached our play. He invented lively projects, like building a double-decker tree house. He would also take us to any fairs and carnivals that were nearby.

Eventually, even Dad was called away to the sickroom to stand watch. Then, we were left with a disinterested <u>babysitter</u>. We seemed to be <u>subordinate</u> to her homework and her friends, and we began to feel lonelier and more scared.

One night, after months of being fed nothing but <u>pap</u>, Aunt Miranda felt ready to try a real meal. When she did, the effect was incredible. After a few bites of chicken and potatoes, Aunt Miranda smiled. After a few more bites, she asked to get up and walk. The months of rest had done their work. Our playroom and, more importantly, our aunt were ours again.

1. Underline the phrase that means close to the same thing as <u>abnormal</u>. Then, use *abnormal* in a sentence.

2. Write about a time when someone tried <u>cajoling</u> to get his or her way.

3. Underline the phrase that tells what the narrator sensed in his or her <u>subconscious</u>. Then, tell what *subconscious* means.

4. Write a sentence about something that someone in your family has spent <u>uncounted</u> hours doing.

5. Describe how an adult who approached play with <u>diligence</u> might behave.

6. Underline the word that describes the <u>babysitter</u> in this passage. Write about a *babysitter* who you know.

7. Describe a babysitter who makes a child's needs <u>subordinate</u> to his or her friends and homework.

8. Circle the words that according to the passage are the opposite of <u>pap</u>. Name two foods that could be served as *pap*.

Name _____ Date _____

"The Sun Parlor" by Dorothy West
Writing About the Big Question

What kind of knowledge changes our lives?

Big Question Vocabulary

adapt   awareness   empathy   enlighten   evolve
growth   history   ignorance   influence   insight
modified   question   reflect   revise   understanding

A. *Use one or more words from the list above to complete each sentence.*

1. Sometimes it takes years to develop _____ into our actions and to understand why we behaved the way we did.

2. Our self-interest can _____ how we treat others.

3. After the death of a beloved family member, people often _____ on their relationship with that person.

B. *Follow the directions in responding to each of the items below.*

1. List two different times that you acquired important self-knowledge.

_____

_____

2. Choose one piece of knowledge you listed and explain whether it changed your life. Use at least two of the Big Question vocabulary words.

_____

_____

C. *Complete the sentence below. Then, write a short paragraph in which you connect this experience to the big question.*

When you gain insight through your mistreatment of others, you often feel

_____

_____

_____

"The Sun Parlor" by Dorothy West
Literary Analysis: Reflective Essay

A **reflective essay** is a brief nonfiction work in which a writer presents the experiences that shaped or inspired his or her thoughts on a topic. In a reflective essay, a writer draws on an event, a time period, or an idea from his or her own life and experience. The writer weaves a connection between personal experience and a point of general interest, such as a lesson about life. The writer's reflections focus on a specific object, scene, occasion, place, or idea.

Dorothy West shares a personal experience and its meaning in her reflective essay "The Sun Parlor." West's unique perceptions and understanding of her own experience lead her to create a new experience for her readers. It is a writer's individual perspective that makes reflective writing engaging and fresh, even when the topic is a familiar one.

DIRECTIONS: *Refer to "The Sun Parlor" to answer the following questions.*

1. What lesson about life does West wish to share with her readers in "The Sun Parlor"?

   _____

   _____

   _____

2. What event does West say she regrets? Why do you think this event stayed in her mind for so many years?

   _____

   _____

   _____

3. What is unique about the way West shares the events of "The Sun Parlor" with her readers?

   _____

   _____

   _____

4. At the end of the essay, West asks Sis if her mother ever let her play in the sun parlor when West was not there. However, she does not want to hear the answer and states that it is enough for her that Sis listened. Why do you think West feels this way? How would you feel in the same situation?

   _____

   _____

   _____

   _____

Name _____ Date _____

"**The Sun Parlor**" by Dorothy West
Reading: Ask Questions to Analyze Main Ideas and Supporting Details

To fully understand an essay, you must **analyze main ideas and supporting details.** To do this, note each main point the writer makes. Then, identify the ideas or facts that explain or illustrate it. To help you analyze, **ask questions** as you read. Ask yourself what the topic of the passage is, what main point is being made, and which details support the point.

A. DIRECTIONS: *Ask yourself the following questions as you read "The Sun Parlor." Then, record your answers on the lines below each question.*

1. What is the topic of the essay?

   _____

   _____

2. What is the main point being made?

   _____

   _____

3. Which details support this point?

   _____

   _____

   _____

   _____

   _____

B. DIRECTIONS: *On the following lines, summarize "The Sun Parlor." Use your answers to the previous questions to help you write your summary.*

   _____

   _____

   _____

   _____

   _____

   _____

   _____

   _____

"The Sun Parlor" by Dorothy West
Vocabulary Builder

Word List

cajoling   convalesce   lavished   rejuvenation   subordinate   succinct

A. DIRECTIONS: *Think about the meaning of the italicized word in each item below. Then, answer the question and explain your answer.*

1. If the director of a school play *lavished* praise on his cast and crew after opening night, did the performance go well or did it go poorly?

   _____

   _____

2. Is a coach *subordinate* to his team?

   _____

   _____

3. Would having an argument with your best friend bring a sense of *rejuvenation*?

   _____

   _____

4. Which person would be more likely to experience *cajoling* in her job: an actress or a firefighter?

   _____

   _____

5. If a family member must *convalesce* for a month after being ill, did she have a severe case of the flu or a mild cold?

   _____

   _____

6. If you gave a *succinct* answer to your father, were you speaking for a long time or did you say just a few words?

   _____

   _____

B. WORD STUDY: The **Latin prefix suc-** means "under" or "less or lower than." Answer each of the following questions using one of these words containing *suc-*: *succor, succumb, successor.*

1. Why would a person give *succor* to someone who was hurt?

2. What will you be doing if you *succumb* to the temptation of chocolate cake?

3. Why might the *successor* to the team captain be unsure of herself?

"The Sun Parlor" by Dorothy West
Enrichment: Studying Families

The family is the basic social unit of most cultures. Family members are the first ones to teach children how to behave and what to believe. In her essay "The Sun Parlor," Dorothy West reflects upon the family's role in shaping children's sense of self-worth.

An anthropologist is a scientist who studies human cultures. One way anthropologists find out what they want to know about a modern culture is to conduct surveys. To do this, they ask many kinds of people questions about their lives. Imagine that you are an anthropologist studying families in the United States today. Conduct a survey to learn more about modern families.

DIRECTIONS: *Ask several people questions such as*: How do you define family? How do you think American families are changing? What role does your family play in your life? What roles should families play in children's lives? *Use the chart below to help you record the questions you ask and the answers you receive. Then, give a brief oral report summarizing your findings for your class.*

Respondent's Name	Question 1:	Question 2:	Question 3:

Name _____ Date _____

"The Sun Parlor" by Dorothy West
Open-Book Test

Short Answer *Write your responses to the questions in this section on the lines provided.*

1. A reflective essay is a brief nonfiction work that reflects on a specific object, scene, place, or idea. Indicate which of these elements are present in "The Sun Parlor" by checking the appropriate boxes in the chart. Then, on the line below, identify two of the elements as they appear in the story.

	Elements of Reflective Essays Present in "The Sun Parlor"
Object	
Scene	
Place	
Idea	

_____

2. Dorothy West begins "The Sun Parlor" with the words, "This is a tale with a moral." What is one of the main morals, or lessons about life, that the story suggests?

_____
_____
_____

3. According to "The Sun Parlor," how does West know that she lives in a beautiful house when she is a child?

_____
_____

4. In "The Sun Parlor," West writes of Sis, "The summer she was eight was the one time I forgot that a child is not subordinate to a house." In what way does West forget this?

_____
_____

5. In "The Sun Parlor," after West tells Sis not to play in the sun parlor, she worries about the effect this will have on Sis. Why is West worried?

_____
_____

6. In "The Sun Parlor," why does the family turn the sun parlor into a special room for West's aunt?

_____

_____

7. During her stay in the sun parlor, the aunt feels afraid and does not sleep well. What do these details suggest is a main idea of "The Sun Parlor"?

_____

_____

_____

8. In the last scene of "The Sun Parlor," why is West reluctant to hear Sis's answer to her question about whether West's mother ever let Sis play in the sun parlor?

_____

_____

_____

9. West writes that her essay is "about houses and children." According to the main idea of the essay, which is *subordinate* to which—houses to children or children to houses? Explain your answer, based on the meaning of *subordinate* in "The Sun Parlor."

_____

_____

10. If you need *cajoling* to do something, are you eager or reluctant to do it? Explain your answer, based on the meaning of *cajoling* in "The Sun Parlor."

_____

_____

Unit 3 Resources: Types of Nonfiction
72

Essay

Write an extended response to the question of your choice or to the question or questions your teacher assigns you.

11. Choose one section of "The Sun Parlor," such as West's memories of her childhood home or her aunt's illness. Then, in an essay, state the main idea of that part of the story. Finally, provide the details that support that idea.

12. A reflective essay like "The Sun Parlor" often makes a connection between personal experiences and a lesson about life. In an essay, explain what lesson West is trying to teach. Why do you think she chose to write a reflective essay to teach this lesson?

13. A key episode of "The Sun Parlor" is West's decision to bar Sis from playing in the parlor. How do you think Sis feels about that decision? How do you think she would have answered West's question at the end of the essay? Develop your response in an essay supported by details from the selection.

14. **Thinking About the Big Question: What kind of knowledge changes our lives?** In an essay, reflect on the knowledge that West gains when she witnesses Sis's great disappointment at not being allowed to play in the sun parlor. How does this knowledge change West, both at the time it happens and later in life? Provide examples from "The Sun Parlor" to support your response.

Oral Response

15. Go back to question 3, 5, or 8 or to the question your teacher assigns you. Take a few minutes to expand your answer and prepare an oral response. Find additional details in "The Sun Parlor" that support your points. If necessary, make notes to guide your oral response.

Name _____ Date _____

"The Sun Parlor" by Dorothy West
Selection Test A

Critical Reading *Identify the letter of the choice that best answers the question.*

_____ 1. What is the focus of the reflective essay "The Sun Parlor"?
   A. the life of a little girl named Sis
   B. a special room in the author's home
   C. the illness of the author's favorite aunt
   D. the importance of having a beautiful home

_____ 2. At the beginning of "The Sun Parlor," West states that this "is a tale with a moral." What is the moral, or lesson, she teaches in this essay?
   A. It is important to know that people listen.
   B. People cannot stop the process of aging.
   C. One must have a beautifully decorated home to impress one's neighbors.
   D. Respect for children is more important than pride in one's home or belongings.

_____ 3. How do visitors react to West's childhood home?
   A. They think it feels very sad.
   B. They think it is quite beautiful.
   C. They are horrified at the awful mess.
   D. They feel it must be a child's paradise.

_____ 4. Each section of "The Sun Parlor" has a main idea. What is the main point of the section about West's childhood home?
   A. The author recalls that there were many visitors to her childhood home.
   B. A house belongs to the children who live there, not the other way around.
   C. West and her siblings were terrified that their mother would throw them out.
   D. Children can destroy a home and its contents if they are allowed to run loose.

_____ 5. In "The Sun Parlor," when does Sis visit the family's cottage in the Highlands of Oak Bluffs?
   A. when she becomes very ill
   B. just once, at Christmastime
   C. during her summer breaks from school
   D. only after she becomes a mother herself

____ 6. How does Sis react to the sun parlor when she first sees it?

A. She runs in excitedly to bounce on the furniture.

B. She runs right past it on her way to play outside.

C. She says that it is the most beautiful room she has ever seen.

D. She says that it looks like a stuffy and boring room for grown-ups.

____ 7. Why does West tell Sis not to play in the sun parlor?

A. because she had just painted it

B. because it is a frightening place

C. because Sis would rather play outside

D. because a sick aunt is using the room

____ 8. Why does West's aunt dislike staying in the sun parlor?

A. It depresses her because someone died there.

B. She cannot sleep because the sun is so bright.

C. She feels separated from the rest of the family.

D. It is difficult to climb the stairs to get there.

____ 9. How does West feel about the sun parlor after her aunt passes away?

A. It makes her sad, so she closes it up.

B. She becomes angry every time she sees it.

C. It reminds her of happy memories of her aunt.

D. She still does not want Sis to play in it.

____ 10. What effect does West fear her actions will have on Sis?

A. Sis will never want to return to the cottage.

B. Sis might sneak into the room and destroy it.

C. Sis will think that West is a stuffy, selfish, and cruel woman.

D. Sis might think that rooms are more important than children.

____ 11. Which of the following details most clearly supports the main idea of "The Sun Parlor"?

A. Sis is one of West's mother's favorite children.

B. West regrets not letting Sis play in the sun parlor.

C. West's generation becomes the oldest in the family.

D. West's aunt keeps a secret from the rest of the family.

____ 12. What makes "The Sun Parlor" a reflective essay?

    A. It tries to persuade readers to take action.

    B. Its purpose is to inform readers about a topic.

    C. It focuses on the writer's personal experiences.

    D. It is a fictional story meant to entertain readers.

Vocabulary and Grammar

____ 13. Which of the following is an example of a person who is *subordinate* to others?

    A. a new military recruit

    B. the owner of a retail store

    C. the principal of a high school

    D. an emergency room doctor

____ 14. Which of the following is the best antonym for the word *lavished*?

    A. pampered

    B. mistreated

    C. cured

    D. withheld

____ 15. Which of the following sentences contains a predicate adjective?

    A. West painted the room.

    B. The sun parlor is special.

    C. It has seven large windows.

    D. Sis wants to play in the room.

Essay

16. Have you ever had a room or a possession of which you were particularly proud? How did you feel about letting others use it? In an essay, explain why West felt protective of her sun parlor. Then state whether you would have forbidden Sis from playing in the sun parlor. Why or why not?

17. Choose one of the events West describes in "The Sun Parlor," such as her memories of her childhood home or her aunt's illness. Then, in an essay, state the main idea and supporting details of the event. Finally, explain what general truth about families the event shows.

18. **Thinking About the Big Question: What kind of knowledge changes our lives?** In "The Sun Parlor," Dorothy West sees Sis's great disappointment at not being allowed to play in the parlor. What lesson does West learn from this incident? Answer this question in a brief essay. Provide examples from "The Sun Parlor" to support your response.

Name _____ Date _____

"**The Sun Parlor**" by Dorothy West
Selection Test B

Critical Reading *Identify the letter of the choice that best completes the statement or answers the question.*

____ 1. What makes "The Sun Parlor" a reflective essay?
  A. It entertains readers with an interesting fictional story about a young girl.
  B. It tries to persuade readers to take action on an issue of social importance.
  C. It includes the writer's personal experiences and what she learned from them.
  D. Its purpose is to inform readers about the facts and details of a particular topic.

____ 2. When she was a child, how did West know that she lived in a beautiful house?
  A. Her mother constantly bragged about how beautiful their house was.
  B. All her mother's friends said so and brought their other friends to see it.
  C. She was not allowed to touch anything for fear of making it less beautiful.
  D. West's friends seemed to be jealous of her house and belongings.

____ 3. How does West's mother respond when visitors ask her how she can let children run loose in such a beautiful house?
  A. She says that she does not mind if the children break a few things.
  B. She says that she intends to send the children away to protect the house.
  C. She says that the children are allowed only in certain areas of the house.
  D. She says that the house belongs to the children, not the other way around.

____ 4. How does Sis feel about the sun parlor when she first sees it?
  A. She loves it and wants to play in it.
  B. She is angry that West has changed it.
  C. She fears it because she senses its sadness.
  D. She finds its decor to be stuffy and unattractive.

____ 5. After West tells Sis not to play in the sun parlor, she worries about the effect this will have on Sis. What is West's concern?
  A. that Sis will think that West is a selfish and cruel woman
  B. that Sis will never learn to appreciate beautiful things
  C. that Sis will have learned that rooms are more important than children
  D. that Sis will sneak into the room and destroy it when West is not home

____ 6. Why does the family turn the sun parlor into a bedroom for West's favorite aunt?
  A. because the aunt loves the room and begs West to let her stay in it
  B. because the cottage is full and there are no more bedrooms available
  C. because the aunt is ill and cannot climb the stairs to the regular bedrooms
  D. because West is trying to persuade her aunt to live with her all year round

____ 7. What lesson is taught by the story of the aunt's stay in the sun parlor?
A. that paint and decorations can become outdated, but a room is still useful for those who live in it
B. that the mood of a room is set by how it is used, so it becomes a sad room instead of the joyful room Sis would have made it
C. that having children playing in the room would have ruined it for the aunt, who needs it more than the children do
D. that large windows and bright decor are totally unsuited to a sickroom for an ill and aging woman

____ 8. Why does West close up the sun parlor?
A. because she is leaving her cottage for the winter
B. because she feels guilty for never letting Sis play in it
C. because her mother tells her it is ugly and she should redecorate it
D. because she feels it is too sad a place after her aunt uses it as a sickroom

____ 9. Why is West hesitant to find out Sis's answer to her question about whether West's mother ever let Sis play in the sun parlor?
A. She does not want to have to punish Sis for going into the sun parlor.
B. She wants to go on believing that Sis did not really care about the sun parlor.
C. She would be angry if she found out that her mother had betrayed her trust.
D. She does not want to find out that she damaged Sis's sense of self-worth.

____ 10. Which of the following is the best statement of the main idea of "The Sun Parlor"?
A. West works hard to repaint and redecorate the sun parlor.
B. West's favorite aunt becomes ill and stays in the sun parlor.
C. West recalls the many visitors who came to admire her childhood home when she was younger.
D. West reflects on the summer when she put her pride in a room ahead of her respect for children.

____ 11. Which of the following details does NOT directly support the main idea of "The Sun Parlor"?
A. West regrets not letting her young relative, Sis, play in her sun parlor.
B. West wonders if her mother ever allowed Sis to play in the sun parlor.
C. As time passed, the author's generation became the oldest in the family.
D. There was no room in West's childhood home that the children could not enter.

____ 12. What lesson about life is West trying to convey in "The Sun Parlor"?
A. It is important to know that people listen.
B. People cannot stop the process of aging.
C. One must have a beautifully decorated home to impress one's neighbors.
D. Respect for children is more important than pride in one's home or belongings.

Vocabulary and Grammar

____ 13. Which of the following is the best antonym for the word *subordinate*?
A. superior
B. dependent
C. military
D. intelligent

_____ **14.** In which of the following sentences is the word *rejuvenation* used correctly?
A. He was *rejuvenation* when he won the game of one-on-one.
B. After taking a long nap, she felt a sense of *rejuvenation*.
C. He felt *rejuvenation* at the end of the day, so all he wanted to do was go to bed.
D. She felt her home was filled with *rejuvenation* because it was soothing and relaxing.

_____ **15.** Which of the following sentences contains a predicate nominative?
A. Dorothy West's sun parlor is a special room.
B. West painted the room with painstaking care.
C. It has seven large windows that let in the sunshine.
D. West does not want children to play in the sun parlor.

_____ **16.** Which of the following sentences contains a predicate adjective?
A. West's favorite aunt is her mother's younger sister.
B. Sis, one of West's young relatives, is energetic and fun-loving.
C. West asks Sis a question, but she does not want to hear the answer.
D. West remembers that she lived in a beautiful home when she was a child.

Essay

17. At the beginning of "The Sun Parlor," West states that this is "a tale with a moral." In an essay, explain what moral, or lesson, West wishes to convey. Why do you think she chose to write a reflective essay to teach this lesson? What other forms of writing might she have chosen? Was a reflective essay her best choice? Why or why not?

18. At the end of "The Sun Parlor," West says to Sis, "It's enough for me that you listened." Why is it important to West that Sis listen? Consider the lesson about children and houses that West learned from her mother. Also think about how, earlier in the essay, West says that she did not really hear what Sis said about the sun parlor.

19. Do you think Sis was deeply affected by West's forbidding her to play in the sun parlor? Use evidence from "The Sun Parlor" and your knowledge of human nature to help you write a short essay. Consider how you think Sis might have answered West's question at the end of the passage about whether her mother ever allowed Sis to play in the sun parlor when West was absent.

20. **Thinking About the Big Question: What kind of knowledge changes our lives?** In an essay, reflect on the knowledge that West gains when she witnesses Sis's great disappointment at not being allowed to play in the sun parlor. How does this knowledge change West, both at the time it happens and later in life? Provide examples from "The Sun Parlor" to support your response.

Vocabulary Warm-up Word Lists

Study these words from In Commemoration: One Million Volumes. *Then, apply your knowledge to the activities that follow.*

Word List A

aimlessly [AYM lis lee] *adv.* without a purpose or goal
The tourist wandered <u>aimlessly</u> through the museum.

budding [BUD ding] *adj.* beginning to show a talent; promising
The <u>budding</u> musicians took classes to improve their playing.

discourse [DIS kawrs] *n.* serious conversation about ideas
The doctors' <u>discourse</u> was so technical that I could barely follow it.

doze [dohz] *v.* to sleep lightly
I began to <u>doze</u> during a slow part of the film, but a loud sound woke me.

enroll [en ROHL] *v.* to register; to become a member
My mother decided to <u>enroll</u> in a pottery class at the community center.

participate [par TI suh payt] *v.* to take part in; to be involved
It is important that all team members <u>participate</u> equally in the project.

tattered [TAT erd] *adj.* torn; ragged; shredded
The pages of the old book were <u>tattered</u>, but its message was still fresh.

volumes [VAHL yoomz] *n.* one of the books of a set
That encyclopedia has twenty-three <u>volumes</u>.

Word List B

ample [AM puhl] *adj.* more than enough; sufficient
We have <u>ample</u> time to finish the project, but we need to use it wisely.

clarify [KLAIR i fy] *v.* to make easier to understand
My teacher's careful explanation helped to <u>clarify</u> the hard math problem.

exhilaration [eg zil uh RAY shuhn] *n.* overwhelming happiness or excitement
The roller coaster ride made me feel pure <u>exhilaration</u>.

haven [HAY vuhn] *n.* safe place; refuge
My favorite park is a quiet <u>haven</u> away from the noise of the city.

idealistic [eye dee uh LIS tik] *adj.* believing perfection is possible
Her <u>idealistic</u> views lead her to believe world peace is possible.

inspiration [in spuh RAY shuhn] *n.* something that sparks creativity
A small flower was the <u>inspiration</u> that led me to paint my room rose red.

labyrinth [LAB uh rinth] *v.* maze
We got lost in the <u>labyrinth</u> of hallways in the hospital's basement.

storehouse [STAWR hows] *n.* place where things are kept; warehouse
Fresh fruit is kept in a cool <u>storehouse</u> before it is shipped.

from In Commemoration: One Million Volumes by Rudolfo Anaya
Vocabulary Warm-up Exercises

Exercise A *Fill in each blank in the paragraph with an appropriate word from Word List A. Use each word only once.*

Jade decided to visit the City Museum because she was a [1] _____

historian. At first, she wandered [2] _____ down many confusing

hallways. Then, she stumbled upon some people talking in the museum library. Their

[3] _____ was about the best way to organize some of the library's

holdings. Jade decided to [4] _____ right away by offering to help.

Together, they arranged hundreds of [5] _____ in the museum's collec-

tion. Some of the books were so old that they were [6] _____ and worn.

By the end of the day, Jade felt a little worn out, too. On the bus home, she started to

[7] _____, but woke up just before her stop. The day had been so much

fun that she decided to [8] _____ in a class at the museum.

Exercise B *Decide whether each statement is true or false. Circle T or F. Then, explain your answers.*

1. A <u>haven</u> is a place that makes people feel nervous and afraid.
   T / F _____

2. A furniture <u>storehouse</u> is probably about the size of a kitchen table.
   T / F _____

3. An <u>idealistic</u> attitude is more positive than a pessimistic one.
   T / F _____

4. You would probably feel <u>exhilaration</u> if you met one of your heroes.
   T / F _____

5. Sources of <u>inspiration</u> for a painting could include a person, a song, or a mood.
   T / F _____

6. If a city has <u>ample</u> food, many people there are certain to starve.
   T / F _____

7. An office that feels like a <u>labyrinth</u> is very open and airy.
   T / F _____

8. The best way to <u>clarify</u> writing is always to use more words.
   T / F _____

from **In Commemoration: One Million Volumes** by Rudolfo Anaya
Reading Warm-up A

Read the following passage. Pay special attention to the underlined words. Then, read it again, and complete the activities. Use a separate sheet of paper for your written answers.

One rainy Saturday morning, Carlos could not think of an interesting way to spend the day. He was wandering <u>aimlessly</u> around the house, drifting from room to room.

"You need somewhere to go," said Grandfather, who was starting to <u>doze</u> but kept getting awakened by Carlos's bored pacing. He went into the attic, and brought down a book. It was old. The cover was <u>tattered</u> and worn. A few pages were held together by tape.

"A book can take you on many journeys," he said, handing the novel to Carlos. "This is one of my favorites. It tells about life during the Mexican Revolution." Carlos looked at it suspiciously, but after reading just a few pages, he was caught up in the story.

By dinnertime, Carlos had finished the novel and was begging his grandfather for more information about the author. His grandfather explained that the author had written at least eight other novels, as well as two <u>volumes</u> of poetry.

The next day, Carlos went to the library to feed his <u>budding</u> interest in Mexican literature. He found two other novels by the same writer and a book on Mexican history.

The next semester, Carlos decided to <u>enroll</u> in a class about Latin American culture. The teacher knew hundreds of fascinating stories, and Carlos loved to share them with his grandfather. Their <u>discourse</u> about Mexico had deepened. They shared information and ideas in long, serious discussions.

One day, Carlos brought the old novel to class to explain how he first became interested in Mexico. After school, Carlos woke his grandfather up from his afternoon nap.

"Our class has been asked to <u>participate</u> in an exchange program!" he shouted. "We're going to go to Mexico for one week!"

His grandfather laughed and tapped the old novel. "You see? A book really can take you on many journeys!"

1. Underline the words that describe how Carlos wandered <u>aimlessly</u>. Then, write a sentence about someone talking *aimlessly*.

2. Circle the word that tells who was starting to <u>doze</u>. Then, tell what *doze* means.

3. Circle a word that has a similar meaning to <u>tattered</u>. Then, describe an item of clothing you have seen that was *tattered*.

4. Circle the word that describes the text found in two <u>volumes</u>. Then, describe a place where you might find *volumes*.

5. Underline the words that describe something that is <u>budding</u>. Then, tell what *budding* means.

6. Circle the words that tell what Carlos decides to <u>enroll</u> in. Then, tell about something you would like to *enroll* in.

7. Underline a sentence that tells what happens in a <u>discourse</u>. Then, tell what *discourse* is.

8. Circle the words that tell what the class is going to <u>participate</u> in. Then, tell something that your class could *participate* in.

from **In Commemoration: One Million Volumes** by Rudolfo Anaya
Reading Warm-up B

Read the following passage. Pay special attention to the underlined words. Then, read it again, and complete the activities. Use a separate sheet of paper for your written answers.

A library can be a vast <u>storehouse</u> for knowledge, holding the wisdom of the ages on every topic. A library can be a doorway to new opportunities, providing people with the information they need to start new projects or careers. A library can also be a quiet <u>haven</u> away from noise and crowds—a safe place to explore a world of ideas. However, a library must be carefully organized in order to be useful. People cannot experience the <u>exhilaration</u> of discovering the perfect book if they do not know where it is. Without a clear order, a library can be a confusing <u>labyrinth</u>, a hopeless maze.

There are two common systems used to organize libraries: the Dewey Decimal Classification and the Library of Congress Classification.

The Dewey Decimal Classification was invented by Melvil Dewey in 1876. At that time, every library used a different classification system. Dewey wanted to create one standard system that would <u>clarify</u> the process of finding a book. His system includes ten main categories. Each category has a three-digit whole number. For example, the 500s include science and mathematics; the 800s include literature. An updated version of Dewey's system is used by many school and public libraries today.

The Library of Congress Classification was developed in 1897 by Herbert Putnam, an <u>idealistic</u> librarian who hoped to create a perfect system for organizing books. Putnam used the alphabet as a source of <u>inspiration</u> rather than decimals. Each book's location code begins with a letter of the alphabet, which stands for a general category. For example, literature is classified under N and science books are found under Q. Today, a modern version of Putnam's system is used by most university and research libraries.

Both of these classification systems are used by millions of people every year. They give <u>ample</u> assistance to all kinds of readers, giving plenty of help to students, researchers, and browsers.

1. Underline the words that describe how a library can be a <u>storehouse</u>. Then, name something else that could be kept in a **storehouse**.

2. Circle the words that have a similar meaning as <u>haven</u>. Then, describe a place that you might call a **haven**.

3. Underline the words that describe something that might cause <u>exhilaration</u>. Then, tell what **exhilaration** is.

4. Circle a word that is a synonym for <u>labyrinth</u>. Then, tell what a **labyrinth** looks like.

5. Underline the words that tell what the Dewey Decimal Classification can <u>clarify</u>. Then, tell how you might **clarify** a recipe you are giving to a friend.

6. Underline the words that tell why Putnam was <u>idealistic</u>. Then, tell what it means to be **idealistic**.

7. Circle the word that names the <u>inspiration</u> for the Library of Congress Classification system. Then, name something that has been an **inspiration** to you.

8. Circle a word that is close in meaning to <u>ample</u>. Then, describe something in your life that is **ample**.

Name _____ Date _____

from **In Commemoration: One Million Volumes** by Rudolfo Anaya
Writing About the Big Question

What kind of knowledge changes our lives?

Big Question Vocabulary

adapt	awareness	empathy	enlighten	evolve
growth	history	ignorance	influence	insight
modified	question	reflect	revise	understanding

A. *Use one or more words from the list above to complete each sentence.*

1. We start out as children who listen to stories, but we _____ into adults who read and sometimes write stories.

2. Reading can _____ people about subjects they never imagined.

3. _____ the importance of books is a necessary trait if you love libraries.

4. Thinking about new ideas that you may have discovered in books is one way to combat _____ .

B. *Follow the directions in responding to each of the items below.*

1. List two times when you read something that made a big impact on you.

   _____

   _____

2. Choose one experience you listed and explain whether it changed your life. Use at least two of the Big Question vocabulary words.

   _____

   _____

C. *Complete the sentence below. Then, write a short paragraph in which you connect this experience to the big question.*

For the author, acquiring information means that _____

   _____

   _____

   _____

Name _____ Date _____

from In Commemoration: One Million Volumes by Rudolfo A. Anaya
Literary Analysis: Reflective Essay

A **reflective essay** is a brief nonfiction work in which a writer presents the experiences that shaped or inspired his or her thoughts on a topic. In a reflective essay, a writer draws on an event, a time period, or an idea from his or her own life and experience. The writer weaves a connection between personal experience and a point of general interest, such as a lesson about life. The writer's reflections focus on a specific object, scene, occasion, place, or idea.

Rudolfo Anaya shares a personal experience and its meaning in the excerpt from *In Commemoration: One Million Volumes*. Anaya's unique perceptions and understanding of his own experience lead him to create a new experience for his readers. It is a writer's individual perspective that makes reflective writing engaging and fresh, even when the topic is a familiar one.

DIRECTIONS: *Refer to the excerpt from* In Commemoration: One Million Volumes *to answer the following questions.*

1. What lesson about life does Anaya wish to share with his readers?

_____

_____

_____

2. Why are libraries so important to Anaya?

_____

_____

_____

3. What is unique about the way Anaya shares the events of the excerpt from *In Commemoration: One Million Volumes* with his readers?

_____

_____

_____

4. Why does Anaya associate books and libraries with freedom? With what do you associate books and libraries? Why?

_____

_____

_____

_____

Name _____ Date _____

from **In Commemoration: One Million Volumes** by Rudolfo A. Anaya
Reading: Ask Questions to Analyze Main Ideas and Supporting Details

To fully understand an essay, you must **analyze main ideas and supporting details.** To do this, note each main point the writer makes. Then, identify the ideas or facts that explain or illustrate it. To help you analyze, **ask questions** as you read. Ask yourself what the topic of the passage is, what main point is being made, and which details support the point.

A. DIRECTIONS: *Ask yourself the following questions as you read the excerpt from* In Commemoration: One Million Volumes. *Then record your answers on the lines below each question.*

1. What is the topic of the excerpt?

   _____

   _____

2. What is the main point being made?

   _____

   _____

3. Which details support this point?

   _____

   _____

   _____

   _____

   _____

B. DIRECTIONS: *On the following lines, summarize the passage from* In Commemoration: One Million Volumes. *Use your answers to the previous questions to help you write your summary.*

   _____

   _____

   _____

   _____

   _____

   _____

   _____

   _____

   _____

Name _____ Date _____

from In Commemoration: One Million Volumes by Rudolfo A. Anaya
Vocabulary Builder

Word List

dilapidated enthralls infinite inherent paradox poignant

A. DIRECTIONS: *Think about the meaning of the italicized word in each item below. Then, answer the question and explain your answer.*

1. Is knowledge of important events in history something that could be *inherent*?

   _____

   _____

2. Would a *dilapidated* courthouse be more or less in need of repair than one that is not dilapidated?

   _____

   _____

3. If a movie *enthralls* the audience, is it likely to make money at the box office?

   _____

   _____

4. Which event would be more *poignant* for those involved: shopping for groceries or graduating from high school?

   _____

   _____

5. Can a library ever have an *infinite* number of books?

   _____

   _____

6. If an answer to a question is a *paradox*, is that answer logical and easy to understand?

   _____

   _____

B. WORD STUDY: The **Greek prefix *para-*** means "beside" or "beyond." Provide an explanation for your answer to each question containing a word with the prefix *para-*.

1. Will a *parasite* choose to live in isolation?

   _____

2. If you *paraphrase* a sentence, are you copying it word for word?

   _____

3. If you wanted to master a science experiment, would you follow or ignore a *paradigm* of that experiment?

   _____

Name _____ Date _____

from In Commemoration: One Million Volumes by Rudolfo A. Anaya
Enrichment: Improving a Library

DIRECTIONS: *How could your community's library be improved to make it more like the library that Anaya commemorates? Interview the librarians at a local library, asking for their "wish list." Then talk to people you know and ask how they would like to see the library improved. Compile a list of what you feel are the most worthwhile ideas, then prepare a proposal you might present to your town's governing body, including suggestions for how these changes might be funded. State your plan as persuasively as possible.*

Wish List:

Needed Improvements:

Proposal:

Name _____ Date _____

"The Sun Parlor" by Dorothy West

from In Commemoration: One Million Volumes by Rudolfo A. Anaya

Integrated Language Skills: Grammar

Subject Complements: Predicate Nominatives and Predicate Adjectives

Predicate nominatives and predicate adjectives are subject complements. They appear after a linking verb and tell something about the subject of the sentence. A **predicate nominative** is a noun or pronoun that appears with a linking verb and renames, identifies, or explains the subject of the sentence. A subject and a predicate nominative are two different words for the same person, place, or thing. The linking verb joins them and equates them. A **predicate adjective** is an adjective that appears with a linking verb and describes the subject of the sentence.

Examples: Dorothy West's special room is her sun parlor. (*Parlor* is a predicate nominative, which renames the subject, *room*.)

Books are fascinating to Rudolfo Anaya. (*Fascinating* is a predicate adjective, which describes the subject, *books*.)

A. PRACTICE: *The following sentences are based on "The Sun Parlor" or the excerpt from* In Commemoration: One Million Volumes. *Underline each predicate nominative or predicate adjective and write* PN *or* PA *on the line before each sentence.*

____ 1. Sis was a young girl who wanted to play in West's sun parlor.

____ 2. West seemed sad and regretful that she did not allow Sis to play in the room.

____ 3. The author and her brothers and sisters were obedient children.

____ 4. Libraries are Anaya's refuge.

____ 5. To Anaya, books are exciting and uplifting.

____ 6. Anaya, a writer, is an intelligent and thoughtful man.

B. Writing Application: *On the lines below, write a paragraph responding to either "The Sun Parlor" or the excerpt from* In Commemoration: One Million Volumes. *Use at least five subject complements in your paragraph. Underline each predicate nominative once and each predicate adjective twice.*

_____

_____

_____

_____

_____

_____

_____

_____

_____

Unit 3 Resources: Types of Nonfiction

Name _____ Date _____

Integrated Language Skills: Support for Writing a Memoir

Before writing your memoir, use the graphic organizer below to help you describe a room or building that has been meaningful to you in your life.

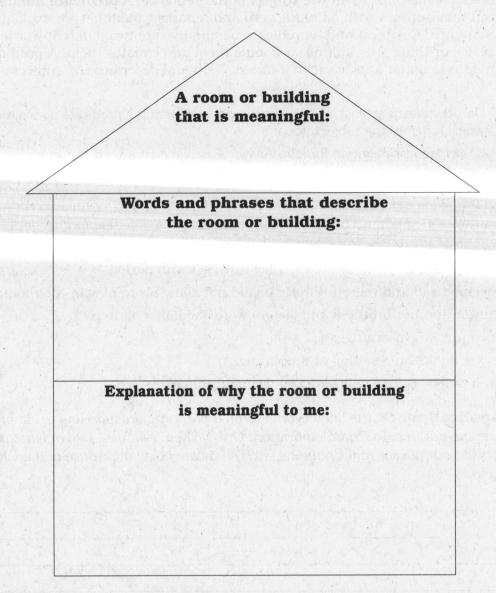

**A room or building
that is meaningful:**

**Words and phrases that describe
the room or building:**

**Explanation of why the room or building
is meaningful to me:**

Now, use your notes to write your memoir about a room or building that has meaning for you.

"The Sun Parlor" by Dorothy West

from **In Commemoration: One Million Volumes** by Rudolfo A. Anaya

Integrated Language Skills: Support for Extend Your Learning

Listening and Speaking: "The Sun Parlor"

Answer the following questions to help you describe a person who is interesting or important to you. Use your answers to help you prepare your oral recollection.

1. Who is someone you know who is interesting or important to you?

   _____

2. Why is this person interesting or important to you?

   _____

   _____

3. What are some details about this person that would help others see him or her the way you do?

   _____

   _____

   _____

4. What is one significant recollection you have of this person?

   _____

   _____

   _____

Listening and Speaking: *from* In Commemoration: One Million Volumes

Answer the following questions to help you describe an organization or institution with which you have been involved. Use your answers to help you prepare your oral recollection.

1. What organization or institution will you describe?

   _____

2. What is the purpose of the organization?

   _____

   _____

3. What are some details about this organization that will help others understand its spirit and its importance to individuals and the community?

   _____

   _____

4. What is one significant recollection you have of this organization?

   _____

   _____

Name _____ Date _____

from **"In Commemoration: One Million Volumes"** by Rudolfo A. Anaya
Open-Book Test

Short Answer *Write your responses to the questions in this section on the lines provided.*

1. A reflective essay is a brief nonfiction work in which a writer presents key experiences that have shaped him or her. In "In Commemoration: One Million Volumes," what are some of Rudolfo Anaya's key experiences? Fill in the graphic organizer. Then, on the line below, provide a summary of Anaya's key experiences.

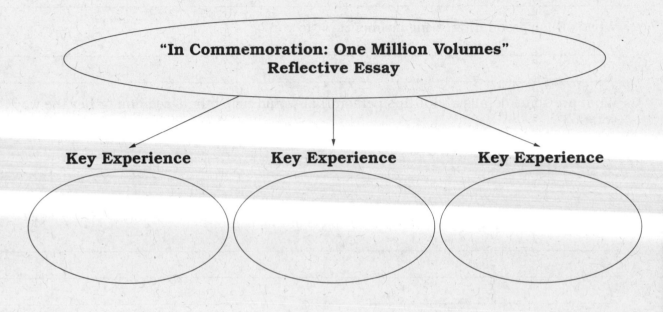

_____

2. One of the main ideas in "In Commemoration: One Million Volumes" is that learning is a magical experience. How does Anaya's retelling of his grandfather's riddle about the Milky Way support this idea?

_____

_____

3. Anaya's grandfather told him that words can be either joyful or deadly. What details from the changing seasons does Anaya present to support this idea in "In Commemoration: One Million Volumes"?

_____

_____

_____

4. In "In Commemoration: One Million Volumes," Anaya recalls that when he began going to school, he "stumbled from sound to word to groups of words." What caused him to stumble with words when he was in school?

_____

_____

5. In "In Commemoration: One Million Volumes," Anaya contrasts his Saturday afternoons as a young boy with the typical Saturdays of other boys in the town. How did he and other boys spend their time differently? What does this tell the reader about Anaya's character?

_____

_____

_____

6. In "In Commemoration: One Million Volumes," Anaya says that freedom was important to his understanding of what his library had to offer. How does his experience connect to a general lesson about life?

_____

_____

_____

7. As Anaya discusses his high school experiences in "In Commemoration: One Million Volumes," what details support his idea that "a library is a place where love begins"?

_____

_____

_____

8. A paradox is a statement that seems to contradict itself. According to Anaya in "In Commemoration: One Million Volumes," why is it a paradox that "a book at once quenches the thirst of the imagination and ignites new fires"?

_____

_____

_____

9. In "In Commemoration: One Million Volumes," Anaya describes his memories of the university library as *poignant*. What emotions does he most likely associate with these *poignant* memories?

_____

_____

_____

10. If you visited a place that *enthralls*, is it likely that you would want to return there? Base your answer on the meaning of *enthralls* as it is used in "In Commemoration: One Million Volumes."

_____

_____

_____

Essay

Write an extended response to the question of your choice or to the question or questions your teacher assigns you.

11. In "In Commemoration: One Million Volumes," Anaya writes about the excitement that reading has brought him throughout his life. In an essay, discuss something you have read—an essay, a story, an article, or a book—that was especially exciting and stimulating for you. Why did this work inspire you? Compare your experience with Anaya's.

12. In "In Commemoration: One Million Volumes," Anaya describes how the older people in his community told stories. He then discusses his love of libraries. In an essay, explain how the stories Anaya heard as a child and the books he later read played a similar role in his life.

13. "In Commemoration: One Million Volumes" is a reflective essay about the joy and inspiration that Anaya has found in books and libraries throughout his life. Today, many people do most of their reading on the Internet rather than in libraries. Some books are available online or in e-book format. In an essay, discuss the consequences of this change in reading habits. Do you think that reading online provides the same experience as holding a book in your hands? Why or why not? Support your answer with specific examples from Anaya's essay and from your own experience.

14. **Thinking About the Big Question: What kind of knowledge changes our lives?** "In Commemoration: One Million Volumes" is a reflective essay about the role of words and books in one man's life. In an essay, reflect on the many ways in which Rudolfo Anaya's life changed as a result of the information he absorbed from a lifetime of devotion to books and libraries.

Oral Response

15. Go back to question 5, 7, or 8 or to the question your teacher assigns you. Take a few minutes to expand your answer and prepare an oral response. Find additional details in "In Commemoration: One Million Volumes" that support your points. If necessary, make notes to guide your oral response.

from **In Commemoration: One Million Volumes** by Rudolfo A. Anaya
Selection Test A

Critical Reading *Identify the letter of the choice that best answers the question.*

____ 1. What is the focus of Anaya's reflective essay from *In Commemoration: One Million Volumes*?

A. stars

B. libraries

C. the author's childhood

D. the author's grandfather

____ 2. What was Anaya's first language?

A. English

B. Creole

C. Spanish

D. Navajo

____ 3. Which of the following is NOT among those who contributed to Anaya's interest in words and learning?

A. his mother

B. his grandfather

C. his childhood friends

D. Miss Pansy, the librarian

____ 4. What did Anaya learn from his grandfather?

A. to love words and learning

B. to speak only the Spanish language

C. to go to libraries and discuss issues with others

D. to value the spoken word over the written word

____ 5. What is the main idea of the following passage from *In Commemoration: One Million Volumes*?

> I was fortunate to have had those old and wise *viejitos* as guides into the world of nature and knowledge. They taught me with their stories; they taught me the magic of words. Now the words lie captured in ink, but the magic is still there, the power inherent in each volume.

A. The stories *los viejitos* told focused on nature and knowledge.

B. Anaya listened to *los viejitos* tell magical stories on summer evenings.

C. The stories told by *los viejitos* inspired Anaya's love of words and books.

D. *Los viejitos* employed an oral tradition; now their stories are told in books.

_____ 6. Where was Anaya's childhood library, the Santa Rosa Library?
    A. in a room above a fire station
    B. in his grandfather's house
    C. in a schoolroom
    D. in a university building

_____ 7. Which of the following is NOT a way Anaya would likely describe a library?
    A. inspirational
    B. comforting
    C. a place for debate
    D. no longer necessary

_____ 8. According to Anaya, what is an interesting effect of reading books?
    A. There are a million books in the world.
    B. The more you read books, the more you want to learn.
    C. You can lose yourself in books and never have to face reality.
    D. You never learn from books as much as you knew when you were a child.

_____ 9. How did Anaya work his way through high school?
    A. He tutored students in writing.
    B. He worked as an assistant librarian.
    C. He wrote love poems.
    D. He wrote for a newspaper.

_____ 10. Which of the following is NOT a main point that Anaya makes in his essay?
    A. A library is a place for people to gather and share ideas.
    B. A library preserves a society's culture and history.
    C. A library is a place where only the most educated people can go to read.
    D. A library represents freedom and the knowledge to create a better future.

_____ 11. What lesson about life does Anaya teach with this essay?
    A. One million is a magical number.
    B. Life is too short to waste in dusty libraries.
    C. The people one meets in a library can become the best of friends.
    D. Libraries offer knowledge, inspiration, and hope for the future.

Vocabulary and Grammar

___ 12. Anaya would value a tiny library in a(n) _____ old building just as much as he values his huge university library that holds over a million volumes.
    A. inherent   **C.** poignant
    B. dilapidated   **D.** infinite

___ 13. Which of the following is the best synonym for the word *enthralls*?
    A. trains   **C.** retains
    B. educates   **D.** fascinates

___ 14. Which of the following sentences contains a predicate nominative?
    A. Anaya is a novelist.
    B. Anaya loves books.
    C. Anaya values his culture.
    D. Anaya reads constantly.

___ 15. Which of the following sentences contains a predicate adjective?
    A. Words have power.
    B. Books are magical.
    C. A library is the heart of a city.
    D. The library has a million volumes.

Essay

16. Most of us think of the library as a place to do research, as a warehouse for books, or a place to use the Internet. In his essay from *In Commemoration: One Million Volumes*, Rudolfo Anaya reflects upon his personal vision of the library and what that has meant to him. How would you explain this essay to someone who has not read it? What is Anaya's vision of the library? In an essay, explain Anaya's perceptions of the purposes of a library. Use examples from the selection to illustrate your points.

17. At the beginning of the selection from *In Commemoration: One Million Volumes*, Anaya describes how the older people in his community told the children stories. Anaya then discusses his experiences in libraries. In an essay, explain how the riddles and stories of Anaya's childhood are similar to the books he read in libraries later in his life.

18. **Thinking About the Big Question: What kind of knowledge changes our lives?**
In Commemoration: One Million Volumes is a reflective essay about how books and stories change one man's life. In an essay, reflect on how Rudolfo Anaya's life changed as a result of the knowledge he gained from stories and books. Support your response with at least three examples from the selection.

from **In Commemoration: One Million Volumes** by Rudolfo A. Anaya
Selection Test B

Critical Reading *Identify the letter of the choice that best completes the statement or answers the question.*

____ 1. What makes this selection from *In Commemoration: One Million Volumes* a reflective essay?
A. It contains the author's memories of his experiences in libraries.
B. Its primary purpose is to inform readers about books and libraries.
C. It is meant to inspire other Mexican Americans to strive for success.
D. It is a fictional story of how a Mexican American boy learns English.

____ 2. Who or what first got Anaya interested in words and learning?
A. the books he read
B. the librarians he befriended
C. the old people he knew
D. the teacher he studied under

____ 3. Which information is NOT given about Anaya's grandfather?
A. He was wise.
B. He was a storyteller.
C. He studied at the university.
D. He spoke many languages.

____ 4. What metaphor does Anaya use to describe his first librarian, Miss Pansy?
A. He compares her to an interesting character in a book.
B. He compares her to a flower that blooms in the desert.
C. He compares her to a pilot who guides him in his reading.
D. He compares her to a mother who feeds him with books.

____ 5. Why do the people of Anaya's childhood town shake their heads and pity his mother?
A. They think she is crazy.
B. They think her son is crazy.
C. She is a very unattractive woman.
D. She is the poorest woman in town.

____ 6. Anaya compares the pleasure of reading to the exhilaration of
A. seeing a beautiful sunset.
B. winning a contest.
C. making money.
D. being in love.

____ 7. According to Anaya, what is a paradox of books?
A. The more you read books, the more you want to learn.
B. You can lose yourself in books without losing your identity.
C. There are more books than you could ever read in a lifetime.
D. You never learn from books as much as you knew when you were a child.

____ 8. What did Anaya learn about libraries when he was in high school?
   A. that a library is a place where love begins
   B. that a library can sometimes feel like a prison
   C. that a library is a good place to get some rest
   D. that a library is a place where one can discuss ideas

____ 9. Why does Anaya associate libraries with freedom?
   A. because people can check books out of libraries free of charge
   B. because the United States is a free country, and it has many libraries
   C. because the availability of books represents freedom from censorship
   D. because he feels carefree in libraries and is able to forget about his daily life

____ 10. Which of the following is NOT a reason why Anaya values libraries?
   A. They preserve a society's culture and history.
   B. They are a place for people to gather and share ideas.
   C. They contain the *cuentos* of his people, as told by his grandfather.
   D. They represent freedom and the knowledge to create a better future.

____ 11. This passage from *In Commemoration: One Million Volumes* is mostly about
   A. how a library can affect people's lives.
   B. why the author writes books.
   C. how the author learned to love reading.
   D. why the author loves freedom.

____ 12. Which of the following details most clearly supports the main idea of the excerpt from *In Commemoration: One Million Volumes*?
   A. In 1981, the university library had one million volumes.
   B. Anaya always knew there were at least a million stars.
   C. When he was a child, Anaya learned his prayers in Spanish.
   D. Anaya believes a library should be the cultural center of a city.

____ 13. What lesson about life does Anaya wish to convey by writing this essay?
   A. One million is a magical number.
   B. Life is too short to waste in libraries.
   C. Libraries contain the collective wisdom of mankind.
   D. One should have great pride in one's culture and heritage.

Vocabulary and Grammar

____ 14. When Anaya says that each volume has *inherent* power, he means that
   A. he inherited the volumes from his grandfather.
   B. each volume or book is naturally powerful or important.
   C. each book is capable of adding to a person's knowledge.
   D. the power of the volumes comes from the author's ancestors.

____ 15. Which of the following is an example of something that is most likely *dilapidated*?
   A. an abandoned warehouse
   B. a new car
   C. an office building
   D. a restored antique chair

___ 16. Which of the following sentences contains a predicate nominative?
   A. Anaya is an inspired novelist.
   B. Anaya loves words, books, and libraries.
   C. Anaya values his culture and heritage.
   D. Anaya finds libraries to be inspiring.

___ 17. Which of the following sentences contains a predicate adjective?
   A. Books contain infinite worlds.
   B. Libraries are relaxing and informative.
   C. A library should be the heart of a city.
   D. There are a million volumes in the library.

Essay

18. In his essay from *In Commemoration: One Million Volumes*, Anaya writes about feeling exhilaration from reading. In an essay of your own, write about something you have read that exhilarated you. Why did you find this particular work to be exciting and inspirational? Has anything inspired you to want to write something of your own? Finally, compare your experience with Anaya's.

19. With the advent of new technologies, the role of the library may change. CD-ROMs can hold entire encyclopedias, and there is almost no limit to the availability of information on the Internet. Every book, newspaper, and video and almost all civic information can be obtained in one's home through the use of a personal computer. What do these changes mean to the library? Will libraries become extinct? Will they serve other purposes? Write an essay in which you assess the role of the library in the twenty-first century. Use principles from Anaya's essay as a guide for your discussion.

20. Anaya begins his essay with memories of his childhood and refers to "the old ones" in his native Spanish. Several times in the essay he uses the original Spanish term for something he is referring to, such as *adivinanzas* for riddles and *cuentos* for stories. How do these references contribute to the selection from *In Commemoration: One Million Volumes*? Write an essay in which you explain the effect of these ethnic references and reminiscences. Use examples from the essay to support your ideas.

21. **Thinking About the Big Question: What kind of knowledge changes our lives?**
In Commemoration: One Million Volumes is a reflective essay about the role of words and books in one man's life. In an essay, reflect on the many ways in which Rudolfo Anaya's life changed as a result of the information he absorbed from a lifetime of devotion to books and libraries.

"A Toast to the Oldest Inhabitant: The Weather of New England" by Mark Twain
"The Dog that Bit People" by James Thurber
Vocabulary Warm-up Word Lists

Study these words from the selections. Then, complete the activities.

Word List A

climax [KLY maks] *n.* point of highest interest or excitement
The <u>climax</u> of the parade was the release of 1,000 red balloons.

compels [kuhm PELZ] *v.* forces to do something
The law <u>compels</u> 18-year-old males to register with the Selective Service.

favorable [FAY ver uh buhl] *adj.* beneficial or advantageous
The clear, warm weather was quite <u>favorable</u> for a picnic.

foliage [FOH lee ij] *n.* leaves of a plant
The <u>foliage</u> of a magnolia tree provides pleasant shade during the summer.

municipal [myoo NIS uh puhl] *adj.* part of a local government
The mayor is one of many <u>municipal</u> officials with an office at City Hall.

residents [REZ i duhnts] *n.* people who live in a place
Many of the <u>residents</u> in our apartment building have lived there for years.

specimens [SPES uh muhnz] *n.* parts of a group to be used as a sample
We tested water <u>specimens</u> from three parts of the stream in our lab.

varying [VAIR ee ing] *v.* differing; changing
The witness and the police officer give <u>varying</u> accounts of the accident.

Word List B

blemished [BLEM isht] *v.* stained; marked with a flaw
The slab of white marble was <u>blemished</u> by a deep crack.

burly [BER lee] *adj.* strong, large, and muscular
Three <u>burly</u> movers lifted the piano with ease.

commences [kuh MENS ez] *v.* begins; starts
Whenever it rains, our dog <u>commences</u> howling.

harmonious [har MOH nee uhs] *adj.* balanced in a pleasing way
Our <u>harmonious</u> home becomes a wild madhouse when my cousins visit.

inconceivable [in kuhn SEE vuh buhl] *adj.* unbelievable; unimaginable
It was <u>inconceivable</u> that the former millionaire was now homeless.

incredulity [in kri DOO li tee] *n.* inability to believe
Even the medal could not shake her <u>incredulity</u> at having won the race.

postscript [POHST skript] *n.* a note added at the end of a piece of writing
Sometimes, my sister will write a <u>postscript</u> that is longer than her letter.

prophecy [PRAHF i see] *n.* prediction of the future
The mysterious <u>prophecy</u> came true, but not in the way we expected.

Name _____ Date _____

"A Toast to the Oldest Inhabitant: The Weather of New England" by Mark Twain
"The Dog that Bit People" by James Thurber
Vocabulary Warm-up Exercises

Exercise A *Fill in each blank in the paragraph with an appropriate word from Word List A. Use each word only once.*

Mia has two parrots. Both are beautiful [1] _____ of their breeds. Unfortunately, they are also quite loud. Some of the [2] _____ in her building have complained about their noise. One neighbor has made many angry calls to the [3] _____ government, though with [4] _____ degrees of success. The situation has become increasingly tense. It reached its ugly [5] _____ yesterday when the neighbor reached across the balcony and set one of the birds free. Luckily, its bright red feathers were easy to see in the green [6] _____ of the tree where it landed, making it easy to catch. Last night, a [7] _____ solution was proposed by the building manager. The agreement [8] _____ Mia to soundproof a room for the parrots.

Exercise B *Write a complete sentence to answer each question. For each item, use a word from Word List B to replace each underlined word without changing its meaning.*

Example: Why is it <u>unbelievable</u> that pigs could fly?
It is <u>inconceivable</u> that pigs could fly because they have no wings.

1. Why might you decide to add an <u>afterthought</u> to a letter?
_____

2. Which room in your home has decorations that feel <u>balanced</u>?
_____

3. What kinds of jobs might require <u>brawny</u> workers?
_____

4. What are some of the changes that occur when spring <u>begins</u>?
_____

5. Why might you leave a movie theater feeling <u>disbelief</u>?
_____

6. Is every <u>prediction</u> equally accurate?
_____

7. What might cause a diamond to be <u>flawed</u>?
_____

"A Toast to the Oldest Inhabitant: The Weather of New England" by Mark Twain
"The Dog that Bit People" by James Thurber
Reading Warm-up A

Read the following passage. Pay special attention to the underlined words. Then, read it again, and complete the activities. Use a separate sheet of paper for your written answers.

Many people associate New England with autumn. When they picture this area, they imagine thousands of red, yellow, and golden brown leaves. Fall <u>foliage</u> attracts many visitors and is an important source of tourism in New England.

Why do leaves turn colors? Living leaves contain a chemical called chlorophyll that gives them their green color. At the end of the growing season, chlorophyll disappears. Then, we can see the other colors that were always in the leaves. Weather also affects fall colors. When conditions are <u>favorable</u>, the colors are much brighter. The most spectacular foliage follows a wet spring, a warm summer, and a fall with sunny days and cool nights.

Local <u>residents</u> can watch the colors change day by day. However, weekend visitors enjoy the thrill of seeing the brilliant hues that appear during peak viewing weekends. As the viewing season approaches its brilliant <u>climax</u>, local populations increase dramatically. A small town of 2,000 residents might host three times as many visitors in one weekend. Many cities hold special events to encourage fall tourism. <u>Municipal</u> governments from Portland, Maine, to Hartford, Connecticut, host fall parades, carnivals, and festivals.

Gardeners often consider leaf color when they select new plants. Some <u>specimens</u> appear to be ordinary during the summer, but burst into unusual colors in the fall. For example, the sugar maple has large leaves that adopt vivid fall colors <u>varying</u> from deep reds to hot oranges and yellows. Consider the smoke bush, whose oval leaves turn a handsome deep maroon. Velvet sumac has lacy leaves that become elegant fingers of yellow and orange every autumn.

Whether you are a year-round New Englander or a weekend traveler, the autumn landscape <u>compels</u> admiration and delight. Like all seasonal things, this autumn show has a limited life. The leaves soon turn brown, and drop off. Luckily, there is always the promise of next year's fall.

1. Circle the word that is a synonym for <u>foliage</u>. Then, describe the *foliage* of one plant.

2. Underline the sentence that describes the <u>favorable</u> conditions for fall color. Then, tell what *favorable* means.

3. Circle the word that means the opposite of <u>residents</u>. Then, tell what *residents* are.

4. Underline the words that tell what happens when the viewing season reaches its <u>climax</u>. Then, describe the *climax* of a movie you have seen.

5. Circle the words that name what the <u>municipal</u> governments sponsor. Then, explain what *municipal* means.

6. Explain how you might collect *specimens* of fall leaves.

7. Underline the words that describe the <u>varying</u> colors of the sugar maple. Then, tell what *varying* means.

8. Circle the words that tell what <u>compels</u> admiration and delight. Then, tell something that *compels* you to study.

Name _____ Date _____

"A Toast to the Oldest Inhabitant: The Weather of New England" by Mark Twain
"The Dog that Bit People" by James Thurber
Reading Warm-up B

Read the following passage. Pay special attention to the underlined words. Then, read it again, and complete the activities. Use a separate sheet of paper for your written answers.

Evidently, life around here was pretty dull until I arrived. The big man is constantly shouting "Look what your dog did now!" at the big woman. This usually occurs after I have pushed over one of the chairs, tables, or children. Once the shouting begins, it is not long before the crying <u>commences</u> and soon after that I am in trouble.

The big man claims that life was <u>harmonious</u> and calm before I got here, but I do not think he understands that sometimes a home should be noisy and chaotic. He does not seem to think that a squirrel is a good reason for barking. Is it so <u>inconceivable</u> that squirrels need to be barked at?

The big woman seems to like me, although sometimes she yells, too. Last week, they left the front door open for a moment, so naturally I ran out to patrol the neighborhood. Apparently, while making my rounds, I knocked over three mailboxes, seven flowerpots, and the mayor's ceramic fountain. "You have <u>blemished</u> our spotless reputation forever," the big woman shrieked. I tried to cheer her up by wagging my tail, but I smashed a glass vase to bits. I hid in the basement for a few hours.

It is not my fault that I am clumsy—I am just a big, <u>burly</u> dog, weighing in at over ninety pounds. I cannot help it if my size disrupts their tiny world once in a while, can I? Yet, every time something new breaks, one of the big people looks at me with <u>incredulity</u>, as if he or she cannot believe I am so clumsy. You would think they could believe it by now.

That is all I have to say about that. Wait—I will add a <u>postscript</u>. Have you ever heard of a self-fulfilling <u>prophecy</u>? Well, if they did not want a dog that breaks things, maybe they should not have named me "Buster."

1. Circle the synonym for <u>commences</u>. Then, name something that *commences* every Monday.

2. Underline the words that describe the opposite of <u>harmonious</u>. Then, describe something you think is *harmonious*.

3. Describe an event so *inconceivable* that it will never happen at your school.

4. Circle the words that tell what has been <u>blemished</u>. Then, explain what *blemished* means.

5. Underline the words that support the description of the narrator as <u>burly</u>. Then, tell how you would feel if you saw a *burly* dog in a dark alley.

6. Underline the words that explain the feeling of <u>incredulity</u>. Then, tell what *incredulity* means.

7. Describe where you might find a *postscript*.

8. Explain what the narrator means by the phrase "self-fulfilling *prophecy*."

Name _____ Date _____

"A Toast to the Oldest Inhabitant: The Weather of New England" by Mark Twain
"The Dog that Bit People" by James Thurber

Writing About the Big Question

What kind of knowledge changes our lives?

Big Question Vocabulary

adapt	awareness	empathy	enlighten	evolve
growth	history	ignorance	influence	insight
modified	question	reflect	revise	understanding

A. *Use one or more words from the list above to complete each sentence.*

1. We used to get upset about the weather, but our _____ response to the weather was to ignore it instead.

2. I have _____ for people who live in cold climates, because I grew up in Alaska.

3. Mother had to _____ her plans for the dog's burial, changing the location and the grave marker.

4. Muggs never did _____ into a dog that was comfortable with strangers.

B. *Follow the directions in responding to each of the items below.*

1. List a time that you faced a challenging situation with the weather or an animal.

   _____

   _____

2. Explain whether you handled the challenge you described seriously or with humor. Use at least two of the Big Question vocabulary words.

   _____

   _____

C. *Complete the sentence below. Then, write a short paragraph in which you connect this experience to the big question.*

To change your attitude toward a bad situation, you should _____

_____

_____

_____

Name _____ Date _____

"A Toast to the Oldest Inhabitant: The Weather of New England" by Mark Twain
"The Dog That Bit People" by James Thurber

Literary Analysis: Humorous Writing

Humorous writing is writing in which people, events, and ideas are presented in unexpected, amusing ways. Techniques for creating humor include the following:

- **Hyperbole** is exaggeration for effect in which a writer describes something as if it were much greater than it is. Describing a creek as a "yawning gorge" is an example of hyperbole.
- A writer uses **understatement** to portray a person, an event, or an idea as if it were much less than it is. Saying that "the avalanche was a minor inconvenience for hikers" is an example of understatement.
- **Satire** is a writer's use of humor to point out the foolishness of a particular type of human behavior. In "The Dog That Bit People," for example, Thurber satirizes the behavior of pet owners who believe their pets can do no wrong.

DIRECTIONS: *Read each of the following passages from "A Toast to the Oldest Inhabitant" and "The Dog That Bit People." Then, identify each passage as an example of hyperbole or understatement, and explain what makes it so.*

"A Toast to the Oldest Inhabitant: The Weather of New England"

1. In the spring I have counted one hundred and thirty-six different kinds of weather inside of four and twenty hours.

   This is an example of _____ because _____

   _____ .

2. You fix up for the drought . . . and ten to one you get drowned. You make up your mind that the earthquake is due . . . and the first thing you know, you get struck by lightning. These are great disappointments. But they can't be helped.

   This is an example of _____ because _____

   _____ .

"The Dog That Bit People"

3. There was a slight advantage to being one of the family, for he didn't bite the family as often as he bit strangers.

   This is an example of _____ because _____

   _____ .

4. Muggs went up the backstairs and down the frontstairs and had me cornered in the living room. I managed to get up onto the mantelpiece above the fireplace, but it gave way and came down with a tremendous crash throwing a large marble clock, several vases, and myself heavily to the floor.

   This is an example of _____ because _____

   _____ .

"A Toast to the Oldest Inhabitant: The Weather of New England" by Mark Twain
"The Dog That Bit People" by James Thurber

Vocabulary Builder

Word List

blemished	choleric	commences	incredulity
indignant	irascible	sumptuous	vagaries

A. DIRECTIONS: *Revise each sentence so that the underlined word is used logically. Be sure to keep the underlined word in your revision.*

Example: The <u>sumptuous</u> meal left the guests hungry.

Answer: The <u>sumptuous</u> meal satisfied everyone.

1. Her perfect day was <u>blemished</u> by a single compliment.

   _____

2. Once the presentation <u>commences</u>, feel free to ask questions.

   _____

3. The <u>vagaries</u> of the weather allow us to plan our outdoor activities in advance.

   _____

4. Jack's mother showed <u>incredulity</u> when he claimed to have cleaned his room in two hours.

   _____

5. The <u>choleric</u> old woman gave the children in her front yard a warm welcome.

   _____

6. Getting a good night's sleep makes me <u>irascible</u> in the morning.

   _____

7. Mia felt <u>indignant</u> after being awarded a part in the play.

   _____

B. DIRECTIONS: *On the line, write the letter of the word that is most nearly similar in meaning to the word in CAPITAL LETTERS.*

____ 1. SUMPTUOUS:
   A. sleepy   B. extravagant   C. rigid   D. conceited

____ 2. INCREDULITY:
   A. awe   B. joyfulness   C. disbelief   D. poverty

____ 3. COMMENCES:
   A. deals   B. enters   C. invites   D. starts

____ 4. BLEMISHED:
   A. smooth   B. damaged   C. cold   D. old

____ 5. VAGARIES:
   A. belief   B. stillness   C. caprice   D. silence

Name _____ Date _____

"A Toast to the Oldest Inhabitant: The Weather of New England" by Mark Twain
"The Dog That Bit People" by James Thurber

Integrated Language Skills: Support for Comparing Literary Works

A humorous essay or speech is a nonfiction composition in which the writer presents people, events, and ideas in unexpected, amusing ways. Identify the techniques—hyperbole, understatement, satire—Twain and Thurber use to create humor in their writing. Record these elements, and examples of each, in the chart. As you write, think about how the comic techniques of these writers are different and similar.

"A Toast to the Oldest Inhabitant: The Weather of New England"	
Comic Technique	**Example in Selection**
1.	1.
2.	2.
3.	3.
4.	4.

"A Toast to the Oldest Inhabitant: The Weather of New England"	
Comic Technique	**Example in Selection**
1.	1.
2.	2.
3.	3.
4.	4.

"A Toast to the Oldest Inhabitant: The Weather of New England" by Mark Twain
"The Dog That Bit People" by James Thurber
Open-Book Test

Short Answer *Write your responses to the questions in this section on the lines provided.*

1. In "A Toast to the Oldest Inhabitant," Mark Twain discusses qualities of the weather in New England. What is the main quality that he discusses?

_____

_____

2. In "A Toast to the Oldest Inhabitant," Twain uses hyperbole to achieve a humorous effect. Using the graphic organizer below, give three examples of Twain's use of hyperbole. Then, on the line below, identify which example of hyperbole you find most effective and why.

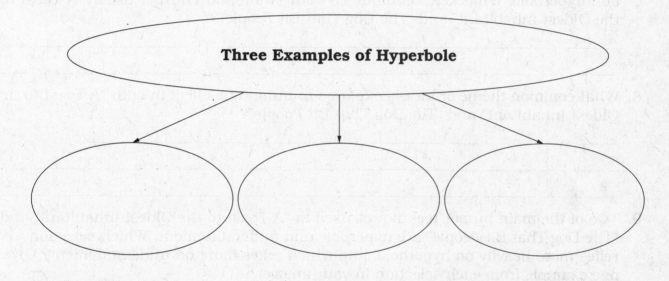

_____

3. If you were dining in *sumptuous* surroundings, would you most likely find yourself in a fancy restaurant or in a corner coffee shop? Explain your answer, based on the meaning of *sumptuous* in "A Toast to the Oldest Inhabitant."

_____

_____

_____

4. Read the following excerpt from "The Dog That Bit People": "Mother . . . told Mrs. Detweiler that it was only a bruise. 'He just bumped you,' she said." Which technique of humorous writing does this excerpt illustrate? Why?

_____

_____

5. The narrator of "The Dog That Bit People" writes, "Mother used to send a box of candy every Christmas to the people the Airedale bit." How is this sentence an example of satire?

_____

_____

6. Would a teacher with a *choleric* temperament most likely show much patience with his or her students? Explain your answer, based on the meaning of *choleric* in "The Dog That Bit People."

_____

_____

7. A humorous essay is a nonfiction composition that presents people or events in an amusing way. Some techniques of humorous writing are understatement, satire, and hyperbole. What key technique do both Twain and Thurber use in "A Toast to the Oldest Inhabitant" and "The Dog That Bit People"?

_____

_____

8. What common theme or idea is explored to humorous effect in both "A Toast to the Oldest Inhabitant" and "The Dog That Bit People"?

_____

_____

_____

9. Two of the main humor techniques used in "A Toast to the Oldest Inhabitant" and "The Dog That Bit People" are hyperbole and understatement. Which selection relies more heavily on hyperbole, and which relies more on understatement? Give one example from each selection in your answer.

_____

_____

_____

_____

10. In "A Toast to the Oldest Inhabitant" and "The Dog That Bit People," what underlying attitude toward their subjects do Twain and Thurber share?

_____

_____

_____

Essay

Write an extended response to the question of your choice or to the question or questions your teacher assigns you.

11. Both Twain and Thurber use humor to make observations about people and their reactions to the world around them. Select a passage that you found especially amusing in either "A Toast to the Oldest Inhabitant" or "The Dog That Bit People." Then, in a short essay, explain why you found the passage funny. Provide specific examples from the passage to support your response.

12. Which of the two selections—"A Toast to the Oldest Inhabitant" or "The Dog That Bit People"—did you find more humorous? Why? Explain your answer in an essay that identifies the techniques of humor used in each selection. Support your answer with specific examples from both selections.

13. In "A Toast to the Oldest Inhabitant" and "The Dog That Bit People," Twain and Thurber use satire to achieve a humorous effect and to point out people's foolish behavior. In an essay, explain how Twain satirizes weather forecasters and how Thurber satirizes pet owners. In your opinion, are the satirical portraits equally effective and funny? Why or why not? Support your response with specific examples from the text.

14. **Thinking About the Big Question: What kind of knowledge changes our lives?** Can humor convey information, and therefore contribute to a reader's body of knowledge? How might the knowledge we gain through "A Toast to the Oldest Inhabitant" and "The Dog That Bit People" change our lives? Develop your thoughts in an essay supported by specific examples from the selections.

Oral Response

15. Go back to question 1, 5, or 8 or to the question your teacher assigns you. Take a few minutes to expand your answer and prepare an oral response. Find additional details in "A Toast to the Oldest Inhabitant" and/or "The Dog That Bit People" that support your points. If necessary, make notes to guide your oral response.

"A Toast to the Oldest Inhabitant: The Weather of New England" by Mark Twain
"The Dog That Bit People" by James Thurber
Selection Test A

Critical Reading *Identify the letter of the choice that best answers the question.*

____ 1. As Mark Twain describes it, which is true of the New England weather?
   A. It is always pleasing.
   B. It is always dark and cold.
   C. It is unpredictable.
   D. It is tropical.

____ 2. Which passage from "A Toast to the Oldest Inhabitant" is an example of hyperbole?
   A. In the spring I have counted one hundred and thirty-six different kinds of weather inside of four and twenty hours.
   B. The people of New England are by nature patient and for-bearing; but there are some things which they will not stand.
   C. These are great disappointments. But they can't be helped.
   D. There—I forgive you, now—the books are square between us.

____ 3. In "A Toast to the Oldest Inhabitant," Twain says the New England rain skips over his tin roof—on purpose. What human quality is he granting the weather?
   A. rudeness
   B. weariness
   C. impatience
   D. mischievousness

____ 4. In "A Toast to the Oldest Inhabitant," Twain says that one kind of New England weather makes up for all the other kinds. What kind of weather is this?
   A. earthquake
   B. lightning storm
   C. wind
   D. ice storm

____ 5. What was Thurber's main reason for writing "The Dog That Bit People"?
   A. to persuade readers not to adopt dogs as pets
   B. to entertain readers with funny stories
   C. to teach readers how to care for dogs
   D. to convince readers that Muggs is guilty

_____ 6. How does Thurber's mother generally deal with conflicts involving Muggs?
A. She punishes him.
B. She trains him to behave.
C. She makes excuses for him.
D. She sends him outside.

_____ 7. What does Thurber's mother do for each of Muggs's victims?
A. She pays their doctor bills.
B. She sends them a box of candy.
C. She invites them to dinner.
D. She sends them to an animal behavior class.

_____ 8. Which sentence from "The Dog That Bit People" is an example of understatement?
A. Muggs was afraid of only one thing, an electrical storm.
B. Muggs would stand on the bench and eat.
C. Muggs at his meals was an unusual sight.
D. Muggs died quite suddenly one night.

_____ 9. Why does Thurber include the story about the thunder machine?
A. to show why neighbors wished the family would get rid of the dog
B. to show how easily animals can be tricked by human beings
C. to show how Muggs would get punished when he bit people
D. to show what lengths the family would go to for Muggs's sake

_____ 10. How do both Twain and Thurber create humor in their essays?
A. They exaggerate ordinary events.
B. They make fun of themselves.
C. They criticize those who hold different beliefs.
D. They ignore the most important part of their topics.

_____ 11. Which idea is explored in both "A Toast to the Oldest Inhabitant" and "The Dog That Bit People"?
A. how people are careless
B. how humans react to non-human forces
C. how most people are impossible to please
D. how humans enjoy the weather

___ **12.** How do both Twain and Thurber make their subjects appear?
 A. worse than they really are
 B. exactly as they really are
 C. better than they really are
 D. opposite of what they really are

___ **13.** Which of these titles would be an appropriate replacement for both "A Toast to the Oldest Inhabitant" and "The Dog That Bit People"?
 A. "Sit!"
 B. "Beware!"
 C. "Welcome!"
 D. "Go Home!"

Vocabulary

___ **14.** What does *choleric* mean in the following sentence from "The Dog That Bit People"?
 A big, burly, <u>choleric</u> dog, he always acted as if he thought I wasn't one of the family.
 A. large
 B. young
 C. confused
 D. angry

___ **15.** Which would be most likely to get *blemished*?
 A. a cloud   **C.** an apple
 B. a pebble   **D.** a river

Essay

16. Both "A Toast to the Oldest Inhabitant" and "The Dog That Bit People" are examples of humorous writing. Choose one passage in each essay that you found particularly funny. Describe the passage. Then, tell what made it humorous. Overall, which essay did you find funnier? Why?

17. Both Twain and Thurber use **satire** in their works. That is, they point out the foolishness of certain types of people. In an essay, explain how Twain satirizes weather forecasters and how Thurber satirizes pet owners. In your opinion, do the portrayals contain any kernels of truth? How so?

18. Thinking About the Big Question: What kind of knowledge changes our lives? How might the knowledge we gain through "A Toast to the Oldest Inhabitant" and "The Dog That Bit People" change our lives? Develop your thoughts in an essay supported by specific examples from both selections. First, identify the knowledge you gained by reading each selection. Then, describe how that knowledge might change your life.

"A Toast to the Oldest Inhabitant: The Weather of New England" by Mark Twain
"The Dog That Bit People" by James Thurber

Selection Test B

Critical Reading *Identify the letter of the choice that best completes the statement or answers the question.*

_____ 1. In "A Toast to the Oldest Inhabitant," Twain says that New England weather must be made by whom?
   A. New Englanders themselves
   B. a weather collector
   C. unskilled apprentices
   D. poets

_____ 2. What is this passage from "A Toast to the Oldest Inhabitant" an example of?
   He not only had weather enough, but weather to spare; weather to hire out; weather to sell;
   to deposit; weather to invest; weather to give to the poor.
   A. hyperbole
   B. conflict
   C. understatement
   D. an unexpected event

_____ 3. According to Twain, New Englanders cannot stand poets because poets
   A. criticize spring weather in New England.
   B. ignore spring weather in New England.
   C. try to change spring weather in New England.
   D. admire spring weather in New England.

_____ 4. In "A Toast to the Oldest Inhabitant," what does Twain imply about weather forecasts?
   A. They are sometimes helpful.
   B. They are so generalized as to be useless.
   C. They are useful only on a beautiful day.
   D. They are usually correct, but only by chance.

_____ 5. In "A Toast to the Oldest Inhabitant," Twain says that there are two things about the weather that New England residents enjoy. What are these two effects of weather?
   A. autumn foliage and rain
   B. rainbows and wind
   C. ice storms and fall foliage
   D. earthquakes and thunder

_____ 6. In "A Toast to the Oldest Inhabitant," when Twain forgives the weather for its "little faults and foibles," what technique is he using?
   A. hyperbole
   B. understatement
   C. satire
   D. conflict

____ 7. Thurber begins "The Dog That Bit People" with a series of anecdotes about other dogs in order to
   A. establish his fondness for dogs and set a humorous tone.
   B. poke fun at people who do not like dogs.
   C. point out that he is easily embarrassed by his dog's behavior.
   D. emphasize his general dislike for dogs.

____ 8. Which sentence from "The Dog That Bit People" helps develop the essay's satire?
   A. But the Airedale, as I have said, was the worst of all my dogs.
   B. That was during the month when we suddenly had mice, and Muggs refused to do anything about them.
   C. It made her so mad to see Muggs lying there, oblivious of the mice. . . .
   D. Mother used to send a box of candy every Christmas to the people the Airedale bit.

____ 9. In "The Dog That Bit People," what does Thurber's mother hope to learn from the lecture on "Harmonious Vibrations"?
   A. how to get people to like Muggs
   B. why Muggs bites people
   C. how to change Muggs's behavior
   D. how to restore Muggs's strength

____ 10. What does the following sentence from "The Dog That Bit People" provide an example of?
   Mother . . . told Mrs. Detweiler that it was only a bruise. "He just bumped you," she said.

   A. hyperbole
   B. comparison
   C. understatement
   D. imagery

____ 11. The author of "The Dog That Bit People" would most likely agree with which statement?
   A. Dog owners tend to indulge their pets.
   B. Most dogs are more trouble than they are worth.
   C. Many dogs are as talented and intelligent as people.
   D. However badly dogs behave, one should try to please them.

____ 12. What human tendency is satirized in both "A Toast to the Oldest Inhabitant" and "The Dog That Bit People"?
   A. the desire to explain or control non-human forces
   B. the desire to avoid confrontation
   C. the need to believe in something
   D. the need to appear knowledgeable

____ 13. Which selection treats an ordinary subject with exaggerated seriousness?
   A. "A Toast to the Oldest Inhabitant"
   B. "The Dog That Bit People"
   C. neither
   D. both

____ 14. Which statement best describes Twain's and Thurber's use of humorous techniques?
   A. Thurber's essay relies more heavily on hyperbole than Twain's does.
   B. Thurber's essay relies more heavily on understatement than Twain's does.
   C. Twain's essay uses only hyperbole, while Thurber's uses only understatement.
   D. Twain's essay uses only understatement, while Thurber's uses only hyperbole.

____ 15. Which is most likely true of Twain and Thurber?
   A. They deeply despise their subjects.
   B. They do not find their subjects humorous.
   C. They harbor a fondness for their subjects.
   D. They secretly believe everything that they are writing.

Vocabulary

____ 16. What does *choleric* mean in the following sentence from "The Dog That Bit People"?
   A big, burly, choleric dog, he always acted as if he thought I wasn't one of the family.
   A. larger than life
   B. untrained
   C. hard to understand
   D. easily angered

____ 17. In "A Toast to the Oldest Inhabitant," what is said to be *sumptuous* about the weather?
   A. its unpredictable nature
   B. its humorous qualities
   C. its beauty
   D. its lavish variety

____ 18. Which sentence from "The Dog That Bit People" best shows mother's *incredulity* when it comes to Muggs?
   A. "He's a large tan-colored Airedale," mother explained.
   B. "He's not strong," she would say, pityingly. . . .
   C. It took a lot out of mother.
   D. My mother had never liked the Congressman. . . .

Essay

19. Both Twain in "A Toast to the Oldest Inhabitant" and Thurber in "The Dog That Bit People" use the techniques of hyperbole and understatement to create humor in their essays. In an essay of your own, define each of these techniques. Then, explain how and to what extent each author uses them in his essay. Provide examples from both works to support your explanation.

20. The authors of both "A Toast to the Oldest Inhabitant" and "The Dog That Bit People" use conflict as a basis for the humor in their writing. In an essay, identify the conflict at the heart of each work. Who or what is portrayed as the underdog? With whom does the author most identify—the stronger party or the weaker party? How does this add to the essay's humor? Use examples from the essays to support your claims.

21. **Thinking About the Big Question: What kind of knowledge changes our lives?** Can humor convey information, and therefore contribute to a reader's body of knowledge? How might the knowledge we gain through "A Toast to the Oldest Inhabitant" and "The Dog That Bit People" change our lives? Develop your thoughts in an essay supported by specific examples from the selections.

Name _____ Date _____

Writing Workshop
Persuasion: Letter to the Editor

Prewriting: Gathering Details

Conduct research to find relevant details and evidence to support your ideas; list the details you find in the proper categories of the following chart.

Facts and Statistics	Real-life Examples	Personal Experience	Expert Opinions

Drafting: Providing Elaboration

Use the graphic organizer below to develop the body of your business letter by filling in the appropriate information on the right; make sure you consider your audience and your tone as you list support.

Introduction	→	

Supporting Detail 1	→	

Supporting Detail 2	→	

Supporting Detail 3	→	

Closing/Thank You	→	

Name _____ Date _____

Writing Workshop
Letter to the Editor: Integrating Grammar Skills

Revising to Combine Choppy Sentences

A series of short sentences can sound choppy and repetitious. To solve the problem, you can sometimes combine sentences by using compound structures. Look for shared elements that you can avoid repeating.

Combined	with Compound Subject	Kay and Kristin are talented musicians.
	with Compound Subject	Neither Kay nor Kristin plays the piano.
	with Compound Verb	Kay plays the violin and composes music.
	with Compound Direct Object	Kay may study the cello or the mandolin.
	with Compound Adjective	The sonata was lovely but difficult.
	with Compound Prepositional Phrase:	Kay practices in the morning and at night.

Identifying Compound Structures for Sentence Combining

A. DIRECTIONS: *Circle the compound structures that you would use to combine each pair of choppy sentences.*

1. Lloyd often goes fishing. His sister Carla does too. (compound subject, compound verb)
2. Ted enjoys fishing in the pond. He also enjoys fishing in the ocean. (compound verb, compound object of a preposition)
3. Carla caught a trout. She also caught two sunfish. (compound subject, compound direct object)
4. Lloyd gave Sandy some fish. He also gave some to Mary. (compound subject, compound indirect object)

Fixing Choppy Sentences Using Compound Structures

B. DIRECTIONS: *For each item, combine the two choppy sentences into a single sentence that uses a compound structure. Write your new sentence on the line provided.*

1. Joel is not in the school play this year. Neither is Delphine.

   _____

2. We rehearse on Mondays. We also rehearse on Thursdays.

   _____

3. We may rehearse in the school auditorium. We may rehearse at Luisa's house.

   _____

4. The rehearsal usually begins at three. It usually ends at five.

   _____

5. The play is long. However, it is also interesting.

   _____

Name _____ Date _____

Unit 3: Types of Nonfiction
Benchmark Test 5

MULTIPLE CHOICE

Literary Analysis *Read the following selection from "Winter Mist" by Robert Palfrey Utter. Then, answer the questions that follow.*

I like pond skating best by moonlight. The hollow among the hills will always have a bit of mist about it, let the sky be clear as it may. The moonlight, which seems so lucid and brilliant when you look up, is all pearl and smoke round the pond and the hills. The shore that was like iron under your heel as you came down to the ice is vague, when you look back at it from the center of the pond, as the memory of a dream. The motion is like flying in a dream; you float free and the world floats under you; your velocity is without effort and without accomplishment, for, speed as you may, you leave nothing behind and approach nothing.

1. From what type of essay was this selection taken?
   A. expository   B. narrative   C. reflective   D. persuasive

2. What is the author's most likely purpose for writing this selection?
   A. to inform   B. to convince   C. to tell a story   D. to describe

3. Which of the following would be an appropriate subject for an expository essay?
   A. My First Day at School   C. Why Watching Television Is Bad for You
   B. How Photosynthesis Works   D. My Crazy Dog

4. What is the main literary technique used in this selection?
   A. dialogue   C. descriptive language
   B. flashback   D. multiple points of view

Read the following selection from Mark Twain's Roughing It. *Then, answer the questions that follow.*

People accustomed to the monster mile-wide Mississippi, grow accustomed to associating the term "river" with a high degree of watery grandeur. Consequently, such people feel rather disappointed when they stand on the shores of the Humboldt or the Carson and find that a "river" in Nevada is a sickly rivulet which is just the counterpart of the Erie canal in all respects save that the canal is twice as long and four times as deep. One of the pleasantest and most invigorating exercises one can contrive is to run and jump across the Humboldt river till he is overheated, and then drink it dry.

5. Which of the following types of essays best describes this selection?
   A. persuasive   B. reflective   C. humorous   D. biographical

6. Which technique is reflected in the final sentence of the selection?
   A. hyperbole   B. understatement   C. satire   D. irony

7. What technique creates humor in this sentence?

   "I'm not sure he likes me," Jim said, leaping back as the frenzied dog charged.

   A. satire   B. wordplay   C. understatement   D. hyperbole

8. Which of the following topics would be the most likely target of satirical writing?
   A. The Life Cycle of a Fern   C. Modern Medical Breakthroughs
   B. America's Obsession With Shopping   D. The History of Air Conditioning

Reading Skills *Read the selection, and answer the questions that follow.*

(1) The earth, as everybody knows nowadays, is a spheroid, a sphere slightly compressed, orange fashion, with a diameter of nearly 8,000 miles. (2) Its spherical shape has been known at least to a limited number of intelligent people for nearly 2,500 years, but before that time it was supposed to be flat, and various ideas which now seem fantastic were entertained about its relations to the sky and the stars and planets. (3) We know now that it rotates upon its axis (which is about 24 miles shorter than its equatorial diameter) every twenty-four hours, and that this is the cause of the alternations of day and night, that it circles about the sun in a slightly distorted and slowly variable oval path in a year.

9. What is the main idea of the selection?
   A. People's ideas about the earth have changed over time.
   B. The earth is a spheroid that rotates on its axis and circles the sun.
   C. Earth's diameter is 8,000 miles, and it is a variable distance from the sun.
   D. People now know that the earth is round.

10. Which of the following details would best support the main idea of the selection?
   A. Because of the earth's shape, part of the planet is always in shadow.
   B. Seventy-one percent of the earth's surface is covered with water.
   C. The earth has only one body orbiting it—the moon.
   D. The ancient Greeks believed the planets and the sun orbited the earth.

11. Which of the following details would be least important to include in a summary of the selection?
   A. The shape of the earth is a spheroid.
   B. The earth rotates on its axis.
   C. Scholars have been aware of the earth's shape for nearly 2,500 years.
   D. The earth traces an oval path around the sun.

12. Which of the following questions would be least helpful to ask in order to understand this particular selection?
   A. What is the author's topic?
   B. What is the author's main point?
   C. What are the author's supporting points?
   D. What is the author's background?

Name _____ Date _____

Read the following selection. Then, answer the questions that follow.

(1) Harriet Beecher Stowe was a highly influential figure in the American anti-slavery movement before the Civil War. (2) Her novel *Uncle Tom's Cabin* launched her from obscurity to fame as a leading opponent of slavery. (3) The chief villain in the book, Simon Legree, became familiar to hundreds of thousands of readers, and the book inflamed anti-slavery passions. (4) Abraham Lincoln famously exclaimed when he met Stowe, "So, you're the little woman who wrote the book that made this great war!" (5) Subsequent historians, however, have assigned her a less important role.

13. What is the main idea of this selection?
    A. Stowe caused the American Civil War.
    B. Stowe was a prominent anti-slavery figure on the eve of the Civil War.
    C. Stowe earned the respect of readers, including President Lincoln.
    D. Stowe's influence in causing the Civil War has been overstated.

14. Which of the following details is least supportive of the main idea?
    A. sentence 2   C. sentence 4
    B. sentence 3   D. sentence 5

15. Which of the following would be a characteristic of an effective summary of this selection?
    A. It would include more detail than the original
    B. It would include information about the author.
    C. It would include less detail than the original.
    D. It would include footnotes and citations.

16. As the author continues writing, how might he or she continue to support the main idea?
    A. by describing Stowe's personality
    B. by describing readers' reactions to *Uncle Tom's Cabin.*
    C. by providing background about the causes of the Civil War
    D. by describing Stowe's childhood

Informational Texts: Follow and Critique Technical Directions

Read this selection from technicial directions. Then answer the questions that follow.

Follow these steps to install this CD drive in your computer
1) Unplug your computer from all power sources. 2) Open an unused bay on your computer.
3) Slide the drive into the computer bay. 4) Attach the green wire on the CD drive to an unused power source in your computer. 5) Plug the audio cable on the CD drive into an unused audio slot in your computer. 6) Plug in the computer.

17. Which statement is accurate according to the directions?
    A. You should leave the computer turned on while you install the CD drive.
    B. You should plug in the CD drive's audio cable before you unplug the computer.
    C. You should connect the drive's green wire before you connect the drive's audio cable.
    D. You should slide the drive into the computer bay after you connect the drive's green wire.

18. Which of the following is an accurate statement about Step 2?
    A. It can be followed easier and faster than all the other steps.
    B. It can be easily followed without a knowledge of computers.
    C. It is not necessary because everyone knows this has to be done.
    D. It is not adequate because it does not say how to open a computer bay.

19. Which of the following is an accurate statement about Step 4?
    A. It does not give enough information about finding an unused computer power source.
    B. It gives too much information about connecting the CD drive's green wire.
    C. It tells you what to do if there is no unused computer power source.
    D. It is well written, very clear, and easy to follow.

Vocabulary

20. What is the meaning of *tactile* in the following sentence?

    Billy liked working with velvet because the material was so tactile.
    A. of or relating to work   C. of or relating to touch
    B. smooth   D. strong

21. Which of the following words has the same root as *configuration*?
    A. disfigure   C. fascination
    B. firefight   D. confuse

22. Which statement is an example of a paradox?
    A. "A penny saved is a penny earned."
    B. "Early to bed and early to rise makes a man healthy, wealthy, and wise."
    C. "Ask not what your country can do for you — ask what you can do for your country."
    D. "The swiftest traveler is he who goes afoot."

23. What does *succinct* mean as it is used in the following sentence?

    The politician's succinct answer was a refreshing change from all the long speeches.
    A. dishonest   C. long
    B. clever   D. short

24. Which of the following pairs of words has the same root?
    A. *transpire* and *training*   C. *community* and *necessity*
    B. *disable* and *readable*   D. *transfigure* and *figuration*

25. What is the opposite of *intact* as it is used in the following sentence?

    Amazingly, the house was intact after the fierce storm.
    A. damaged   C. on high ground
    B. clean   D. full of water

Grammar

26. Which part of speech is the italicized word in this sentence?

    Sheila told her *friends* the news.

    A. direct object
    B. indirect object
    C. object of the preposition
    D. predicate nominative

27. What part of speech is the italicized word in this sentence?

    The state has wonderful *mountains*.

    A. direct object
    B. indirect object
    C. object of the preposition
    D. predicate nominative

28. What part of speech is the italicized word in this sentence?

    The most beautiful girl on the beach is *Claire*.

    A. direct object
    B. indirect object
    C. predicate adjective
    D. predicate nominative

29. What part of speech is the italicized word in this sentence?

    All the choices on the menu are *delicious*.

    A. direct object
    B. indirect object
    C. predicate adjective
    D. predicate nominative

30. How were these short sentences combined?

    I sold my bike. / I put the money in the bank. / *I sold my bike and put the money in the bank.*

    A. using compound verbs
    B. using compound objects
    C. using predicate nominatives
    D. using predicate adjectives

31. How were these short sentences combined?

    He studied French. / He studied Latin. / *He studied French and Latin.*

    A. using compound verbs
    B. using compound objects
    C. using predicate nominatives
    D. using predicate adjectives

32. Which statement is accurate?
   A. A direct object answers the question to whom.
   B. An indirect object answers the question to whom.
   C. A direct object answers the question to what.
   D. An indirect object answers the question what.

33. Which statement is accurate?
   A. Predicate nominatives appear before a linking verb.
   B. Predicate nominatives appear after an action verb.
   C. Predicate adjectives appear before an action verb.
   D. Predicate adjectives appear after a linking verb.

34. How were these short sentences combined?

The room is large. It is airy. It is colorful. = The room is large, airy, and colorful.

   A. using compound objects   C. using predicate nominatives
   B. using compound verbs   D. using predicate adjectives

ESSAY

35. Your high school needs funds for band uniforms. Write a business letter to a local firm soliciting a donation to help pay for the uniforms. Remember to explain why the uniforms are important. Include relevant information such as the cost of the uniforms and how many you need. Use both logical and persuasive arguments.

36. Even the most ordinary life includes a few surprises. Write a brief memoir that describes a time when a person or event surprised you. Use vivid details and precise words to help readers re-create your experience in their minds as they read.

37. Take a stand! Write a letter to your local paper in which you state your position on an issue under debate in your community. State your opinion clearly and support it with persuasive facts, statistics, or examples. Be sure to use polite language and correct formatting.

Name _____

Unit 3: Types of Nonfiction Skills Concept Map—2
What kind of knowledge changes our lives?

Literary Analysis:

Nonfiction Writing

includes → **persuasive compositions, including speeches** and → **analytic and interpretive essays**

(demonstrated in this selection)
Selection name: _____

(demonstrated in this selection)
Selection name: _____

Reading Skills and Strategies:
Evaluating Persuasive Texts

You can **evaluate the writer's argument and appeals**

by → **determining whether techniques are used effectively** → and by → **distinguishing between fact and opinion**

(demonstrated in this selection)
Selection name: _____

Informational Text:
Course Catalog

you can analyze text structures → to → **understand the organization of the text**

Comparing Literary Works:
Author's Purpose

might be to →

- persuade or pay tribute
- inform or entertain

(demonstrated in these selections)
Selection names:
1.
2.

Words you can use to discuss the Big Question

_____
_____
_____
_____
_____

Basic Elements of Essay and Speeches

- Style
- Tone
- Perspective
- Purpose

Types of Essays

- Narrative
- Descriptive
- Expository
- Persuasive
- Reflective

Types of Speeches

- Address
- Talk
- Oration
- Lecture

Student Log

Complete this chart to track your assignments.

Writing	Extend Your Learning	Writing Workshop	Other Assignments

Study these words from "Keep Memory Alive." Then, complete the activities.

Word List A

behalf [bee HAF] *n.* in the interest of
  She accepted the honor on <u>behalf</u> of her mother, who could not attend.

bewilderment [be WIL duhr muhnt] *n.* the state of being very confused
  The maze looked simple, but soon I was lost and felt utter <u>bewilderment</u>.

endure [en DOOR] *v.* to suffer pain or hardship for a long time
  With no power after the storm, we had to <u>endure</u> many difficulties.

ghetto [GET oh] *n.* an impoverished part of a city
  By the early 1940s, the Nazis had confined the Polish Jews to a <u>ghetto</u>.

guilty [GIL tee] *adj.* having broken a law or a rule
  The court found the criminals <u>guilty</u> of robbing the neighborhood store.

identified [eye DEN ti fyd] *v.* having understood someone else's feelings
  Because I am so clumsy, I <u>identified</u> with those picked last for the team.

mankind [man KYND] *n.* all humans, considered as a group
  Throughout the history of <u>mankind</u>, there has rarely been peace for long.

perished [PER isht] *v.* died
  Li's grandfather <u>perished</u> in a battle years ago.

Word List B

anguish [AN gwish] *n.* suffering caused by extreme pain or worry
  Linda was overcome with <u>anguish</u> when her kitten was missing.

committed [kuh MIT tid] *v.* having done something wrong or illegal
  Anyone who uses biological weapons has <u>committed</u> a serious crime.

deportation [dee pawr TAY shuhn] *v.* to make a person leave a country
  The <u>deportation</u> of Jews from the land of their birth was a cruelty of war.

destiny [DES ti nee] *n.* fate; predetermined future
  The unfortunate shoulder injury changed the star pitcher's <u>destiny</u>.

humiliation [hyoo mil ee AY shuhn] *n.* shame
  The comedian left the stage in <u>humiliation</u> after being booed by the crowd.

multitudes [MUL ti toods] *n.* very large numbers of things or people
  There was almost a stampede as <u>multitudes</u> of fans saw the star's limo pull up.

naïve [nye EEV] *adj.* lacking any experience of life
  You would have to be very <u>naïve</u> to think that things will always go as planned.

profound [pruh FOWND] *adj.* very great, important, or strong
  Seeing the Mona Lisa made a <u>profound</u> impression on her.

Name _____   Date _____

"Keep Memory Alive" by Elie Wiesel
Vocabulary Warm-up Exercises

Exercise A *Fill in each blank in the paragraph with an appropriate word from Word List A.
Use each word only once.*

Johann was surprised to see the name of his grandfather's street in the historical

novel he was reading. It was even more shocking to read that people had once

[1] _____ in that neighborhood. Those in power had forced a minority

group to live in a [2] _____, apart from the rest of the city. Johann felt

confusion and [3] _____ as he tried to unravel truth from fiction. How

could people have been [4] _____ of such cruelty? Johann was also a

member of a minority group, so he [5] _____ with the victims. What

hardships they had been made to [6] _____! He wanted to write about

what happened on [7] _____ of those who had died. It was important

that everyone, indeed that all of [8] _____, learn from the past.

Exercise B *Revise each sentence so that the underlined vocabulary word is used in a logical
way. Be sure to keep the vocabulary word in your revision.*

Example: We experienced the <u>humiliation</u> with no feeling of shame.
We experienced the <u>humiliation</u> with a great sense of shame.

1. Because the people faced <u>deportation</u>, they knew they could stay in the country.

   _____

2. <u>Multitudes</u> of people live in the city, so it is not a bit crowded.

   _____

3. Evidence showed that he had <u>committed</u> the crime, so we found him innocent.

   _____

4. When Eve became a painter, she fulfilled her <u>destiny</u> to be a great musician.

   _____

5. After working so hard for the prize, he felt great <u>anguish</u> when he won it.

   _____

6. The <u>naïve</u> boy had a sophisticated, worldly sense of humor.

   _____

7. Nell had a <u>profound</u> desire to help people, so she kept putting herself first.

   _____

"Keep Memory Alive" by Elie Wiesel
Reading Warm-up A

Read the following passage. Pay special attention to the underlined words. Then, read it again, and complete the activities. Use a separate sheet of paper for your written answers.

During World War II, some remarkable people risked their own lives to save others. A woman named Irene Sendler rescued 2,500 Jewish children in Poland. In 1942, the Nazis made several hundred thousand Jews live in a small <u>ghetto</u> in the Polish city of Warsaw. Once there, people had to <u>endure</u> starvation and disease. During this awful time, Irene Sendler sacrificed her own safety to help others.

Irene Sendler was not Jewish, so she could travel freely. She was able to enter the ghetto, where she went daily to give people food and medicine. As the situation worsened, Sendler decided to try to help children escape the ghetto. It was difficult to convince parents to give up their children. As a mother herself, Sendler <u>identified</u> with the parents' grief. However, she knew that the children had no hope of staying alive if they stayed. After the parents agreed, Sendler found places for the children to hide in homes, orphanages, or convents. The children must have felt great confusion and <u>bewilderment</u> as they were smuggled out of the ghetto, sometimes in potato sacks and other times in coffins.

After Sendler had rescued about 400 children, the Nazis found her out. They arrested her and tortured her, believing that she was <u>guilty</u> of a terrible crime. Yet, she never gave them information about the children. Sendler escaped from prison, and managed to help over 2,000 more children leave the ghetto.

After the war, most of these children learned that their families had <u>perished</u> in concentration camps. They were among the millions killed by the Nazis in one of the darkest chapters in the history of <u>mankind</u>. Yet, one woman's courage saved 2,500 children.

In 2003, at the age of 93, Irene Sendler was awarded one of Poland's highest honors. She accepted it on <u>behalf</u> of all of the others who had sacrificed their own safety to save others.

1. Circle the words that tell where the <u>ghetto</u> was. Then, write what *ghetto* means.

2. Circle the words that tell what people in the ghetto had to <u>endure</u>. Then, explain what *endure* means.

3. Underline the phrase that explains why Sendler <u>identified</u> with the parents so easily. Use the phrase *identified with* in a sentence.

4. Circle the word that means something close to <u>bewilderment</u>. Use *bewilderment* in a sentence.

5. Underline the phrase that tells what the Nazis believed that Sendler was <u>guilty</u> of. Then, explain what *guilty* means.

6. Circle the words that tell where the rest of the children's families had <u>perished</u>. Use *perished* in a sentence.

7. Underline the sentence in which the word <u>mankind</u> appears. Then, rewrite the sentence, using a synonym for *mankind*.

8. Underline the phrase that tells on whose <u>behalf</u> Sendler accepted the honor. Then, explain what *behalf* means.

"Keep Memory Alive" by Elie Wiesel
Reading Warm-up B

Read the following passage. Pay special attention to the underlined words. Then, read it again, and complete the activities. Use a separate sheet of paper for your written answers.

Perhaps it seems unsophisticated or <u>naïve</u> to believe in the possibility of peace on Earth. Certainly, the goal of attaining peace for the <u>multitudes</u> of people in the world may seem impossibly out of reach. Yet, every year, a prize is given to the person or persons doing the most to achieve that goal. This remarkable award is called the Nobel Peace Prize. The prize is named for Alfred Nobel, a nineteenth-century chemist. Nobel invented dynamite and became very wealthy because of that and other major inventions. In his will, he asked that his money be used for annual prizes in physics, chemistry, literature, and peace.

From 1901 to the present, the Peace Prize has been given annually. Winners have included world leaders, like American president Woodrow Wilson, who work to negotiate peace. It has been given to activists, like members of Amnesty International, who work to end crimes <u>committed</u> by the powerful against the powerless. It has also been given to humanitarians, like Mother Theresa of India, who work to improve the lives of suffering people. All the winners have worked to make the world a better place.

Some winners, like Elie Wiesel, have experienced shame and <u>humiliation</u> as they went through agonizing ordeals early in their lives. These experiences made them vow to work to end the suffering and <u>anguish</u> of other people. Other winners, like the International Committee of the Red Cross, work to protect ordinary civilians during wartime. Such protections now shield people from <u>deportation</u>, or forced removal from their countries.

The political leaders, humanitarians, and activists who have won the Nobel Peace Prize share a <u>profound</u> desire to change the world. They also share a belief in their ability to make a difference in the <u>destiny</u> of suffering peoples.

1. Circle the word that is a synonym of <u>naïve</u>. Then, use *naïve* in a sentence.

2. Underline the words that tell what is being counted as <u>multitudes</u>. Why is it easier to achieve peace for a few people than for *multitudes*?

3. Circle the word that tells who <u>committed</u> crimes against the powerless. Explain what *committed* means.

4. Circle the word that is similar in meaning to <u>humiliation</u>. Then, use *humiliation* in a sentence.

5. Circle the synonym for <u>anguish</u>. Then, write about a time when you felt *anguish*.

6. Write a sentence about how you would feel or what you would do if faced with <u>deportation</u>.

7. Write a sentence about something you have a <u>profound</u> desire to do.

8. Underline the phrase that tells about whose <u>destiny</u> the peace prize winners work to change. Explain what *destiny* means.

Name _____ Date _____

"Keep Memory Alive" by Elie Wiesel

Writing About the Big Question

What kind of knowledge changes our lives?

Big Question Vocabulary

adapt	awareness	empathy	enlighten	evolve
growth	history	ignorance	influence	insight
modified	question	reflect	revise	understanding

A. *Use one or more words from the list above to complete each sentence.*

1. Elie Wiesel experienced one of the most painful moments in world _____ .

2. It was impossible to gain _____ into the cruel hearts of those who persecuted him.

3. Claiming _____ about the suffering and mistreatment of others is never a good excuse.

4. Wiesel wants to _____ others to stand up for the rights of the oppressed.

B. *Follow the directions in responding to each of the items below.*

1. List two different times in which you learned about or experienced an unjust situation.

   _____

   _____

2. Write two sentences explaining one of the situations you listed, and describe how it made you feel. Use at least two of the Big Question vocabulary words.

   _____

   _____

C. *Complete the sentence below. Then, write a short paragraph in which you connect this experience to the big question.*

When you learn that people are capable of brutality against others, you can choose to _____ .

_____

_____

_____

Unit 3 Resources: Types of Nonfiction

"Keep Memory Alive" by Elie Wiesel
Literary Analysis: Persuasive Writing

Persuasive writing is nonfiction intended to convince people to take a particular action or agree with the author's point of view. Persuasive writers present **arguments,** using reason to support their positions. They also use **rhetorical devices,** or patterns of words that create emphasis and stir emotion. Rhetorical devices include the following:

- **Repetition**—the reuse of a key word or idea for emphasis
- **Parallelism**—similar grammatical structures used to express related ideas
- **Slogans and saws**—short, catchy phrases
- **Rhetorical questions**—questions that are intended to have obvious answers and that are asked for effect

Examples of persuasive writing include persuasive essays, speeches, advertisements, political writings, legal arguments, sales brochures, and fund-raising letters.

A. DIRECTIONS: *Answer the following about Elie Wiesel's speech "Keep Memory Alive."*

1. What sentence in Weisel's speech sums up the point with which he wants his listeners to agree?

   _____

   _____

2. List three reasonable, persuasive elements Wiesel uses to support his main point. Identify the type of argument or rhetorical device used in each.

   _____

   _____

   _____

   _____

   _____

3. Why is this message more powerful coming from Elie Wiesel than from someone else?

   _____

   _____

   _____

4. Why is it important to Wiesel to keep the memory of what happened to him and his people alive?

   _____

   _____

   _____

Name _____ Date _____

Reading: Test the Writer's Logic to Evaluate Persuasive Appeals

When reading persuasive writing, **evaluate the writer's appeals** to decide whether the writer makes a good case for his or her point of view. If a writer calls for a particular action or makes a specific claim, **test the writer's logic.** To do this, consider whether the evidence and reasoning the writer presents supports the point. For example, if a writer claims that fish make better pets than dogs, he or she needs to support this opinion with evidence and reasoning. A good supporting point might be that fish cannot dig up one's yard. An illogical or poor argument might be that mice have a tendency to bite. This argument does not support the point that fish make better pets than dogs.

DIRECTIONS: *First, fill in the main point with which Elie Wiesel wants his audience to agree. Then, list four appeals he uses in his speech and evaluate the logic of each.*

1. What is the main point with which Wiesel wants his audience to agree?

   _____

   _____

2. List four appeals from "Keep Memory Alive" and test the logic of each.

   A. _____

   _____

   _____

   B. _____

   _____

   _____

   C. _____

   _____

   _____

   _____

   D. _____

   _____

   _____

   _____

"**Keep Memory Alive**" by Elie Wiesel
Vocabulary Builder

Word List

accomplices   bewilderment   naïve   presumptuous   profound   transcends

A. DIRECTIONS: *Write a sentence that demonstrates the meaning of each of the vocabulary words.*

1. A situation that might cause *bewilderment*: _____

_____

2. People who are *accomplices*: _____

_____

3. Characteristics of someone who is *naïve*: _____

_____

4. Someone who might make a *profound* statement: _____

_____

5. Feelings a person might have when he or she *transcends* expectations: _____

_____

B. WORD STUDY: The **Latin root -scend-** means "climb." Revise each sentence so that the underlined word containing the root -scend- is used logically. Be sure not to change the underlined word.

1. We knew that to *ascend* the mountain, we would have to climb down slowly.

_____

2. The mountaineer's *descent* took her higher and higher until she could see across the valley.

_____

3. The ballerina's dance was *transcendent*, and the audience walked out in disappointment.

_____

"**Keep Memory Alive**" by Elie Wiesel
Enrichment: Connecting to Art

Imagine a postal system in which the person who *receives* the letter is responsible for paying the postage. That is how postal systems worked throughout Europe during the seventeenth and eighteenth centuries. An English schoolmaster first proposed, in 1837, that postage be prepaid by the sender of the letter.

Now, more than 150 years later, postage stamps do more than move the mail. They send messages in and of themselves. In particular, commemorative stamps—by means of their art— publicize a nation's successes, praise its heroes, and pay tribute to achievements both large and small. Almost no topic has been left untouched. Here is just a brief list: anniversaries of the births and deaths of writers, artists, media celebrities, presidents, and scientists; anniversaries of inventions, battles, and other events, such as statehood; "first" accomplishments, such as space travel; war; peace; human rights; and nature and the environment. The only "rule" with regard to U.S. commemorative stamp subjects is that living persons are not depicted.

Postal administrations receive hundreds of suggestions each year for commemorative stamp subjects. Once the subject for a stamp design is decided upon by a committee, the design is rendered, or drawn. An artist or illustrator may render an original design, or an image may be reproduced from an existing painting, portrait, or photograph. Designs are carefully constructed for color balance and composition, or overall impression. The picture, the words, and any other elements must balance and work together if the stamp is to convey an effective message.

Postage stamps have become an art form in themselves. The miniature art on a commemorative stamp is expected to reflect its age, its issuing nation, and the subject it commemorates all at once. That is a great deal to ask of a piece of paper approximately one inch square.

DIRECTIONS: *Review "Keep Memory Alive" by Elie Wiesel. Then, in the following space or on a separate piece of paper, design a postage stamp that commemorates the victims of the Holocaust. Your design may be abstract or realistic. Include an identifying phrase, the name of the issuing nation, and the value of the stamp.*

Name _____ Date _____

"Keep Memory Alive" by Elie Wiesel
Open-Book Test

Short Answer *Write your responses to the questions in this section on the lines provided.*

1. A rhetorical question is a question that is intended to have obvious answers. Use the chart to list the two rhetorical questions that Elie Wiesel asks in the second paragraph of "Keep Memory Alive." Write the questions in your own words. Then, on the lines below, provide the "obvious" answer to the questions.

	Rhetorical Questions in "Keep Memory Alive"
Question 1	
Question 2	

_____

_____

2. Would it be *presumptuous* for an experienced lawyer to give advice about a legal matter? Base your answer on the meaning of *presumptuous* in "Keep Memory Alive."

_____

_____

3. In the fourth paragraph of "Keep Memory Alive," Wiesel writes, "It all happened so fast. The ghetto. The deportation. The sealed cattle car." How does this passage illustrate the rhetorical device of parallelism?

_____

_____

_____

4. What does Wiesel mean in the first paragraph of "Keep Memory Alive" when he says of the honor bestowed upon him, "your choice transcends me." If the honor transcends, or goes beyond, Wiesel, then to whom is the honor really dedicated?

_____

_____

5. In "Keep Memory Alive," Wiesel begins several sentences in a row with the words "I remember." What rhetorical device is he using in these sentences—saws, repetition, or rhetorical questions?

_____

6. In "Keep Memory Alive," Wiesel recalls asking his father about the world's response to the Holocaust. What feeling does he express to his father?

_____

_____

_____

7. In "Keep Memory Alive," Wiesel states that the Holocaust "happened yesterday or an eternity ago." What does he mean by this statement?

_____

_____

_____

8. What is Wiesel's main argument in "Keep Memory Alive"?

_____

_____

_____

9. In "Keep Memory Alive," Wiesel appeals to his audience never to forget the crimes of the Holocaust. On what basic argument does he base this appeal?

_____

_____

_____

10. If you felt constant *bewilderment* while taking a math test, would you most likely have done well or poorly on the test? Explain your answer, based on the meaning of *bewilderment* in "Keep Memory Alive."

_____

_____

Essay

Write an extended response to the question of your choice or to the question or questions your teacher assigns you.

11. Elie Wiesel has dedicated his life to writing and talking about the horrors of the Holocaust so that the world will never forget about this terrible crime against humanity. In an essay, explain why Wiesel believes that memory is such a powerful force. Why is he concerned that people will forget about the Holocaust?

12. "Keep Memory Alive" is both an acceptance speech and a persuasive speech. In an essay, explain what Wiesel tries to convince his audience to do or to believe. Then discuss the rhetorical techniques he uses to persuade his listeners. Did he convince you? Why or why not? Support your answer with at least two examples from Wiesel's speech.

13. Toward the end of "Keep Memory Alive," Wiesel argues that "we must always take sides" when we become aware of examples of human "suffering and humiliation." Do you agree with him? Why or why not? In an essay, explain what you think Wiesel is saying about a person's obligation to the community. Provide examples from the speech to support your response.

14. **Thinking About the Big Question: What kind of knowledge changes our lives?** As we learn in "Keep Memory Alive," Wiesel has devoted his whole life to keeping alive the memory of the horrors and injustices of the Holocaust. In an essay, reflect on how the lives of people around the world most likely have changed by the knowledge spread by Wiesel's speeches and books on this topic. What does Wiesel claim is the effect of keeping knowledge of the Holocaust alive?

Oral Response

15. Go back to question 4, 5, or 7 or to the question your teacher assigns you. Take a few minutes to expand your answer and prepare an oral response. Find additional details in "Keep Memory Alive" that support your points. If necessary, make notes to guide your oral response.

"Keep Memory Alive" by Elie Wiesel
Selection Test A

Critical Reading *Identify the letter of the choice that best answers the question.*

____ 1. What feelings does Wiesel say he has about receiving the Nobel Prize?
   A. fear and pleasure
   B. excitement and happiness
   C. regret and humiliation
   D. surprise and dismay

____ 2. On whose behalf does Wiesel accept the Nobel Prize?
   A. himself and his family members
   B. those who remained silent
   C. those who died in the Holocaust
   D. Holocaust survivors and their children

____ 3. Wiesel writes, "How could the world remain silent?" What rhetorical device is he using?
   A. repetition
   B. parallelism
   C. slogans and saws
   D. rhetorical question

____ 4. What does the adult Wiesel tell the "boy" in his essay?
   A. that he has won the Nobel Prize for his achievements
   B. that he has tried to keep memory alive for others
   C. that he has almost forgotten those who died so long ago
   D. that he has gotten revenge for the Holocaust

____ 5. Wiesel begins several sentences in a row with the words "I remember." What rhetorical device is he using?
   A. repetition
   B. parallelism
   C. slogans and saws
   D. rhetorical question

____ 6. In "Keep Memory Alive," Wiesel recalls asking his father about the world's response to the Holocaust. What feeling does he express to his father?
   A. surprise that the world did not know about the Holocaust
   B. pleasure that the world acted so quickly to stop the Holocaust
   C. shock that the world remained silent and allowed it to happen
   D. fear that the world actively helped the Nazis commit mass murder

____ 7. Why does Wiesel say that the Holocaust "happened yesterday or an eternity ago"?

    A. to show that he remembers the Holocaust clearly and always will

    B. to let the audience know that the Holocaust is still happening

    C. to remind others that he knows the Holocaust happened years ago

    D. to admit that he does not remember the Holocaust very well

____ 8. Wiesel says that forgetting the Holocaust makes us guilty. How does he support this claim?

    A. by stating that forgetting makes it possible for it to happen to us

    B. by explaining that forgetting encourages new torments to occur

    C. by saying that forgetting makes us accomplices to the crime

    D. by pointing out that forgetting does not honor those who died

____ 9. What does Wiesel say about neutrality in the final statements of "Keep Memory Alive"?

    A. Neutrality helps keep people out of trouble.

    B. Neutrality helps the oppressor, never the victim.

    C. Neutrality is a sign of indecision and should be avoided.

    D. Neutrality keeps people from getting involved.

____ 10. What is Wiesel trying to persuade his audience to believe or do?

    A. fight against current Nazi oppression

    B. take sides when they see injustice

    C. give him the Nobel Peace Prize for his writing

    D. find out more about the victims of the Holocaust

____ 11. What is a rhetorical device?

    A. a way to test the writer's reasoning and logic

    B. a badly written translation from another language

    C. a question intended to have an obvious answer

    D. a word-pattern that creates emphasis and emotion

____ 12. Why should you test the logic of a writer's appeals?

    A. to decide whether a writer should receive the Nobel Prize

    B. to reach a conclusion about the entertainment value of an essay

    C. to decide whether a writer makes a good case for a point of view

    D. to reach a decision about whether to speak out against injustice

Vocabulary and Grammar

____ 13. Which of the following is an example of being *presumptuous*?
   A. writing a letter of complaint
   B. disagreeing with a friend
   C. intruding into a conversation
   D. speaking publicly to persuade people to act

____ 14. Which of the following is the best synonym for *bewilderment*?
   A. personality
   B. wilderness
   C. confusion
   D. violence

____ 15. Which of the following is the correct way to form the superlative of the adverb *sadly*?
   A. sadly
   B. sadliest
   C. more sadliest
   D. most sadly

Essay

16. Wiesel has made it his personal mission to remind others about the horrors of the Holocaust. In an essay, explain why Wiesel feels so strongly about keeping the memory of the Holocaust alive. Why does he feel that memory is such a powerful force? What are his concerns about people forgetting the Holocaust? Use at least two examples from his speech to support your explanation of his point of view.

17. "Keep Memory Alive" is an acceptance speech, but it is also a persuasive speech. In an essay, explain what Wiesel calls upon his audience to do. Then, discuss the persuasive techniques he uses to convince his listeners to agree with him. Did he convince you? Why or why not? Use at least two examples from Wiesel's speech to support your answer.

18. **Thinking About the Big Question: What kind of knowledge changes our lives?** Elie Wiesel has devoted his life to keeping the memory of the Holocaust alive by writing books and delivering speeches. In an essay, explain how the knowledge spread by Wiesel's work might change people's lives. Keep in mind the following question: What might happen if we forget about the Holocaust?

Name _____ Date _____

"Keep Memory Alive" by Elie Wiesel

Selection Test B

Critical Reading *Identify the letter of the choice that best completes the statement or answers the question.*

____ 1. Why does receiving the Nobel Prize frighten Wiesel?
  A. because he thinks his fellow survivors will be jealous
  B. because he is worried that Nazis will find out and punish him
  C. because he had taken a vow of silence and will have to break it
  D. because he does not feel entitled to represent those who died

____ 2. How does Wiesel represent those who have died?
  A. He is trying to find their descendants.
  B. He is calling for revenge for their deaths.
  C. He is dedicating his Nobel Prize to the survivors.
  D. He is telling the story of what happened to them.

____ 3. Why does Wiesel feel that he does not have the right to speak for the dead?
  A. They would be angry at him.
  B. He did not know any of them.
  C. No one remembers them.
  D. No one can interpret his or her dreams.

____ 4. Why does Wiesel say his Nobel Prize belongs to all Holocaust survivors and their children?
  A. He is relating their story as well as his own.
  B. He did not do anything to deserve the award.
  C. They would be angry if he did not mention them.
  D. They are more capable of speaking for those who died.

____ 5. As a boy, what shocked Wiesel about the world's response to the Holocaust?
  A. The world did not know about the Holocaust.
  B. The world acted so quickly to stop the Holocaust.
  C. The world remained silent and allowed it to happen.
  D. The world actively helped the Nazis commit genocide.

____ 6. What does the "boy" ask the adult Elie Wiesel?
  A. He asks what Elie Wiesel has done with the boy's future.
  B. He asks why Elie Wiesel is receiving the Nobel Prize.
  C. He asks about how many people died in the Holocaust.
  D. He asks how the world could let the Holocaust happen.

____ 7. Wiesel claims that we all have a moral duty to remember what happened during the Holocaust. How does he support this claim?
  A. by stating that the Holocaust might happen again if we forget
  B. by explaining that silence encourages torments to occur
  C. by saying that if we forget, we are accomplices to the crime
  D. by pointing out that the dead would want to be remembered

Name _____ Date _____

____ 8. What is the "fiery altar" Wiesel mentions in his speech?
   A. Jewish ghettos
   B. cattle cars
   C. gas chambers
   D. concentration camps

____ 9. Wiesel mentions the "fiery altar upon which the history of our people and the future of mankind were meant to be sacrificed." What persuasive appeal is embedded in these words?
   A. Wiesel is indicating his distaste for all established religions and institutions.
   B. Wiesel is trying to make his audience sympathize with the plight of the Jewish people.
   C. Wiesel is attempting to scare his audience with frightening imagery and ideas.
   D. Wiesel is suggesting that the loss of Jews has affected the future of the world.

____ 10. Why does Wiesel repeat the words "I remember" several times near the end of his speech?
   A. to entertain listeners with recollections of his youth
   B. to emphasize that he wants his audience to remember, too
   C. to point out that it does not matter if anyone else remembers
   D. to make it clear that he is not losing his ability to think clearly

____ 11. What assumption does Wiesel make about a person's main obligation to the community?
   A. We are all obligated to speak out against injustice.
   B. Each person is obligated to manage his or her life.
   C. Everyone is obligated to find out more about the Holocaust.
   D. Everyone is obligated to know what is going on in the world.

____ 12. Wiesel writes, "Neutrality helps the oppressor, never the victim. Silence encourages the tormentor, never the tormented." What rhetorical device is he using?
   A. repetition
   B. parallelism
   C. slogans and saws
   D. rhetorical question

____ 13. What is Wiesel's central argument in "Keep Memory Alive"?
   A. People must speak out against all oppression and injustice.
   B. People must stay neutral in arguments that do not concern them.
   C. People must speak for the dead, who cannot speak for themselves.
   D. People must remember what happened when they were children.

____ 14. Which of the following best describes the persuasive technique Wiesel uses?
   A. He rages passionately about the awful things that happened during the Holocaust.
   B. He logically relates historical events from the twentieth century about the Holocaust.
   C. He describes his experience to bring home to others the horrors of the Holocaust.
   D. He explains that if others forget the Holocaust, they will share responsibility for it.

____ 15. How can a reader test the logic of Wiesel's appeals?
   A. by thinking about how another writer might support the same claims
   B. by identifying which rhetorical devices he uses most frequently
   C. by eliminating opinions from the essay and analyzing the facts for logic
   D. by considering whether the evidence he presents supports his points

Vocabulary and Grammar

____ 16. Which of the following is the best antonym for *presumptuous*?
   A. modest   C. talkative
   B. arrogant   D. hospitable

____ 17. Which of the following is an example of people who are behaving as *accomplices*?
   A. sisters planning a surprise get-together for a friend
   B. two nations working together to achieve peace
   C. a couple getting married after dating for many years
   D. teenagers competing for a place on a basketball team

____ 18. Which of the following is the correct way to form the superlative of the adverb *forcefully*?
   A. forceful   C. more forcefully
   B. forcefullest   D. most forcefully

____ 19. In which of the following sentences is the comparative adverb formed correctly?
   A. Elie Wiesel will speak to our group soon, when we have set a date.
   B. Elie Wiesel will speak to our group sooner than we expected.
   C. Elie Wiesel will speak to our group the soonest of all our guests.
   D. Elie Wiesel will speak to our group more sooner than we had hoped.

Essay

20. Consider why the author works to "keep memory alive." In an essay, explain why he believes that people must remember the Holocaust and what effect remembering the atrocities experienced by the Jews has on us. In your essay, analyze the power that Wiesel attributes to memory. Use at least two examples from his speech to support your ideas.

21. Wiesel warns his listeners that silence helps the oppressors but never the victims. He says we must always take action against injustice. In an essay, describe a current situation in which being a silent witness might be unhelpful. Use at least two examples from Wiesel's speech to support your position that people should take action to change this situation.

22. "Keep Memory Alive" is both an acceptance speech and a persuasive speech. What is Wiesel hoping to convince his audience to believe or do? In an essay, identify Wiesel's central argument and evaluate the effectiveness of his supporting logic. Cite at least two specific arguments and supporting details from Wiesel's speech, and state whether Wiesel succeeds in persuading his audience.

23. **Thinking About the Big Question: What kind of knowledge changes our lives?** As we learn in "Keep Memory Alive," Wiesel has devoted his life to keeping alive the memory of the Holocaust. In an essay, reflect on how the lives of people around the world most likely have changed by the knowledge spread by Wiesel's speeches and books on this topic. What does Wiesel claim is the effect of keeping knowledge of the Holocaust alive?

Unit 3 Resources: Types of Nonfiction
144

Vocabulary Warm-up Word Lists

Study these words from the excerpt of Solzhenitsyn's Nobel Lecture. Then, apply your knowledge to the activities that follow.

Word List A

acute [uh KYOOT] *adj.* very powerful; sharp
  The dog's barking showed its <u>acute</u> awareness of an approaching stranger.

analysis [uh NAL i sis] *n.* the careful examination of something
  We set our budget after a careful <u>analysis</u> of our monthly expenses.

essentially [i SEN shuhl lee] *adv.* relating to the most basic qualities of something
  The fat in foods fried in vegetable oil or olive oil is <u>essentially</u> the same.

expelled [ek SPELD] *v.* officially made someone leave
  Gina was <u>expelled</u> from school after she admitted to cheating on the exam.

internal [in TER nuhl] *adj.* relating to matters within a country
  With a global oil crisis, energy usage is no longer just an <u>internal</u> concern.

organizations [or guh ni ZAY shuhnz] *n.* groups formed for a particular purpose
  Our school has <u>organizations</u> for both choral and instrumental musicians.

unity [YOO ni tee] *n.* togetherness; being at one with others
  The <u>unity</u> of the members of the jury helped them reach a speedy verdict.

violence [VY uh luhns] *n.* behavior that is intended to hurt others
  Young children cannot distinguish real <u>violence</u> from acting on TV.

Word List B

advocated [AD vuh kayt ed] *v.* supported a certain way of doing things
  Not all Southerners <u>advocated</u> slavery before the Civil War.

colleagues [KAHL eegz] *n.* people with whom one works
  The young attorney's <u>colleagues</u> took her to lunch for her birthday.

exclusively [eks KLOO siv lee] *adv.* only
  If runners train <u>exclusively</u> for speed, their endurance may be poor.

translations [trans LAY shuhnz] *n.* writings put into another language
  <u>Translations</u> of the American bestseller appeared in French and Spanish.

literary [LIT uh rer ee] *adj.* of books, poems, and other literature
  Our <u>literary</u> society meets monthly to discuss great works of fiction.

nominated [NOM uh nay tid] *v.* named someone to compete or run for something
  Ian was honored to be one of the few people <u>nominated</u> for the award.

persecution [per si KYOO shuhn] *n.* the act of treating someone cruelly
  A free society cannot allow <u>persecution</u> of people because of their ideas.

unanimous [yoo NAN i muhs] *adj.* with everyone in agreement
  One dissenting vote kept us from making a <u>unanimous</u> decision.

from **"Nobel Lecture"** by Alexander Solzhenitsyn
Vocabulary Warm-up Exercises

Exercise A *Fill in each blank in the paragraph with an appropriate word from Word List A. Use each word only once.*

Freida had an [1] _____ awareness that she needed to make an impact on the world around her. She wanted to work with [2] _____ with which she could make a difference. She went to a library and did an [3] _____ of a number of such groups so she could choose wisely where to invest her time. One international group offered assistance to families who had been [4] _____ from their country because of their beliefs. The countries had [5] _____ problems such as poverty or political unrest. Some of the children of these families had witnessed [6] _____ or had relatives who were jailed because of their political beliefs. Freida liked the global [7] _____ that the organization stood for. No matter where they live or what their beliefs, deep down inside, people everywhere are [8] _____ the same.

Exercise B *Answer the questions with complete explanations.*

1. If a group expresses <u>unanimous</u> support in favor of an idea, has anyone disagreed?
   _____

2. If someone has experienced <u>persecution</u>, will he or she want to experience it again?
   _____

3. If an author complains of bad <u>translations</u> of her work, does she mean that she is unhappy with the artwork?
   _____

4. If an action was <u>advocated</u> by members of a political party, do you think they would be angry when it took place?
   _____

5. If Mary is a <u>literary</u> agent, does she most likely represent musicians?
   _____

6. If Ted has been <u>nominated</u> for a prize, does that mean he has won the prize?
   _____

7. If an actor is famous <u>exclusively</u> for comedic roles, does he also do serious drama?
   _____

8. If Barb is meeting her <u>colleagues</u> for lunch, whom is she meeting?
   _____

from **"Nobel Lecture"** by Alexander Solzhenitsyn
Reading Warm-up A

Read the following passage. Pay special attention to the underlined words. Then, read it again, and complete the activities. Use a separate sheet of paper for your written answers.

Maria was <u>essentially</u> a dreamer. She had visions of justice and peace for all people. Art, she believed, was a means of achieving those dreams. As a writer and performer, Maria believed in the importance of freedom of expression. She wanted to write and act in plays all over the world, and she wanted to teach others to do the same.

Maria's plays were not simple stories. They were satires that used humor to criticize the culture. She mocked the brutality and <u>violence</u> of the national media. She also showed an <u>acute</u> awareness of the inequality between the rich and the poor. She wanted to make a difference in the world.

In college, Maria joined several playwrights' <u>organizations</u>. Through these, she hoped to gain opportunities to travel, to learn, and to have her plays produced. After college, she hoped to teach theater in developing countries. She wanted to learn about the <u>internal</u> issues of different countries that most outsiders would not understand. At home, she knew that the worst she might face for making bold statements would be being <u>expelled</u> from school, but in other countries, artists could face prison or worse. Yet, Maria held on to her belief that art could make a difference.

One drama teacher made a huge contribution to Maria's development as an artist when she made this critical <u>analysis</u> of Maria's work: "Remember that theater exists not only to teach, but also to entertain. Your lessons are sound, but your theater is not."

At first, Maria was crushed, but then she realized just what the teacher meant. Maria worked harder to make her acting livelier, her writing wittier, and her stagecraft more impressive. By the time she finished college, Maria's drama teacher wrote her glowing recommendations. Maria was committed to the idea of advancing the <u>unity</u> of artists and dreamers everywhere so that they could work together to achieve their dreams.

1. Circle the words that tell what Mary <u>essentially</u> was. Then, tell what *essentially* means.

2. Circle the word that means close to the same thing as <u>violence</u>. Then, use *violence* in a sentence.

3. Underline the phrase that tells what Maria's plays showed an <u>acute</u> awareness of. Then, explain what *acute* means.

4. Circle the word that tells what kind of <u>organizations</u> Maria belonged to. Then, tell what *organizations* are.

5. Underline the phrase that tells who would not understand <u>internal</u> issues. Then, explain what *internal* means.

6. Circle the word that tells where Maria could be <u>expelled</u> from. Then, tell what *expelled* means.

7. Underline the sentences that quote the drama teacher's critical <u>analysis</u> of Maria's work. Then, use *analysis* in a sentence.

8. Maria wants to advance <u>unity</u> of specific groups of people. Circle the names of these groups. Then, use *unity* in a sentence.

from **"Nobel Lecture"** by Alexander Solzhenitsyn
Reading Warm-up B

Read the following passage. Pay special attention to the underlined words. Then, read it again, and complete the activities. Use a separate sheet of paper for your written answers.

Writers often try to influence other people through their writing. Writers who are part of the international <u>literary</u> organization known as PEN go a step further. They try to change the world.

PEN started in England in 1921. The letter *P* stands for poets and playwrights, *E* for editors and essayists, and *N* for novelists. It was established with three main goals. First, to advance understanding among the world's writers. PEN members believed that their ideal of a peaceful world was attainable <u>exclusively</u> through such understanding. Second, they wanted to promote the idea that literature is central to international culture. They believed that even in wartime, libraries and museums should be preserved. Third, members of PEN sought to protect their <u>colleagues</u>—other writers who faced lack of freedom, discrimination, or harassment from their governments. The founders of PEN were <u>unanimous</u> in their agreement with these goals.

Today, PEN has over 10,000 members globally. In America alone, there are 3,700 members. All are accomplished in the field of literature. These members can be <u>nominated</u> or selected for PEN's many awards and honors. They can take part in campaigns for free expression for all of the world's writers. They can also ensure that literary <u>translations</u> are available and well publicized. In that way, important works in one culture are read and appreciated in another.

Throughout its history, PEN has <u>advocated</u> and campaigned for full freedom of expression for writers and artists everywhere. There is a Rapid Response program, through which PEN members learn of injustices, such as the curbing of freedom of the press in a specific country or the imprisonment of a journalist. After learning the facts, members write an appeal, asking for justice and an end to <u>persecution</u>. As Alexander Solzhenitsyn discovered, prominent writers exerting their influence can change the life of one writer in trouble.

1. Underline the name of the <u>literary</u> organization. Explain what interests members of a *literary* organization might share.

2. In your own words, rewrite the sentence containing the word <u>exclusively</u>. Then, write what *exclusively* means.

3. Underline the phrase that tells who the <u>colleagues</u> are that PEN members want to protect. Use *colleagues* in a sentence.

4. If the founders of PEN were <u>unanimous</u> in agreement, how many objected to the goals?

5. Circle the synonym for <u>nominated</u>. Then, write a sentence using the word *nominated*.

6. Explain why PEN works to make sure that <u>translations</u> are available.

7. Circle the synonym for <u>advocated</u>. Then, use *advocated* in a sentence.

8. Underline the name of PEN's program to help stop <u>persecution</u>. Write what kinds of *persecution* an outspoken journalist in another country might face.

Name _____ Date _____

from "Nobel Lecture" by Alexander Solzhenitsyn
Writing About the Big Question

What kind of knowledge changes our lives?

Big Question Vocabulary

adapt	awareness	empathy	enlighten	evolve
growth	history	ignorance	influence	insight
modified	question	reflect	revise	understanding

A. *Use one or more words from the list above to complete each sentence.*

1. Throughout _____ writers have been a uniting force for freedom.

2. Writers often _____ repressive governments and write critically about them.

3. Solzhenitsyn wants to banish lies and _____ the world with the truth.

4. Getting rid of _____ and providing the truth about society is a writer's greatest challenge.

B. *Follow the directions in responding to each of the items below.*

1. List two situations in which you had to tell the truth but did not want to.

   _____

   _____

2. Write two sentences explaining one of the situations you listed, and describe how it made you feel. Use at least two of the Big Question vocabulary words.

   _____

   _____

C. *Complete the sentence below. Then, write a short paragraph in which you connect this experience to the big question.*

   Writers who present the truth about society help people _____

   _____

   _____

   _____

from "**Nobel Lecture**" by Alexander Solzhenitsyn
Literary Analysis: Persuasive Writing

Persuasive writing is nonfiction intended to convince people to take a particular action or agree with the author's point of view. Persuasive writers present **arguments,** using reason to support their positions. They also use **rhetorical devices,** or patterns of words that create emphasis and stir emotion. Rhetorical devices include the following:

- **Repetition**—the reuse of a key word or idea for emphasis
- **Parallelism**—similar grammatical structures used to express related ideas
- **Slogans and saws**—short, catchy phrases
- **Rhetorical questions**—questions that are intended to have obvious answers and that are asked for effect

Examples of persuasive writing include persuasive essays, speeches, advertisements, political writings, legal arguments, sales brochures, and fund-raising letters.

A. DIRECTIONS: *Answer the following questions.*

1. What sentence in Solzhenitsyn's speech sums up the point with which he wants his listeners to agree?

   _____

2. List three reasonable, persuasive elements Solzhenitsyn uses to support his main point. Identify the type of argument or rhetorical device used in each.

   _____

   _____

   _____

   _____

3. Why is this message more powerful coming from Alexander Solzhenitsyn than from someone else?

   _____

   _____

4. Why is it important to Solzhenitsyn to establish the idea of "world literature"?

   _____

   _____

B. DIRECTIONS: *In a brief essay, explain whether or not you were persuaded by this speech to agree with Solzhenitsyn. Be very specific about which words, phrases, points, arguments, and rhetorical devices impressed you most or failed to effectively persuade you, and explain why.*

   _____

   _____

   _____

   _____

Name _____ Date _____

from **"Nobel Lecture"** by Alexander Solzhenitsyn
Reading: Test the Writer's Logic to Evaluate Persuasive Appeals

When reading persuasive writing, **evaluate the writer's appeals** to decide whether the writer makes a good case for his or her point of view. If a writer calls for a particular action or makes a specific claim, **test the writer's logic.** To do this, consider whether the evidence and reasoning the writer presents supports the point he or she is trying to make. For example, if a writer claims that fish make better pets than dogs, he or she needs to support this opinion with evidence and reasoning. A good supporting point might be that fish cannot dig up one's yard. An illogical or a poor argument might be that mice have a tendency to bite. This argument does not support the point that fish make better pets than dogs.

DIRECTIONS: *First, fill in the main point with which Solzhenitsyn wants his audience to agree. Then, list four appeals he uses in his speech and evaluate the logic of each.*

1. What is the main point with which Solzhenitsyn wants his audience to agree?

   _____

   _____

2. List four appeals from Solzhenitsyn's "Nobel Lecture" and test the logic of each.

   A. _____

   _____

   _____

   _____

   B. _____

   _____

   _____

   _____

   C. _____

   _____

   _____

   _____

   D. _____

   _____

   _____

   _____

Name _____ Date _____

from **"Nobel Lecture"** by Alexander Solzhenitsyn
Vocabulary Builder

Word List

aggregate   condemn   inexorably   jurisdiction   oratory   reciprocity

A. DIRECTIONS: *Write a sentence that demonstrates the meaning of each of the words.*

A situation in which *reciprocity* is usually expected: A person giving a ride to a friend might expect *reciprocity* if he or she ever needs a ride.

1. Something that happens *inexorably*: _____

   _____

2. Things that can be an *aggregate*: _____

   _____

3. Someone who has *jurisdiction*: _____

   _____

4. Something or someone that people can *condemn*: _____

   _____

5. A situation that would involve *oratory*: _____

   _____

B. WORD STUDY: The Latin root *-jur-* means "law" or "right." Answer each of the following questions. Explain your answers.

1. Is a *jury* interested in breaking the law?

   _____

2. If you had an *injury* to your leg, would you go see a doctor or go play a football game?

   _____

3. Would a *juror* report to a courtroom or to a cafeteria?

   _____

from **"Nobel Lecture"** by Alexander Solzhenitsyn
Enrichment: Current Events

In his "Nobel Lecture," Solzhenitsyn states that literature and art can vanquish lies. He is referring to the power of words and images to stir people to take action against an unjust government. Solzhenitsyn wrote against his government, and his writings were banned in his country. His words found a global audience instead. He helped educate the world about injustices committed by the Soviet government.

DIRECTIONS: *Answer the following questions.*

1. What is one example of a time in the history of the United States or another country when artists or writers were able to stir people to take action against an unjust government?

   _____

   _____

   _____

   _____

2. **A.** What is one example of government injustice happening in the world today?

   _____

   _____

   _____

   _____

   B. How might writers and artists use their skills to fight against this particular example of injustice?

   _____

   _____

   _____

   _____

3. **A.** What is one example of injustice that you think is happening in the United States?

   _____

   _____

   _____

   _____

   B. In the following space or on a separate piece of paper, write or draw a sketch that might help make people aware of this injustice so they will take action.

   _____

   _____

   _____

   _____

"Keep Memory Alive" by Elie Wiesel
from *"Nobel Lecture"* by Alexander Solzhenitsyn

Integrated Language Skills: Grammar

Degrees of Adverbs

Most adverbs have three different forms to show degrees of comparison—the *positive*, the *comparative*, and the *superlative*. There are different ways to form the comparative and superlative degrees of adverbs. Notice how the forms of the adverbs in the chart change to show degrees of comparison.

Positive	Comparative	Superlative
People fighting injustice want change to come *early*.	Those who speak out can make change occur *earlier* than we think.	The *earliest* time that change can come is when leaders listen to their people.
Solzhenitsyn *firmly* believes in the power of writing to change nations.	Solzhenitsyn believed this fact *more firmly* when people around the world read his work.	Solzhenitsyn probably believed in his work *most firmly* when he witnessed the fall of the Soviet Union.
Wiesel speaks very *well*.	Wiesel speaks *better* than most people.	Wiesel is the *best* speaker I have ever heard.

A. PRACTICE: *The following sentences are based on Wiesel's "Keep Memory Alive" or the excerpt from Solzhenitsyn's "Nobel Lecture." On the line before each sentence, identify the degree of comparison of each italicized adverb or adverb phrase.*

_____ 1. Wiesel speaks *most passionately* about the danger of remaining silent.

_____ 2. Wiesel delivered his acceptance speech *skillfully*.

_____ 3. Solzhenitsyn *strongly* urges his listeners to speak out against violence.

_____ 4. The Soviet Union fell *sooner* than Solzhenitsyn might have expected.

B. Writing Application: *On the following lines, write a paragraph responding to either "Keep Memory Alive" or the excerpt from "Nobel Lecture." Underline the adverbs that have a positive degree of comparison once, underline the adverbs or adverb phrases that are comparative twice, and underline the adverbs or adverb phrases that are superlative three times. Use at least six adverbs that show degrees of comparison.*

_____

_____

_____

_____

_____

Name _____ Date _____

"Keep Memory Alive" by Elie Wiesel
from "Nobel Lecture" by Alexander Solzhenitsyn
Integrated Language Skills: Support for Writing a Letter

For your letter to Elie Wiesel or Alexander Solzhenitsyn, use the following graphic organizer to help you take a position on the writer's claim, choose a principle, and plan your logical arguments to support it.

Position	General Principle	Arguments

Now, use your notes to write your letter to Elie Wiesel or Alexander Solzhenitsyn. Remember to use language that is appropriate to your reader. Wiesel and Solzhenitsyn are respected and educated men whom you have not met, so use formal language and avoid slang or jargon.

Unit 3 Resources: Types of Nonfiction
© Pearson Education, Inc. All rights reserved.

"Keep Memory Alive" by Elie Wiesel
from **"Nobel Lecture"** by Alexander Solzhenitsyn
Integrated Language Skills: Support for Extend Your Learning

Listening and Speaking: "Keep Memory Alive"

Use this diagram to help you prepare arguments for your group debate about Wiesel's claim that silence makes people accomplices to crime.

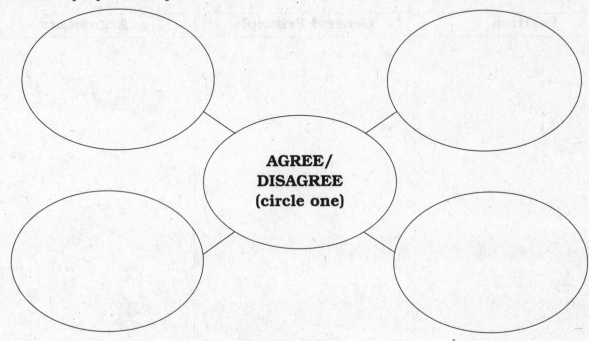

Listening and Speaking: *from* "Nobel Lecture"

Use this diagram to help you prepare arguments for your group debate about Solzhenitsyn's claim that truth will bring down an unjust government.

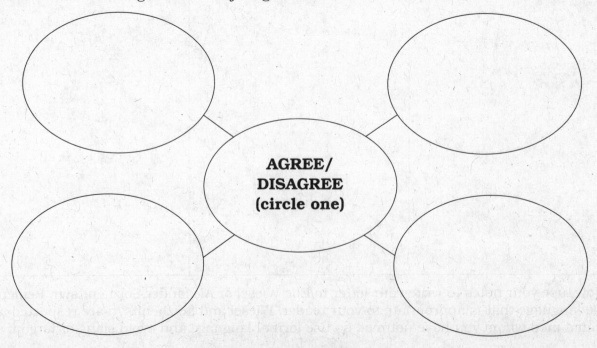

Name _____ Date _____

from **"Nobel Lecture"** by Alexander Solzhenitsyn
Open-Book Test

Short Answer *Write your responses to the questions in this section on the lines provided.*

1. A rhetorical question is a question that is intended to have obvious answers. Use the chart below to list two of the three rhetorical questions that Solzhenitsyn asks in "Nobel Lecture." Use your own words to write the questions. Then, on the line below, identify the main effect that these questions have on listeners and readers.

	Rhetorical Questions in "Nobel Lecture"
Question 1	
Question 2	

_____

_____

2. Solzhenitsyn's "Nobel Lecture" is both an acceptance speech and a persuasive speech. What are the main two things that Solzhenitsyn wants his audience to think or to do?

_____

_____

_____

_____

3. In the first paragraph of "Nobel Lecture," what catchy image does Solzhenitsyn use to convey the idea that world literature is a great unifying force for all people?

_____

_____

4. In "Nobel Lecture," what key difference between times past and the modern world does Solzhenitsyn use to support his claim that world literature can be a unifying force for humanity?

_____

_____

_____

_____

5. Read this passage from "Nobel Lecture": "Mankind's salvation lies exclusively in . . . the people of the East being anything but indifferent to what is thought in the West, and in the people of the West being anything but indifferent to what happens in the East." What rhetorical device does Solzhenitsyn use in this passage? Which specific phrase is the main example of this device?

_____

_____

6. In "Nobel Lecture," what does Solzhenitsyn suggest about the relationship between violence and lying?

_____

_____

7. In "Nobel Lecture," Solzhenitsyn claims that lies cannot stand against great works of art. What reasoning does he use to support this claim?

_____

_____

8. In "Nobel Lecture," Solzhenitsyn writes that "no such thing as INTERNAL AFFAIRS remains on our crowded Earth." How does Solzhenitsyn feel about this development? What does it suggest about how mankind can achieve a better future?

_____

_____

_____

9. In "Nobel Lecture," Solzhenitsyn writes, "It demands of its victims only allegiance to the lie, only complicity in the lie." What rhetorical device is he using in this sentence?

_____

_____

10. If you were listening to someone's *oratory*, would you most likely be in a concert hall or in someone's living room? Explain your answer, based on the meaning of *oratory* in "Nobel Lecture."

_____

_____

Essay

Write an extended response to the question of your choice or to the question or questions your teacher assigns you.

11. In "Nobel Lecture," Solzhenitsyn says that writers are the best people to stand up against unjust governments and violent acts. In an essay, discuss his reasons for this claim. Do you agree with him? Why or why not? Provide examples from the speech to support your points.

12. In "Nobel Lecture," Solzhenitsyn states that it is the duty of artists and writers to stand up for truth and against injustice and violence. Think about a current issue involving injustice or violence. In an essay, express what you believe is the truth behind this issue. Support your points by applying examples from "Nobel Lecture."

13. In an essay, identify Solzhenitsyn's central claim in the excerpt from "Nobel Lecture." Then explain whether you believe that he adequately supports his claim with facts and logic. Do you agree or disagree with Solzhenitsyn's argument? Why? Use specific examples from the speech to support your opinion.

14. **Thinking About the Big Question: What kind of knowledge changes our lives?** In "Nobel Lecture," Solzhenitsyn speaks of the role that world literature can play in getting rid of lies and violence in the world. In an essay, explore Solzhenitsyn's argument that violence and lying are "intertwined." Describe how knowledge gained by reading literature can combat violence and lies.

Oral Response

15. Go back to question 3, 5, or 8 or to the question your teacher assigns you. Take a few minutes to expand your answer and prepare an oral response. Find additional details in "Nobel Lecture" that support your points. If necessary, make notes to guide your oral response.

Name _____ Date _____

from **"Nobel Lecture"** by Alexander Solzhenitsyn
Selection Test A

Critical Reading *Identify the letter of the choice that best answers the question.*

____ 1. Solzhenitsyn's "Nobel Lecture" is an acceptance speech. It is also a persuasive speech. What is the main thing Solzhenitsyn wants his audience to think or do?
   A. begin reading world literature
   B. speak out against unjust governments
   C. give him the Nobel Prize for Literature
   D. help him to escape from the Soviet Union

____ 2. Who nominated Solzhenitsyn for the Nobel Prize?
   A. the Soviet government
   B. fellow Russian writers
   C. François Mauriac, a French writer
   D. Heinrich Böll, a German writer

____ 3. Solzhenitsyn refers to something he calls the "one great heart" of the world. What is it?
   A. truth
   B. world literature
   C. communism
   D. global unity

____ 4. How does Solzhenitsyn feel about other writers around the world?
   A. He is hesitant to approach them due to a language barrier.
   B. He has been isolated and does not know any of them.
   C. He feels they do not understand his experiences.
   D. He respects them and feels they have a shared literature.

____ 5. Solzhenitsyn claims that world literature allows people to reach across national borders to understand and help one another. How does he logically support this claim?
   A. by thanking his audience for the honor of receiving the Nobel Prize for Literature
   B. by stating that violence does not accomplish anything except bring more violence and lies
   C. by encouraging other governments to go to war with corrupt and unjust governments
   D. by pointing out that people around the world read his work and offered him support

_____ 6. How did Norwegian writers show support for Solzhenitsyn?

A. They declared a national holiday to honor Solzhenitsyn.

B. They published his work and made it available to Soviet citizens.

C. They urged their government to go to war with the Soviet Union.

D. They had a place for him in case of his exile from the Soviet Union.

_____ 7. What does Solzhenitsyn believe writers and artists can do?

A. eliminate lies

B. express their feelings

C. serve their governments

D. stop all forms of violence

_____ 8. Solzhenitsyn writes, "What can literature do against the pitiless onslaught of naked violence?" What rhetorical device is he using?

A. repetition

B. parallelism

C. slogans and saws

D. rhetorical question

_____ 9. Solzhenitsyn says, "Once lies have been dispelled [taken away] . . . hollow violence will collapse." How does he support this claim?

A. by saying that governments never lie to their citizens

B. by saying that writers and artists never lie to the public

C. by saying that writers and artists can be violent if angered

D. by saying that violence only exists if it is supported by lies

_____ 10. What is the most likely reason Solzhenitsyn's writing was not published in his own country?

A. because it was not very good

B. because it was written in English

C. because in it, he spoke out against the Soviet government

D. because people in the Soviet Union could not afford to buy it

_____ 11. According to Solzhenitsyn, why can't lies stand up against art?

A. because art expresses truth

B. because art has unique beauty

C. because artists are incapable of lying

D. because governments cannot ban art

___ 12. Why do writers use rhetorical devices?
- A. to help readers appreciate their art
- B. to express ideas about government
- C. to create emphasis and stir emotions
- D. to make their writing more complicated

Vocabulary and Grammar

___ 13. Which of the following is the best synonym for *inexorably*?
- A. haltingly
- B. joyfully
- C. cooperatively
- D. relentlessly

___ 14. Which of the following is an example of something being *assimilated*?
- A. college students learning new information in a class
- B. a mother going on vacation without her family
- C. a writer publishing articles protesting his or her government
- D. a writer nominating someone for a literary award

___ 15. What is the correct way to form the comparative of the adverb *surprisingly*?
- A. surprisinger
- B. more surprisingly
- C. surprisinglyer
- D. most surprisingly

Essay

16. In the excerpt from "Nobel Lecture," Solzhenitsyn states that "Lies can stand up against much in the world, but not against art." In an essay, explain why you agree or disagree with this statement. Did Solzhenitsyn say anything that either convinced you or failed to convince you that this statement is true? Use at least two examples from his writing to support your explanation.

17. Solzhenitsyn says that writers are the best people to stand up against unjust governments. In an essay, express your opinion regarding the appropriate role of writers and artists in a nation. Are they responsible for speaking out about their beliefs? Or, should writers and artists be independent from any responsibility as citizens? Use at least two examples from Solzhenitsyn's writing to support your opinion.

18. **Thinking About the Big Question: What kind of knowledge changes our lives?**
In "Nobel Lecture," Solzhenitsyn writes that literature can help to end lies and violence in the world. In an essay, describe how literature can fight violence and lies. Provide at least two details from the selection to support your response.

from "Nobel Lecture" by Alexander Solzhenitsyn
Selection Test B

Critical Reading *Identify the letter of the choice that best completes the statement or answers the question.*

____ 1. What was Solzhenitsyn's main purpose in writing "Nobel Lecture"?
A. to praise the European community of writers
B. to denounce the horrors of Soviet oppression
C. to make a gracious acceptance for a major award
D. to articulate his understanding of the writer's role

____ 2. According to Solzhenitsyn, what is the main difference between world literature today and that of the past?
A. isolationist tendencies
B. quality of writing
C. lack of censorship
D. instantaneous reciprocity

____ 3. According to Solzhenitsyn, what is the world's most powerful force?
A. literature
B. truth
C. friendship
D. violence

____ 4. Solzhenitsyn says, "Mankind's salvation lies exclusively in everyone's making everything his business." How does he support this claim?
A. by stating that world literature is a powerful unifying tool that cannot be stopped by ministries of internal affairs
B. by asserting that lies cannot stand for long against people who investigate each other's business
C. by establishing the fact that corrupt governments have the power to silence dissenting writers and artists
D. by thanking his European peers for the great honor of nominating him for the Nobel Prize in Literature

____ 5. Which of the following best characterizes Solzhenitsyn's relationship to other European writers mentioned in the excerpt from "Nobel Lecture"?
A. appreciative
B. uncomprehending
C. uncomfortable
D. supportive

____ 6. What is the central argument of Solzhenitsyn's speech?
A. Literacy critics have devalued world literature.
B. Writers all over the world form a writing fraternity.
C. The writer must be a force for political and social reform.
D. We are moving toward international language and literature.

_____ 7. Which of the following influenced Solzhenitsyn's writing the most?
   A. literary critics who liked his work
   B. his desire for fame and fortune
   C. winning the Nobel Prize in literature
   D. his need to condemn his government

_____ 8. In the excerpt from "Nobel Lecture," what kind of relationship does Solzhenitsyn suggest exists between violence and lying?
   A. casual
   B. unknowing
   C. incompatible
   D. interconnected

_____ 9. Solzhenitsyn claims that lies cannot stand against art. What reasoning does he use to support this claim?
   A. Artists and writers are incapable of lying under any circumstances.
   B. Artists and writers can expose lies and tell the truth in conspicuous ways.
   C. Artists and writers must be loyal to governments under difficult conditions.
   D. Artists and writers have a wider audience for their work than politicians.

_____ 10. Solzhenitsyn writes, "It demands of its victims only allegiance to the lie, only complicity in the lie." What rhetorical device is he using?
   A. repetition
   B. parallelism
   C. slogans and saws
   D. rhetorical question

_____ 11. Which of these would probably bring the greatest pain to Solzhenitsyn?
   A. permanent exile from Europe
   B. creation of a world government
   C. an end to his ability to write
   D. lack of recognition as an artist

_____ 12. What is Solzhenitsyn's belief about how humankind will be saved?
   A. He believes that all forms of communism must end.
   B. He believes that national boundaries must be eliminated.
   C. He believes that world literature must be available to all.
   D. He believes that people must recognize their interdependence.

_____ 13. What is a rhetorical device?
   A. a way to test a writer's logic and reasoning
   B. a translation that is difficult for readers to understand
   C. a question intended to have an obvious answer
   D. a word-pattern that creates emphasis and emotion

_____ 14. How can a reader test the logic of a writer's appeals?
   A. by thinking about how another writer might support the same claims
   B. by identifying which rhetorical devices the author uses most frequently
   C. by eliminating opinions from the essay and analyzing the facts for logic
   D. by considering how the writer's evidence supports his or her points

Vocabulary and Grammar

____ 15. Which of the following is an example of *reciprocity*?
   A. a government banning free speech by political writers
   B. a boy doing something nice for a friend who did him a favor
   C. a country attempting to stay out of a conflict between neighbors
   D. a man becoming angry at someone who takes his parking space

____ 16. Which of the following is the best antonym for *inexorably*?
   A. haltingly
   B. joyfully
   C. cooperatively
   D. relentlessly

____ 17. What is the correct way to form the superlative of the adverb *soon*?
   A. sooner
   B. soonest
   C. most soon
   D. more soonest

____ 18. In which of the following sentences is the comparative adverb formed correctly?
   A. Writers can present truth powerfully to others.
   B. Writers can present truth powerful than others.
   C. Writers can present truth the most powerfully of all.
   D. Writers can present truth more powerfully than others.

Essay

19. In the excerpt from "Nobel Lecture," Solzhenitsyn states that writers are the spokespersons of their countries and can be helpful in a world full of injustice and suffering. In an essay, explain Solzhenitsyn's position on violence, injustice, and suffering. Discuss the ways in which he thinks writers can make a contribution. Use at least two examples from the lecture to support your explanation.

20. In an essay, identify Solzhenitsyn's central claim in the excerpt from his "Nobel Lecture." Then, explain whether you believe he adequately supported his claim with logic. Did you agree with his argument? Why or why not? What reasons seemed most logical to you, and which ones seemed least logical? Use at least two examples from his lecture to support your position.

21. What is a current issue about which you feel strongly? Write an essay in which you state your opinion about this issue in a way that would make Alexander Solzhenitsyn proud. State the truth as you see it. Use your writing to let people know what is going on and how they can help to bring about positive change. Be sure to support your claims with logical reasoning. Use Solzhenitsyn's lecture as a model to find ways to best support your position.

22. **Thinking About the Big Question: What kind of knowledge changes our lives?** In "Nobel Lecture," Solzhenitsyn speaks of the role that world literature can play in getting rid of lies and violence in the world. In an essay, explore Solzhenitsyn's argument that violence and lying are "intertwined." Describe how knowledge gained by reading literature can combat violence and lies.

"The American Idea" by Theodore H. White
Vocabulary Warm-up Word Lists

Study these words from "The American Idea." Then, complete the activities.

Word List A

anniversary [an uh VER suh ree] *n.* a date on which a special event happened
  The elderly couple celebrated their fiftieth wedding <u>anniversary</u>.

continental [kahn tuh NEN tl] *adj.* relating to a continent
  The railroad reached across the <u>continental</u> United States.

correspondence [kawr i SPAHN duhns] *n.* letters between people
  The <u>correspondence</u> between the two authors was published as a book.

couriers [KOOR ee erz] *n.* people who deliver packages and documents
  The bicycle <u>couriers</u> raced across the city to deliver their packages.

pursuit [per SOOT] *n.* trying to achieve something in a determined way
  All people have a right to the <u>pursuit</u> of their dreams.

relentlessly [ri LENT lis lee] *adv.* continuing without stopping
  The child begged <u>relentlessly</u> for the popular new toy.

rivalry [RYE vuhl ree] *n.* competition over a long period of time
  The <u>rivalry</u> between the Yankees and the Red Sox is famous.

traditional [truh DISH uhn uhl] *adj.* customary; following old ways
  It is <u>traditional</u> in this country to have a large dinner on Thanksgiving.

Word List B

administrations [ad min i STRAY shuhnz] *n.* countries' governments
  The Clinton and Bush <u>administrations</u> have had little in common.

divine [di VYN] *adj.* having the qualities of God, or coming from God
  Some people believe there is a <u>divine</u> plan for each human being.

edited [ED it ed] *v.* revised and fixed errors in a book or an article
  After Kim <u>edited</u> her draft, it was transformed into an outstanding paper.

embodied [em BAH deed] *v.* was the best example of an idea or a quality
  The athlete <u>embodied</u> skill, discipline, and grace.

emigrants [EM i gruhnts] *n.* people who leave their own country for another
  The colonies were soon filled with <u>emigrants</u> from Great Britain.

endowed [en DOWD] *v.* having a good quality, feature, or ability
  The senator was <u>endowed</u> with the gift of strong leadership.

revolutionaries [rev uh LOO shuhn air eez] *n.* people who revolt
  The French <u>revolutionaries</u> rose up against the rule of their king.

universal [yoo nuh VER suhl] *adj.* consistently true or appropriate
  Humans have a <u>universal</u> instinct to protect themselves from harm.

"The American Idea" by Theodore H. White
Vocabulary Warm-up Exercises

Exercise A *Fill in each blank in the paragraph with an appropriate word from Word List A. Use each word only once.*

As the American colonists considered their separation from England, they formed a

[1] _____ government to represent them. We can learn much about

these early politicians by reading their [2] _____. Some letters describe

the [3] _____ between political factions. Others show that though their

strategies differed, most politicians were in [4] _____ of the same

goals. Although it often seemed that they argued [5] _____ over

political matters, these leaders also made time for their families. In those days, it was

[6] _____ to send gifts for many occasions, and politicians showered

their loved ones with presents. Their [7] _____ were often dispatched to

deliver packages for a birthday or a wedding [8] _____.

Exercise B *Revise each sentence so that the underlined vocabulary word is used in a logical way. Be sure to keep the vocabulary word in your revision.*

Example: The <u>revolutionaries</u> wanted the government to stay the same.
The <u>revolutionaries</u> wanted the government to change.

1. She <u>embodied</u> grace when she tripped down the stairs.
   _____

2. Because clean water is a <u>universal</u> right, only our country should enjoy it.
   _____

3. The <u>emigrants</u> traveled across town to find a home.
   _____

4. The writer <u>edited</u> the draft before she wrote it.
   _____

5. They believed their ruler's <u>divine</u> power was granted by his mother.
   _____

6. The two <u>administrations</u> never governed.
   _____

7. He was <u>endowed</u> with natural intelligence, so he could not learn anything.
   _____

Name _____ Date _____

"The American Idea" by Theodore H. White
Reading Warm-up A

Read the following passage. Pay special attention to the underlined words. Then, read it again, and complete the activities. Use a separate sheet of paper for your written answers.

One fun way to learn about the Second <u>Continental</u> Congress is to watch the acclaimed musical *1776*. In the late 1960s, America was getting ready to celebrate the Bicentennial, the two hundredth <u>anniversary</u> of the founding of the United States. One former history teacher named Sherman Edwards decided to put the story of the signing of the Declaration of Independence to music. Produced in 1969 on Broadway, *1776* was an immediate success.

Unlike most <u>traditional</u> musicals, *1776* has long sections with no singing or dancing. In these sections, the arguments for and against the signing of the declaration are dramatized. The musical also shows the friendship and <u>rivalry</u> between John Adams and Thomas Jefferson and depicts the influence of the pragmatic Benjamin Franklin. While Adams badgered his colleagues <u>relentlessly</u>, Jefferson was quieter. Though chosen to write the declaration, he seemed at times to be more interested in the <u>pursuit</u> of his lovely wife than in writing about the inalienable rights of man.

While the play is a wonderful history lesson, the songs provide wit and emotional energy. "But Mr. Adams" is a comical song about the Founding Fathers, each one trying to avoid the job of writing the declaration. John Adams seems more human in "Yours, Yours, Yours." This number brings to life his <u>correspondence</u> with his wife, Abigail. The most moving ballad, "Mama Look Sharp," is sung by one of the <u>couriers</u> who brings news of the war to the congress. It tells the story of a young soldier dying on the battlefield. This reminds the characters and audience alike of the real cost of a revolution.

While you may not find a local stage production of *1776*, there is a movie version of the musical that features many of the original Broadway cast members. Watch it and learn!

1. Circle the word that tells what <u>Continental</u> describes. Explain what *continental* means.

2. Circle the words that tell what <u>anniversary</u> the Bicentennial marked. Then, define *anniversary*.

3. Underline the phrase that tells how *1776* is different from many <u>traditional</u> musicals. Then, tell what *traditional* means.

4. Underline the word that means the opposite of <u>rivalry</u>. Then, write a sentence about a *rivalry*.

5. Circle the word that tells what Adams did <u>relentlessly</u>. Then, in your own words, describe his behavior.

6. Underline the phrase that tells what Jefferson was in <u>pursuit</u> of. Tell what *pursuit* means.

7. Circle the words that tell with whom Adams had a <u>correspondence</u>. Write about a *correspondence* you have had with a friend.

8. Circle the words that tell what <u>couriers</u> did in *1776*. Tell what job *couriers* do today.

"The American Idea" by Theodore H. White
Reading Warm-up B

Read the following passage. Pay special attention to the underlined words. Then, read it again, and complete the activities. Use a separate sheet of paper for your written answers.

Of all the Founding Fathers, the one with the most fascinating life is Alexander Hamilton. Born in the West Indies during the 1750s, Hamilton <u>embodied</u> the American dream. As a child, he had few advantages—his parents were not married, and his father abandoned the family. Still, Alexander Hamilton made a name for himself.

After a terrible storm hit the West Indies, he wrote a letter to a newspaper that told of the enormity of <u>divine</u> power. This letter showed the community that Hamilton was <u>endowed</u> with an amazing intelligence. A few prominent men sent him to study in New York City. Like many <u>emigrants</u> then and now, Hamilton found success there.

After college he joined a militia and fought alongside other <u>revolutionaries</u> in battles against Great Britain. Later, he served as a staff officer with General George Washington and eventually became a field commander.

When he married Elizabeth Schuyler, he joined a prominent New York family and entered an elite circle. He also began to practice law, and he became extremely well regarded in the legal field.

Hamilton was elected to the Continental Congress in 1782, where he advocated a strong national government. With James Madison and John Jay, Hamilton wrote *The Federalist,* in which he argued in favor of a constitution. Hamilton asserted that there was a <u>universal</u> need for wise political <u>administrations</u>, and his arguments proved persuasive. Hamilton's son eventually <u>edited</u> a later edition of this important document.

After Washington became president, Hamilton became the Secretary of the Treasury. Some of his monetary policies were controversial.

Hamilton retired, but stayed active. He offended Aaron Burr, with whom he had once shared a law practice, by calling him "despicable." Burr challenged Hamilton to a duel. When the two faced one another, Hamilton fired into the air, not meaning to harm his rival, but Burr shot Hamilton. Thus ended an extraordinary life.

1. Underline what Hamilton <u>embodied</u>. Then, tell what *embodied* means.

2. Explain why a storm could be described in terms of <u>divine</u> power.

3. Circle the words that tell what Hamilton was <u>endowed</u> with. Name a special quality that someone whom you admire is *endowed* with.

4. Underline the way in which Hamilton was like many <u>emigrants</u>. Who is a famous *emigrant* whom you admire?

5. Hamilton fought on the side of <u>revolutionaries</u>. Use a definition of the word to explain whether Hamilton believed that the colonies should be governed by Great Britain.

6. Name three rights that you believe should be <u>universal</u>. Define *universal*.

7. Write a sentence identifying the presidential <u>administrations</u> that have existed in your lifetime.

8. What were some of the things Hamilton's son might have done as he <u>edited</u> *The Federalist*?

Name _____ Date _____

"The American Idea" by Theodore H. White
Writing About the Big Question

What kind of knowledge changes our lives?

Big Question Vocabulary

adapt	awareness	empathy	enlighten	evolve
growth	history	ignorance	influence	insight
modified	question	reflect	revise	understanding

A. *Use one or more words from the list above to complete each sentence.*

1. The Declaration of Independence has served the United States from its
_____ as a tiny nation to a global power.

2. The _____ of America is filled with tough, smart
people who helped create a successful government.

3. Thomas Jefferson _____ his thoughts enough
to please both John Adams and Benjamin Franklin.

4. Although archrivals for much of their lives, Jefferson and Adams did
_____ into friends once more as they grew
older.

B. *Follow the directions in responding to each of the items below.*

1. List two situations in which a compromise you made produced an important result.

_____

_____

2. Write two sentences explaining one of the situations you listed, and describe the
impact it made on your life. Use at least two of the Big Question vocabulary words.

_____

_____

C. *Complete the sentence below. Then, write a short paragraph in which you connect this
experience to the big question.*

People who left their countries to live in the United States developed an
awareness of _____

_____

_____

_____

Name _____ Date _____

Literary Analysis: Analytic and Interpretive Essays

In an **analytic essay,** a writer explores a subject by breaking it into parts. In an **interpretive essay,** a writer offers a view of the meaning or significance of an issue of general interest. The author of an interpretive essay introduces an issue and then addresses it, presenting his or her ideas and analysis based on his or her own ideas, values, and beliefs. A single essay may combine features of both types of essay.

Writers of analytic and interpretive essays might use any of the following types of appeals to support their points:

- Appeals to authority, which call on the opinions of experts or other respected people
- Appeals to reason, which call on logic
- Emotional appeals, which tap a reader's fears, sympathy, or pride
- Appeals to shared values, which call on beliefs shared by many about what is good, right, or fair

A. DIRECTIONS: *Fill in the following table with one or more examples of each type of appeal from "The American Idea." If there are no examples of a particular appeal, write NONE.*

Appeals to Authority	
Appeals to Reason	
Emotional Appeals	
Appeals to Shared Values	

B. DIRECTIONS: *On the following lines, write a short essay in which you explain whether "The American Idea" is an analytic essay, an interpretive essay, or both. How do you know?*

_____

_____

_____

_____

_____

Name _____ Date _____

"The American Idea" by Theodore H. White
Reading: Distinguish Between Fact and Opinion
to Evaluate Writers' Appeals

To **evaluate a writer's appeals,** decide whether the writer makes a good case for his or her point of view. First, **distinguish between fact and opinion** to determine what kind of support a writer should provide. A statement of fact can be proven true or false. A statement of opinion expresses a belief or a viewpoint and should be supported by facts or logical reasoning.

DIRECTIONS: *In the following chart, list ten facts and five opinions White includes in his essay about the American idea. Then, list facts or logical reasons the author gives to support each opinion.*

Facts	
1. _____	6. _____
2. _____	7. _____
3. _____	8. _____
4. _____	9. _____
5. _____	10. _____

Opinions	Support for Opinions
1. _____	1. _____
2. _____	2. _____
3. _____	3. _____
4. _____	4. _____
5. _____	5. _____

Name _____ Date _____

"The American Idea" by Theodore H. White
Vocabulary Builder

Word List

embodied   emigrants   relentlessly   subversion   successive   universal

A. DIRECTIONS: *Provide an explanation for your answer to each question.*

1. If you were thinking about an animal, would your thoughts be *embodied* by a soft toy that looked like a dog?

   _____

2. Would *emigrants* be packed and ready to travel or settling into a future in their home country?

   _____

3. If the wind blew *relentlessly*, would there be a break when everything was still?

   _____

4. If your school had *universal* hat day, would everyone wear a hat?

   _____

5. If your cousin had three *successive* gray cats, did she have three cats at the same time?

   _____

6. If the dictator was worried about *subversion*, did he feel secure in the loyalty of the citizens?

   _____

B. WORD STUDY: The **Greek prefix em-** means "in." Answer each of the following questions using one of these words containing *em-*: *empathy, emperor, embrace.*

1. Is an *emperor* someone who is in power or who serves those in power?

   _____

2. If someone has *empathy*, does that person disregard the feelings of others?

   _____

3. If you give a person an *embrace*, are you putting your arms around that person or running away from that person?

   _____

"The American Idea" by Theodore H. White
Enrichment: Current Events

In the late 1700s and early 1800s, Thomas Jefferson and John Adams debated about the meaning and application of the American idea. According to Theodore H. White, Adams saw it as the call for American independence, while Jefferson came to believe that it was a call to the world, a universal promise of freedom.

The debate about what the American idea means to Americans and to the rest of the world continues today. In his State of the Union address in January of 2005, President George W. Bush established a policy that called for the United States to take action to spread freedom throughout the world. Many people agreed with him and many did not. Think about your opinion of President Bush's position. How have recent world events influenced your opinion? What future events might change your mind?

DIRECTIONS: *Find a newspaper or magazine article about a recent world event that has to do with how the American idea figures into national or world politics and culture. For example, you might find an article about the United States assisting another nation in conducting free elections, one about people in another country resenting the United States' efforts to spread democracy, or one about the U.S. government placing economic pressure on a foreign government that disrespects human rights. Then, in the following space, draw a political cartoon that expresses your opinion about the issue. Look at several examples of published political cartoons to help you create your own. Remember that the drawings in political cartoons are symbolic—they stand for other things. Political cartoonists often use labels to help show readers what the drawings represent.*

Name _____ Date _____

"The American Idea" by Theodore H. White
Open-Book Test

Short Answer *Write your responses to the questions in this section on the lines provided.*

1. In "The American Idea," Theodore H. White appeals to the reader by using a combination of facts and opinions. Use the chart to provide an example of a fact and an opinion from the essay. Then, on the line below, briefly explain the difference between a fact and an opinion.

Fact	
Opinion	

_____

2. According to White, what is "The American Idea"?

_____

_____

_____

3. In the fourth paragraph of "The American Idea," White argues that the American idea reached all over the world, "unsettling all traditional civilizations." What type of appeal is White using when he lists various countries that have been inspired by American ideals?

_____

_____

4. In the fifth paragraph of "The American Idea," White describes the Statue of Liberty as "the great statue that looks down the Narrows of New York Harbor." What type of appeal is White using in this passage—an emotional appeal, an appeal to authority, or an appeal to reason?

_____

_____

5. According to White in "The American Idea," how did the freedom of the wilderness affect American colonists? In other words, what did this type of freedom cause them to want?

_____

_____

6. White believes the American idea has had "explosive power." On what fact or idea does White base this interpretation of the American idea?

_____

_____

7. In "The American Idea," White states his opinion that it was an idea, not a place, that gave birth to the United States. On what fact does White base this opinion?

_____

_____

8. In "The American Idea," White supports his points with quotations from Thomas Jefferson. By including these quotations, what type of persuasive appeal is White using?

_____

_____

9. In "The American Idea," White notes that, according to legend, John Adams's last words were, "Thomas Jefferson still survives." Why might it have been important to the dying Adams that Jefferson survive?

_____

_____

_____

10. If a lecturer were making her point *relentlessly*, would you most likely be enjoying the lecture? Explain your answer, based on the meaning of *relentlessly* in "The American Idea."

_____

_____

_____

Essay

Write an extended response to the question of your choice or to the question or questions your teacher assigns you.

11. In "The American Idea," White says that even though the American idea is based on certain key values, it can mean different things to different people. In an essay, describe the key truths that White identifies. Then, explain what the American idea means to you. Provide at least two examples from White's essay to support your response.

12. White concludes "The American Idea" with a story about Adams and Jefferson. In an essay, explain the message White is trying to send through this story. Does he favor one man's ideas over the other's, or does he think they are equally important? Support your response with specific examples from White's essay.

13. Based on White's interpretation of the American idea, write an essay in which you explain what role the American idea has played in the world, both at home and abroad. Do you think this role has been positive, negative, or neither? Provide examples from "The American Idea" to support your response.

14. **Thinking About the Big Question: What kind of knowledge changes our lives?** In an essay, reflect on White's argument that people around the world have learned enough from the American idea to have been changed by it in "explosive" ways. Do you agree? Why or why not? Support your response with specific examples from "The American Idea."

Oral Response

15. Go back to question 3, 4, or 10 or to the question your teacher assigns you. Take a few minutes to expand your answer and prepare an oral response. Find additional details in "The American Idea" that support your points. If necessary, make notes to guide your oral response.

"**The American Idea**" by Theodore H. White
Selection Test A

Critical Reading *Identify the letter of the choice that best answers the question.*

____ 1. What is the American idea?
A. a call to freedom
B. the American Revolution
C. Jefferson's and Adams's debate
D. a global superpower

____ 2. According to White, who first put the American idea into words?
A. Thomas Jefferson
B. Benjamin Franklin
C. John Adams
D. Horace Greeley

____ 3. Which of the following is NOT one of the groups of people White says heard the call of the American idea?
A. Irish
B. Europeans
C. Mexicans
D. Chinese

____ 4. According to White, how did "the freedom of the wilderness" affect American colonists?
A. It inspired them to want more freedoms.
B. It encouraged them to dislike government.
C. It frightened them into obeying British rulers.
D. It convinced them to hide from soldiers.

____ 5. In "The American Idea," White calls the American rebels "tough men fighting for a very tough idea." This is meant to make modern Americans feel proud of those who fought for our freedom. What type of persuasive appeal is he using?
A. appeal to authority
B. appeal to reason
C. emotional appeal
D. appeal to shared values

_____ 6. Why does White describe the American idea as having "explosive power"?
   A. It was a spectacular failure but a good effort.
   B. It makes Americans seem prideful and angry.
   C. People have been arguing about it for many years.
   D. It inspired people all over the world to seek freedom.

_____ 7. White states his opinion that it was an idea, not a place, that gave birth to the United States. Which of the following is a FACT that he uses to support his opinion?
   A. The American people came from all over the world.
   B. The American idea had power undreamed of in 1776.
   C. The United States government is the best in the world.
   D. The American idea represented a promise to Jefferson.

_____ 8. Why does White say the American idea means different things to different people?
   A. to show that it is a growing and changing idea
   B. to avoid having to define the American idea clearly
   C. to prove that it is not a good basis for governing
   D. to show that it should guide the world's conduct

_____ 9. What was Thomas Jefferson's interpretation of the American idea?
   A. It was probably doomed to eventual failure.
   B. It was a call of freedom to the whole world.
   C. It was an expression of the need for independence.
   D. It was not a practical basis for a new government.

_____ 10. Which of the following is a FACT White included in "The American Idea"?
   A. Thomas Jefferson won his long debate with John Adams.
   B. Thomas Jefferson wrote the Declaration of Independence.
   C. Jefferson was the most intelligent of the nation's early leaders.
   D. Jefferson could not imagine the reach of his call across the world.

_____ 11. What was unusual about the deaths of Thomas Jefferson and John Adams?
   A. They died on the same day—July 4, 1826.
   B. They both died in Philadelphia, Pennsylvania.
   C. The Continental Congress had just met.
   D. They had finally decided to end their debate.

_____ 12. Is "The American Idea" an analytic essay or an interpretive essay?

    A. It is an analytic essay only.

    B. It is an interpretive essay only.

    C. It is both an analytic and an interpretive essay.

    D. It is neither an analytic nor an interpretive essay.

Vocabulary and Grammar

_____ 13. Which is an example of *subversion*?

    A. a declaration

    B. a vacation

    C. an election

    D. a revolution

_____ 14. Who are *emigrants*?

    A. people who enter a country from elsewhere

    B. people who believe strongly in the American idea

    C. people who leave one country to settle elsewhere

    D. people who fought for the American Revolution

_____ 15. Which is the correct way to form the superlative of the adjective *proud*?

    A. prouder

    B. proudest

    C. more proud

    D. most proud

Essay

16. White says in his essay that the American idea means different things to different people. In an essay, describe what the American idea means to you. Explain your response by giving at least two examples from White's essay that relate to how the American idea has affected you, your community, the nation, or the world.

17. In an essay, explain what White's concluding story about Adams and Jefferson is meant to show. Does he favor one person's position over the other, or does he think that both men's opinions are important to the concept of the American idea? Explain your response, using at least two details from White's essay to support your explanation.

18. **Thinking About the Big Question: What kind of knowledge changes our lives?** In "The American Idea," White writes that the American idea has changed people around the world in "explosive" ways. In an essay, provide three examples of how the American idea has changed people. Support your response with details from "The American Idea."

"The American Idea" by Theodore H. White
Selection Test B

Critical Reading *Identify the letter of the choice that best completes the statement or answers the question.*

_____ 1. Which of the following is the best statement of the American idea as White presents it?
   A. Debate between friends is healthy.
   B. Immigrants build a strong nation.
   C. The founders of America were brave.
   D. All people should have freedom.

_____ 2. According to White, what whetted the American colonists' appetite for freedom?
   A. their hatred of English soldiers
   B. the freedom of the wilderness
   C. the Statue of Liberty
   D. the Declaration of Independence

_____ 3. White states his opinion that "it was not puffed-up rhetoric" for colonial leaders to pledge their lives in pursuit of independence. Which of the following is a FACT that he uses to support his opinion?
   A. Many of them did die in the war for independence.
   B. They were wrapped in myths by historians and poets.
   C. They intended to surrender if it looked like they might lose.
   D. If they lost the Revolution, they would be judged as traitors.

_____ 4. According to White, how is the origin of the United States different from the origins of other nations in the world?
   A. The United States beat the British.
   B. The United States was in one location.
   C. The United States declared its independence.
   D. The United States was born from an idea.

_____ 5. What was Thomas Jefferson's belief about the meaning of the American idea?
   A. It was the call for American independence.
   B. It was a call of freedom to the whole world.
   C. It was a slogan used to encourage people to fight.
   D. It was the folly of a group of hotheaded young men.

_____ 6. Why did the rivalry between Jefferson and Adams finally begin to fade after many years?
   A. They both agreed that Adams won the debate.
   B. They both agreed that Jefferson won the debate.
   C. They simply got tired of arguing about the American idea.
   D. They realized that there was glory enough for both of them.

_____ 7. Based on the facts contained in "The American Idea," why might it have been impor-
tant to John Adams as he lay dying to believe that Thomas Jefferson was still alive?
   A. Adams knew Jefferson would make sure that he was honored after his death.
   B. Adams respected Jefferson and knew he would keep the American idea alive.
   C. Adams would win their debate if he died before Jefferson could reply to his letter.
   D. Jefferson would publish Adams's writings so people would know about him.

_____ 8. What is significant about the date on which both Jefferson and Adams died?
   A. It was the day after Benjamin Franklin's birthday.
   B. It was the day after they declared their debate over.
   C. It was the fiftieth anniversary of the signing of the Declaration of Independence.
   D. It was the day the Continental Congress approved the Declaration of Independence.

_____ 9. In White's opinion, what would define a person as American?
   A. emigrating to live on American soil
   B. being born in the United States
   C. fighting soldiers of other nations
   D. believing in freedom and equality

_____ 10. In what way is "The American Idea" an analytic essay?
   A. It examines two founders' differing interpretations of the American idea.
   B. It entertains readers with interesting fictional accounts of historical figures.
   C. It expresses White's point of view about the meaning of the American idea.
   D. It attempts to persuade people around the world to adopt the American idea.

_____ 11. In what way is "The American Idea" an interpretive essay?
   A. It examines two founders' differing interpretations of the American idea.
   B. It entertains readers with interesting fictional accounts of historical figures.
   C. It expresses White's point of view about the meaning of the American idea.
   D. It attempts to persuade people around the world to adopt the American idea.

_____ 12. In "The American Idea," White supports his interpretation of the American idea with
the words of Thomas Jefferson. What type of persuasive appeal is he using?
   A. appeal to authority
   B. appeal to reason
   C. emotional appeal
   D. appeal to shared values

_____ 13. Which of the following is a FACT that White includes in "The American Idea"?
   A. In the debate between Jefferson and Adams, Jefferson was right in the end.
   B. The American idea has the ability to bring freedom to all nations of the world.
   C. The Continental Congress approved the Declaration of Independence on
      July 4, 1776.
   D. Thomas Jefferson was able to capture the American idea in ringing words of
      inspiration.

Vocabulary and Grammar

_____ 14. Which of the following is an example of *subversion*?
   A. a child pretending to be a superhero and trying to fly
   B. a high school student dreaming about graduation
   C. freedom fighters circulating pamphlets against a dictator
   D. a father leaving work to take his children to the beach for the day

_____ 15. Which set of numbers is *successive*?
   A. 5, 6, 7, 8, 9
   B. 4, 15, 23, 8, 16
   C. 10, 6, 8, 12, 4
   D. 8, 7, 4, 6, 5

_____ 16. What is the correct way to form the comparative of the adjective *inspiring*?
   A. inspiringer
   B. more inspiring
   C. more inspiringer
   D. most inspiring

_____ 17. In which of the following sentences is the superlative of the adjective *proud* formed correctly?
   A. Early American leaders were proud to fight for their freedom and equality.
   B. Early American leaders were more proud after they defeated the British.
   C. Early American leaders were proudest of their accomplishments after the war.
   D. Early American leaders were most proudest of the Constitution they wrote.

Essay

18. White writes that Thomas Jefferson and John Adams had an ongoing debate about their interpretations of the meaning of the American idea. In an essay, explain why you agree with Jefferson's or Adams's point of view. Use at least two examples from White's writing to support your explanation.

19. White says in his essay that the American idea means different things to different people. In an essay, express what the American idea means to you. Support your response with persuasive appeals and factual details. Use examples from events in your community, the United States, or the world to support your interpretation. Explain how your ideas do or do not relate to the position White takes in his essay.

20. In an essay, explain what role you think the American idea should play in the United States and the world. Give examples of recent events that have to do with the American idea at work. Give your opinion about how effective or appropriate the American idea is as a foreign policy tool and what responsibilities you believe America should adopt with respect to other nations. Use White's essay as a jumping-off point for your opinion.

21. **Thinking About the Big Question: What kind of knowledge changes our lives?** In an essay, reflect on White's argument that people around the world have learned enough from the American idea to have been changed by it in "explosive" ways. Do you agree? Why or why not? Support your response with specific examples from "The American Idea."

Vocabulary Warm-up Word Lists

Study these words from "What Makes a Degas a Degas?" Then, apply your knowledge to the activities that follow.

Word List A

backstage [BAK stayj] *adj.* behind the stage of a theater
   Molly was nervous as she waited in the <u>backstage</u> area for her cue.

ballerina [bal uh REE nuh] *n.* a girl or woman ballet dancer
   In her tutu, tights, and toe shoes, Erin looked like a professional <u>ballerina</u>.

conveyed [kuhn VAYD] *v.* communicated by words or actions
   Ed's secretive actions <u>conveyed</u> that he was hiding something.

dimpled [DIM puhld] *adj.* having natural indentations on the skin
   Carlotta's smile revealed her <u>dimpled</u> cheeks.

enthusiastic [en thoo zee AS tik] *adj.* having intense or eager interest
   It was clear from his cheering that Ben was an <u>enthusiastic</u> baseball fan.

lifelong [LYF lawng] *adj.* lasting or continuing throughout one's life
   Since meeting in preschool, Kim and Sally have been <u>lifelong</u> friends.

sheen [sheen] *n.* brightness; shininess; luster
   Kenneth's hair has a natural <u>sheen</u> that makes it look healthy.

silhouette [sil oo ET] *n.* a dark shape seen against a light background
   Through the curtain, Sara saw the <u>silhouette</u> of a tall man.

Word List B

backdrop [BAK drahp] *n.* scenery hung at the back of a stage; setting
   The <u>backdrop</u> suggested that the actors were by the seashore.

inspiration [in spuh RAY shuhn] *n.* something that sparks creativity
   The vivid dream Maura had served as an <u>inspiration</u> for her short story.

intimacy [IN tuh muh see] *n.* the state or fact of being close
   The <u>intimacy</u> of their quiet conversation was disrupted by the phone.

intimate [IN tuh muht] *adj.* very close or friendly; familiar
   The twins' relationship is <u>intimate</u> and loving.

lacquered [LAK uhrd] *adj.* covered with a shiny varnish
   The <u>lacquered</u> jewelry box contained many lovely treasures.

masterpieces [MAS tuhr pees ez] *n.* great works of art
   You can view <u>masterpieces</u> of painting and sculpture at the Louvre.

overlaps [oh vuhr LAPS] *v.* lies or extends partly over
   Each of the boards on the side of the house <u>overlaps</u> an adjacent board.

profile [PROH fyl] *n.* the outline of a human face as seen from the side
   Rex's <u>profile</u> reveals a bump on his nose.

184

"What Makes a Degas a Degas?" by Richard Mühlberger
Vocabulary Warm-up Exercises

Exercise A *Fill in each blank in the paragraph with an appropriate word from Word List A. Use each word only once.*

Cynthia was a very [1] _____ fan of the ballet. Seeing her first ballet at the age of seven was the start of her [2] _____ interest in the art. In fact, she wanted to be a [3] _____ when she grew up. On the wall of her bedroom was a [4] _____ of a ballet dancer cut out of black paper. Next to that was a photograph of Cynthia herself in her own toe shoes, their satin [5] _____ captured in the light. It had been taken while she waited [6] _____, just before her recital last year. Her mother had told her that her [7] _____ cheeks added to the charm of the picture. Cynthia thought the picture [8] _____ her true personality, her hopes, and her dreams.

Exercise B *Answer the questions with complete sentences or explanations.*

1. Would you share an *intimate* secret with someone whom you just met?
   _____

2. Describe an item of *lacquered* furniture or art that you would like to have.
   _____

3. How might a grandmother enjoy a moment of *intimacy* with her grandchild?
   _____

4. Name two *masterpieces* of art, literature, or music that you would recommend to a friend.
   _____

5. Describe a possible *backdrop* for a play set in a big city.
   _____

6. Each tile on a roof *overlaps* the ones near it. Is this a good idea? Explain.
   _____

7. If you had a photograph of your friend's *profile*, would you see both eyes?
   _____

8. Who has been an *inspiration* to you?
   _____

"What Makes a Degas a Degas?" by Richard Mühlberger
Reading Warm-up A

Read the following passage. Pay special attention to the underlined words. Then, read it again, and complete the activities. Use a separate sheet of paper for your written answers.

The *Nutcracker* is an annual event for <u>enthusiastic</u> ballet lovers. The ballet opens as guests are entering the parlor of Dr. Stahlbaum; his children, Clara and Fritz, are excited as the Christmas Eve party begins. Clara, sometimes portrayed as <u>dimpled</u> and shy, is a girl with a lively imagination.

Then, another guest enters from <u>backstage</u>—it is Drosselmeyer, Clara's godfather. Everyone likes Drosselmeyer, but through his mysterious bearing it is <u>conveyed</u> that he has unusual powers. His gift to Clara is a nutcracker in the shape of a little man, which Clara loves immediately.

After the party ends, the children are sent to bed. Unable to sleep, Clara tiptoes downstairs to see her nut-cracker again. Hugging it, she curls up on the couch and falls asleep. The clock striking midnight wakens Clara, who gets the feeling that the parlor is strangely changed. A shadowy <u>silhouette</u> in the corner seems like a monster, and scary forms cross the floor. Suddenly, the room is overrun by mice who begin to attack Clara. Next, Drosselmeyer appears, telling Clara that the Nutcracker will be her <u>lifelong</u> protector. He then disappears.

Amazingly, the Nutcracker comes to life. A strange glow fills the room, casting a <u>sheen</u> over all the Christmas decorations. The Nutcracker leads a battle against the mice, but he is overpowered. Clara saves him, and he turns into a handsome prince who promises to take Clara to his kingdom.

The second act takes place in the Palace of the Sugar-plum Kingdom, where Clara is rewarded with grand entertainment. One exotic <u>ballerina</u> after another dances on the stage, with and without partners. However, even a magical party must come to an end, and at last the Sugarplum Fairy tells Clara it is time to return home. Immediately, Clara is back on the couch in the parlor. Has it all been a dream?

1. Circle the word that tells who is <u>enthusiastic</u>. What does *enthusiastic* mean?

2. Underline the name of the person who is sometimes portrayed as <u>dimpled</u>. Use *dimpled* in a sentence.

3. Circle the words that describe who enters from <u>backstage</u>. Can a person in the audience see what's happening *backstage*? Explain.

4. Underline the words that tell what is <u>conveyed</u> through Drosselmeyer's bearing. What does *conveyed* mean?

5. Circle the word that describes <u>silhouette</u>. What is a *silhouette*?

6. Underline the word that <u>lifelong</u> describes. What is another way of saying *lifelong*?

7. Circle the words that tell what had a <u>sheen</u>. Use *sheen* in a sentence.

8. Underline the words that tell what each <u>ballerina</u> did. What is a *ballerina*?

Name _____   Date _____

Read the following passage. Pay special attention to the underlined words. Then, read it again, and complete the activities. Use a separate sheet of paper for your written answers.

One of the <u>masterpieces</u> of Impressionist paintings is *La Bal au Moulin de la Galette* by Pierre August Renoir (1841–1919). It is set against the <u>backdrop</u> of a popular outdoor café in Paris. Here, a throng of Sunday revelers enjoys the day in various ways. Some crowd the benches and tables, chatting and sipping drinks from tall glasses. Others dance energetically on the outdoor dance floor, dressed in their Sunday best. Some of the men and women wear straw hats, which catch the light in interesting ways, appearing almost <u>lacquered</u>. The golden color of the straw hats repeats the golden color of the chair in the foreground and the clothing and hair of some of the subjects. Blues, greens, and blacks, along with a few spots of red, complete the color palette.

Sunlight dapples the entire scene. This light <u>overlaps</u> areas of shade, producing that effect of fleeting light that is such an <u>inspiration</u> to the Impressionists. Circular spots of sunlight on the floor and on various articles of clothing are echoed by the circular lamps on the chandeliers and other light fixtures.

The viewer seems to be eavesdropping on an <u>intimate</u> conversation taking place in the foreground. A woman dressed in blue, seen in <u>profile</u>, could just as easily be eavesdropping on the conversation taking place near her. No one in the scene seems aware of an observer. They are not posing. Rather, they are simply going about their activities.

The casual placement of the figures suggests that the scene could easily go on beyond the frame, and we are curious about what that scene might reveal. Renoir has captured moments of <u>intimacy</u> between the various subjects that will never be repeated in just the same way.

1. Underline the name of one of the <u>masterpieces</u> of Impressionist paintings. Use *masterpieces* in a sentence.

2. Circle the words that further explain the <u>backdrop</u>. What does *backdrop* mean?

3. Underline the words that tell what seems almost <u>lacquered</u>. Name two things that might be *lacquered*.

4. Circle the words that tell what the sunlight <u>overlaps</u>. Use *overlaps* in a sentence.

5. Underline the words that tell what is an <u>inspiration</u> to the Impressionists. Name someone who has been an *inspiration* to you, and explain why.

6. Circle the word that is described by the adjective <u>intimate</u>. What is another word for *intimate*?

7. Underline the words that tell what is seen in <u>profile</u>. If you were going to pose for a *profile*, how would you sit in relation to the artist?

8. Circle the words that describe who is having moments of <u>intimacy</u>. How could you paint a moment of *intimacy* between a mother and a child?

Name _____ Date _____

"What Makes a Degas a Degas?" by Richard Mühlberger
Writing About the Big Question

What kind of knowledge changes our lives?

Big Question Vocabulary

adapt	awareness	empathy	enlighten	evolve
growth	history	ignorance	influence	insight
modified	question	reflect	revise	understanding

A. *Use one or more words from the list above to complete each sentence.*

1. Painting can help us _____ on the beauty of the world by presenting a new perspective.

2. Degas' _____ of painting, drawing, and photography allowed him to use various techniques in his own work.

3. Degas could _____ his painting style to look as though he had drawn with pastels.

4. An understanding of art _____ allows an artist to learn from past masters.

B. *Follow the directions in responding to each of the items below.*

1. List two encounters you have had with art (a painting, drawing, or sculpture) that made an impact on you.

   _____

   _____

2. Write two sentences explaining one of the experiences you listed, and describe the effect it had on your life. Use at least two of the Big Question vocabulary words.

   _____

   _____

C. *Complete the sentences below. Then, write a short paragraph in which you connect this experience to the Big Question.*

Understanding how to interpret art is valuable because you gain insight into

_____

Artists can influence us by _____

_____

_____

"What Makes a Degas a Degas?" by Richard Mühlberger
Literary Analysis: Analytic and Interpretive Essays

In an **analytic essay,** a writer explores a subject by breaking it into parts. In an **interpretive essay,** a writer offers a view of the meaning or significance of an issue of general interest. The author of an interpretive essay introduces an issue and then addresses it, presenting his or her ideas and analysis based on his or her own ideas, values, and beliefs. A single essay may combine features of both types of essay.

Writers of analytic and interpretive essays might use any of the following types of appeals to support their points:

- Appeals to authority, which call on the opinions of experts or other respected people
- Appeals to reason, which call on logic
- Emotional appeals, which tap a reader's fears, sympathy, or pride
- Appeals to shared values, which call on beliefs shared by many about what is good, right, or fair

A. DIRECTIONS: *Fill in the following table with one or more examples of each type of appeal from "What Makes a Degas a Degas?" If there are no examples of a particular appeal, write NONE.*

Appeals to Authority	
Appeals to Reason	
Emotional Appeals	
Appeals to Shared Values	

B. DIRECTIONS: *On the following lines, write a short essay in which you explain whether "What Makes a Degas a Degas?" is an analytic essay, an interpretive essay, or both. How do you know?*

_____

_____

_____

_____

_____

_____

_____

Name _____   Date _____

"What Makes a Degas a Degas?" by Richard Mühlberger
Reading: Distinguish Between Fact and Opinion to Evaluate Writers' Appeals

To **evaluate a writer's appeals,** decide whether the writer makes a good case for his or her point of view. First, **distinguish between fact and opinion** to determine what kind of support a writer should provide. A statement of fact can be proven true or false. A statement of opinion expresses a belief or a viewpoint and should be supported by facts or logical reasoning.

DIRECTIONS: *In the following chart, list ten facts and five opinions Mühlberger includes in his essay about Degas. Then, list facts or logical reasons the author gives to support each opinion.*

Facts	
1. _____ _____	6. _____ _____
2. _____ _____	7. _____ _____
3. _____ _____	8. _____ _____
4. _____ _____	9. _____ _____
5. _____ _____	10. _____ _____

Opinions	Support for Opinions
1. _____ _____	1. _____ _____
2. _____ _____	2. _____ _____
3. _____ _____	3. _____ _____
4. _____ _____	4. _____ _____
5. _____ _____	5. _____ _____

Name _____ Date _____

"What Makes a Degas a Degas?" by Richard Mühlberger
Vocabulary Builder

Word List

immaterial   lacquered   recalls   silhouette   simulating   spontaneous

A. DIRECTIONS: *Provide an explanation for your answer to each question.*

1. Does a *lacquered* table feel like rough logs just cut from a tree?

   _____

2. Are your ideas about the school recycling program *immaterial* or concrete?

   _____

3. If your mother *recalls* your first day of kindergarten, is she thinking about the past or trying to forget the past?

   _____

4. Would you submit a *silhouette* of your family if you wanted to show a detailed, colorful representation of their appearance?

   _____

5. If you had to tie bandages because your health class was *simulating* an accident, was anyone actually hurt?

   _____

6. If your class was *spontaneous* and sang to your teacher on her birthday, had you planned that moment for a long time?

   _____

B. WORD STUDY: The **Latin prefix *im-*** means "not" or "without." Answer each of the following questions using one of these words containing *im-*: *immense, immortal, improbable.*

1. If something is *immense*, is it easy to carry in your pocket?

   _____

2. If something is *immortal*, does it have a short lifespan?

   _____

3. When your team registered an *improbable* victory, were people expecting you to win?

   _____

Name _____   Date _____

"What Makes a Degas a Degas?" by Richard Mühlberger
Enrichment: Art and Photography

Artists have been creating fine art—paintings, drawings, sculptures, and prints—for many centuries. By comparison, photography is a "new" art medium, having been around only since the early 1800s. Since photography's invention, however, painting and photography have greatly influenced each other. Artists of both mediums frequently borrow freely from one another. What elements are unique to each medium? What elements do they share? How is their influence "seen"? In Degas's paintings, for example, the influence of photography can be seen in the effect of a candid moment captured on canvas and in the way Degas uses the frame of the canvas to "cut off" figures and forms, as if they were moving beyond the "film" frame.

The elements of painting, which may be combined by the artist in any number of ways, include line, form, color, tone, and texture. Photographers use the art of light to transmit images onto paper.

A. DIRECTIONS: *Find a contemporary photograph of a ballet dancer taken in the midst of a performance. Then, complete the following chart by comparing and contrasting the photograph with* Dancers, Pink and Green *or with another Degas painting of ballet dancers.*

	Title of Degas Painting:	Title of Photograph:
Artist and Year Created		
Subject		
Medium		
Technique		
Composition		
Design -line -form -color -tone -texture		
Overall Impression Created		

B. DIRECTIONS: *In a paragraph, summarize how the photograph and the painting of ballet dancers are similar and how they are different. Draw upon the details you have gathered in your chart for your summary.*

_____

_____

_____

"What Makes a Degas a Degas?" by Richard Mühlberger
"The American Idea" by Theodore H. White
Integrated Language Skills: Grammar

Degrees of Adjectives

Most adjectives have three different forms to show degrees of comparison—the *positive*, the *comparative*, and the *superlative*. The positive is used to describe one item, group, or person. The comparative is used to describe two items, groups, or people. The superlative is used when describing three or more items, groups, or people.

There are different ways to form the comparative and superlative degrees of adjectives. Add *-er*, *more*, or *less* to form the comparative and *-est*, *most*, or *least* to form the superlative of most one- and two-syllable adjectives. Add *more* and *most* or *less* and *least* to adjectives of three or more syllables to form the comparative and superlative.

> Impressionist paintings seem *spontaneous*. (Positive)
>
> Impressionist paintings seem *more spontaneous* than other styles. (Comparative)
>
> The Impressionist paintings looked the *most spontaneous* of all the paintings I saw in the art museum. (Superlative)

A. PRACTICE: *The following sentences are based on "What Makes a Degas a Degas?" or "The American Idea." On the line before each sentence, identify the degree of comparison of each underlined adjective or adjective phrase.*

(Comparative) Degas mimicked pastels using oil paints to create a *fresher* look.

_____ 1. Degas's *greatest* thrill as a child was looking at art.

_____ 2. Degas found photography to be *more inspirational* than traditional painting styles.

_____ 3. The *simple* idea of freedom inspired Americans to fight for their own country.

_____ 4. Jefferson believed the American call to freedom was a *universal* promise to the world.

B. Writing Application: *On the following lines, write a paragraph responding to either "What Makes a Degas a Degas?" or "The American Idea." Underline the adjectives that have a positive degree of comparison, underline the adjectives or adjective phrases that are comparative twice, and underline the adjectives or adjective phrases that are superlative three times. Use at least six adjectives that show degrees of comparison.*

_____

_____

_____

_____

_____

"The American Idea" by Theodore H. White
"What Makes a Degas a Degas?" by Richard Mühlberger
Integrated Language Skills: Support for Writing a Critique

For your critique of White's or Mühlberger's essay, use the following graphic organizer to help you identify one of the author's central claims and evaluate the evidence he uses to support it. In the ovals, write facts and opinions the author uses as evidence and jot down ideas about the effectiveness of each.

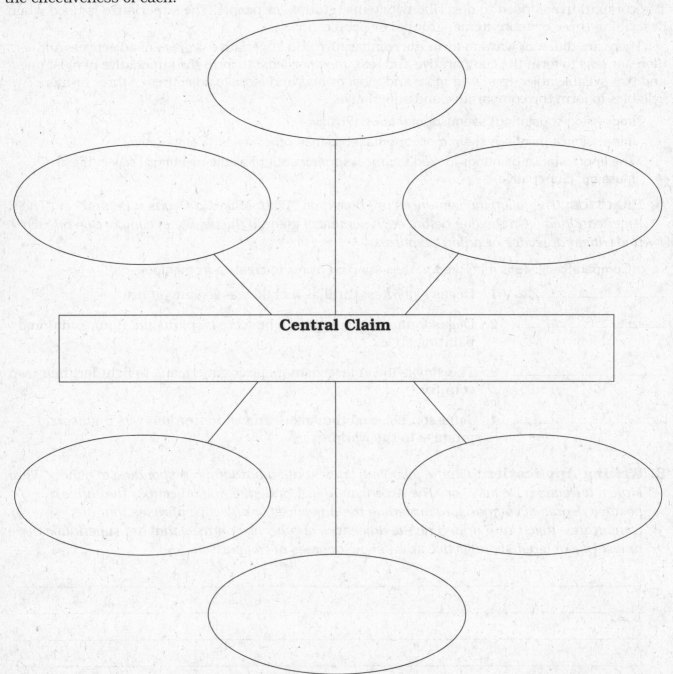

Central Claim

Now, use your notes to write your critique of "The American Idea" or "What Makes a Degas a Degas?"

"The American Idea" by Theodore H. White
"What Makes a Degas a Degas?" by Richard Mühlberger

Integrated Language Skills: Support for Extend Your Learning

Research and Technology: "The American Idea"

Choose one of the nation's founders and find some information about that person to include in each of the following categories. Use these categories and facts as the basis of your résumé and cover letter.

Education/Training	Experience	Awards/Honors	References

Research and Technology: "What Makes a Degas a Degas?"

Choose a French impressionist painter and find some information about that person to include in each of the following categories. Use these categories and facts as the basis of your résumé and cover letter.

Education/Training	Experience	Special Skills	References

"What Makes a Degas a Degas?" by Richard Mühlberger
Open-Book Test

Short Answer *Write your responses to the questions in this section on the lines provided.*

1. Most essay writers use appeals, or support, to strengthen the points they make. In the first sentence of "What Makes a Degas a Degas?" Mühlberger speaks of Degas's "famous ballet paintings." What basic kind of appeal is contained in this phrase?

   _____

   _____

2. In "What Makes a Degas a Degas?" Richard Mühlberger uses a combination of facts and opinions to appeal to the reader. A fact is something that can be proven. An opinion is someone's point of view; it is neither right nor wrong. Fill in the chart with one example of a fact and one example of an opinion from the essay. Then, on the line below, describe the difference between a fact and an opinion in your own words.

Fact	
Opinion	

   _____

3. In the painting *Dancers, Pink and Green,* why did Degas outline his figures with thin black lines? Base your answer on "What Makes a Degas a Degas?"

   _____

   _____

4. In "What Makes a Degas a Degas?" Mühlberger argues that one of Degas's goals was "to make paint look spontaneous." On what key idea does Mühlberger base this opinion?

   _____

   _____

   _____

5. According to "What Makes a Degas a Degas?" Degas was always searching for ways to make his paintings seem more realistic. What aspect of Japanese prints inspired Degas to accomplish this goal?

   _____

   _____

6. In "What Makes a Degas a Degas?" Mühlberger expresses the opinion that Degas's painting *Carriage at the Races* seems lopsided. On what fact does Mühlberger base this opinion?

_____

_____

7. In "What Makes a Degas a Degas?" Mühlberger describes qualities that might make Degas's paintings seem careless or incomplete. How does Mühlberger's interpretation of the paintings make these qualities seem admirable?

_____

_____

8. How are characters' actions in video games an example of *simulating* movement? Base your answer on the meaning of *simulating* as it is used in "What Makes a Degas a Degas?"

_____

_____

9. If you suddenly decided to drop your math homework and rush out to buy a milk shake from a passing ice-cream truck, would your action be *spontaneous*? Base your answer on the meaning of *spontaneous* as it is used in "What Makes a Degas a Degas?"

_____

_____

_____

10. Some artists carefully follow established traditions, while others try to express themselves in new ways. Based on "What Makes a Degas a Degas?" do you think Mühlberger sees Degas as a traditionalist or an experimental artist? Why?

_____

_____

_____

Name _____ Date _____

Essay

Write an extended response to the question of your choice or to the question or questions your teacher assigns you.

11. In an essay, discuss which Degas painting—*Dancers, Pink and Green* or *Carriage at the Races*—you think is more true to life. Provide specific details from "What Makes a Degas a Degas?" to support your ideas.

12. In an essay, give your own interpretation of the title of the essay: "What Makes a Degas a Degas?" Cite at least two details from Degas's paintings and Mühlberger's essay to support your opinion of what characterizes Degas's work.

13. "What Makes a Degas a Degas?" is both an analytic and an interpretive essay. In an essay of your own, explain which elements of Mühlberger's essay are analytic and which are interpretive. Use at least four details from the essay to support your response.

14. **Thinking About the Big Question: What kind of knowledge changes our lives?** In "What Makes a Degas a Degas?" Mühlberger emphasizes the originality and uniqueness of Degas's paintings. In an essay, discuss the kinds of information that inspired Degas to develop a more original painting style.

Oral Response

15. Go back to question 1, 8, or 10 or to the question your teacher assigns you. Take a few minutes to expand your answer and prepare an oral response. Find additional details in "What Makes a Degas a Degas?" that support your points. If necessary, make notes to guide your oral response.

"What Makes a Degas a Degas?" by Richard Mühlberger
Selection Test A

Critical Reading *Identify the letter of the choice that best answers the question.*

____ 1. According to "What Makes a Degas a Degas?" what theme does Degas repeat in hundreds and hundreds of his drawings, prints, pastels, and oil paintings?
   A. ballet
   B. opera
   C. horse racing
   D. mother and child

____ 2. What kind of effect did Degas try to convey with oil paint?
   A. surprising
   B. moody
   C. spontaneous
   D. planned

____ 3. What is the setting for the painting *Dancers, Pink and Green*?
   A. an elegant horse race
   B. Degas's private art studio
   C. backstage at the Paris Opéra
   D. a box seat at a famous theater

____ 4. Mühlberger claims that Degas made *Dancers, Pink and Green* look like it was done hastily and a little sloppily on purpose. Which of the following is a fact he uses to support this opinion?
   A. Degas thought ballerinas were very beautiful and talented.
   B. The rest of Degas's paintings all looked much more careful.
   C. Degas spent a great deal of time at the ballet.
   D. Degas took time planning and creating this painting.

____ 5. What is the main focus of the painting *Carriage at the Races*?
   A. ballet dancers
   B. running horses
   C. baby Henri Valpinçon
   D. the French countryside

____ 6. Which of the following is probably NOT a reason why Degas painted *Carriage at the Races*?

A. because he loved horses and the French countryside

B. because he wanted to paint his lifelong friend and his family

C. because he wanted to experiment with ways to arrange a painting

D. because he wanted to show that he could use pastels as well as oil

____ 7. In "What Makes a Degas a Degas?" what characteristic in Degas's paintings shows the influence of photography?

A. the simulated matte finish

B. the cut-off figures and forms

C. the sketchy outlines of figures

D. the large areas of brilliant color

____ 8. What is the main way in which Japanese prints were different from most Western art during Degas's time?

A. Japanese prints were very quickly and poorly done.

B. Japanese prints looked like they were done in pastels.

C. Dancers were a very popular subject in Japanese prints.

D. Figures were cut off at the edges in Japanese prints.

____ 9. From reading "What Makes a Degas a Degas?" what would you say might be a viewer's first impression of the composition of a Degas painting?

A. balanced

B. bare

C. busy

D. lopsided

____ 10. Which of the following is a FACT that Mühlberger includes about Degas?

A. Degas was very talented.

B. Degas often painted dancers.

C. Degas was one of the greatest painters.

D. Degas was an excellent photographer.

____ 11. Which of the following is the best summary of how Mühlberger probably feels about Degas's work?

A. Degas's work tended to be boring because it repeated the same themes.

B. Degas was a bold pioneer into a new artistic style, with a unique approach.

C. Degas was an excellent student of traditional and classical painting styles.

D. Degas's painting is unique, but it also can feel crude and unfinished-looking.

____ 12. What kind of persuasive appeal does Mühlberger use most to support the idea
that Degas achieved his goal of making viewers feel like they are present along
with him?
A. appeals to authority
B. appeals to reason
C. emotional appeals
D. appeals to shared values

Vocabulary and Grammar

____ 13. In *Dancers, Pink and Green*, Degas painted a man's *silhouette*. What does a sil-
houette look like?
A. an outline filled in with solid color
B. a highly detailed, realistic drawing
C. a well-lit face in profile
D. a simplified, stick-like figure

____ 14. Which of the following is *immaterial*?
A. a music box
B. a statue
C. a shadow
D. a fountain

____ 15. What is the correct way to form the superlative of the adjective *beautiful*?
A. beautifuller   C. more beautiful
B. beautifullest   D. most beautiful

Essay

16. In "What Makes a Degas a Degas?" the author states that Degas wanted viewers to
see a scene as if they were actually part of it. In an essay, identify elements in
Degas's paintings that demonstrate his attempts to create this effect. Explain how
these techniques make viewers feel like they are present with Degas. Use at least
two details from the essay and from Degas's paintings to support your answer.

17. In an essay, explain which Degas painting—*Dancers, Pink and Green* or *Carriage at
the Races*—you respond to more, and why. Be specific in your reasons, using at
least two details from the painting you have chosen to support your opinion.

18. **Thinking About the Big Question: What kind of knowledge changes our lives?**
In "What Makes a Degas a Degas?" Mühlberger discusses the people and traditions
that influenced Degas as an artist. In an essay, discuss at least two types of
knowledge that helped Degas develop his style of painting. Provide examples from
the selection to support your response.

Name _____ Date _____

"What Makes a Degas a Degas?" by Richard Mühlberger
Selection Test B

Critical Reading *Identify the letter of the choice that best completes the statement or answers the question.*

_____ 1. Which of the following words would Mühlberger most likely use to describe Degas?
   A. traditionalist
   B. amateur
   C. follower
   D. innovator

_____ 2. According to Mühlberger, what was Degas's "lifelong quest"?
   A. to impress his close friend Paul Valpinçon
   B. to become a well-known professional photographer
   C. to make viewers feel that they were beside him
   D. to paint more dancers than anyone had before

_____ 3. According to "What Makes a Degas a Degas?" which techniques did Degas invent?
   A. painting with pastels and oils
   B. impressionistic approaches to painting
   C. simulated matte finish of pastels with oils
   D. painting using photographs as sources

_____ 4. Why does Degas outline his figures with thin black lines?
   A. to imitate the look of charcoal
   B. to make them look more realistic
   C. to create light and shadows
   D. to make them look like photographs

_____ 5. How do you know that the baby, Henri, is the focus of the painting *Carriage at the Races*?
   A. He is dressed in very bright colors that show up well.
   B. He is the largest figure in the entire painting.
   C. All the people in the foreground are looking at him.
   D. The carriage and its occupants are centered in the work.

_____ 6. What is surprising about the central image in *Carriage at the Races*?
   A. It looks like it was drawn hastily.
   B. It is off-center and cut off.
   C. It has extremely bright, clashing colors.
   D. It is very abstract and unrealistic.

_____ 7. Mühlberger expresses the opinion that *Carriage at the Races* seems lopsided. Which of the following is a FACT that he uses to support this opinion?
   A. There are horses racing in the background.
   B. The horse farms in Normandy are beautiful.
   C. Degas was enchanted with little Henri Valpinçon.
   D. The largest and darkest objects are in one corner.

____ 8. Which of the following is an OPINION implied by the essay "What Makes a Degas a Degas?"

    A. Degas was inspired by Japanese prints and photographs.

    B. Degas remained close to his friend Paul Valpinçon all his life.

    C. Degas attended many ballet performances at the Paris Opéra.

    D. Degas succeeded in creating a spontaneous look with oil paints.

____ 9. Based on facts included in "What Makes a Degas a Degas?" which of the following conclusions is most likely to be true?

    A. Degas was probably a good photographer.

    B. Degas never pestered dancers backstage.

    C. Degas wanted to have children but never did.

    D. Degas hoped his work would influence others.

____ 10. Mühlberger's descriptions of Degas's paintings might make them seem careless or incomplete. How does Mühlberger's interpretation of Degas's paintings make these qualities seem valuable?

    A. He explains that Degas used these qualities to make him a better photographer.

    B. He explains that all art critics and fans know that this style is the best way to paint.

    C. He explains that Degas intended for his paintings to seem more spontaneous.

    D. He explains that Degas was not very good at finishing out the details of his paintings.

____ 11. What is the purpose of an analytical essay?

    A. to entertain and inform the reader

    B. to narrate the story of the subject's life

    C. to break down a large idea into smaller parts

    D. to convey the larger significance of a subject

____ 12. What is the purpose of an interpretive essay?

    A. to entertain and inform the reader

    B. to narrate the story of the subject's life

    C. to break down a large idea into its smaller parts

    D. to convey the larger significance of a subject

Vocabulary and Grammar

____ 13. Which of the following could not possibly be determined from a *silhouette*?

    A. coloring

    B. body type

    C. height

    D. gender

____ 14. Which of the following is the best synonym for the word *simulating*?

    A. pretending

    B. innovating

    C. pestering

    D. observing

_____ 15. Which of the following describes something that is *immaterial*?
   A. a photograph of a mountain range
   B. the face of a clock
   C. time
   D. the ocean

_____ 16. In which of the following sentences is the superlative of the adjective *expressive* formed correctly?
   A. Degas's paintings are very expressive forms of artwork.
   B. Degas's paintings are more expressive than other artists' work.
   C. Degas's paintings are the most expressive ones I have seen.
   D. Degas's paintings are the expressivest ones I have seen.

Essay

17. In an essay, answer the title's question: "What Makes a Degas a Degas?" Explore the unique aspects of this artist's work. Cite at least two details from Degas's paintings and Mühlberger's essay to support your interpretation.

18. "What Makes a Degas a Degas?" is both an analytic and an interpretive essay. In an essay of your own, explain which elements of Mühlberger's work are analytic and which are interpretive. Use at least two details from his writing to support your explanation of each aspect of his essay.

19. In an essay, identify one of Mühlberger's opinions about Degas's work. Then, list two persuasive appeals he uses to support his claim. Explain how Mühlberger uses each appeal to subtly try to get readers to agree with his point of view. The four kinds of persuasive appeals are appeals to authority, appeals to reason, emotional appeals, and appeals to shared values.

20. **Thinking About the Big Question: Can information change us?** In "What Makes a Degas a Degas?" Mühlberger emphasizes the originality and uniqueness of Degas's paintings. In an essay, discuss the kinds of information that inspired Degas to develop a more original painting style.

Vocabulary Warm-up Word Lists

Study these words from the selections. Then, complete the activities.

Word List A

alliance [uh LYE uhns] *n.* a partnership between groups
  Despite their disagreements, the United States and Canada have a strong alliance.

assuage [uh SWAYJ] *v.* to provide relief from something painful
  To assuage my guilt, I confessed to my mother that I had broken her vase.

cautioning [KAW shuhn ing] *v.* warning against something
  The ads cautioning young people against smoking have been successful.

competition [kahm pi TISH uhn] *n.* contest; display of skill
  There was fierce competition between the rival football teams.

confronted [kuhn FRUHNT ed] *v.* having been faced with
  When we confronted the intruder, he turned and fled at top speed.

culture [KUHL cher] *n.* customs, beliefs, and other expressions of a society
  Anthropologists rely on artifacts to study the culture of ancient peoples.

disperse [dis PURS] *v.* to make something scatter in different directions
  The police sprayed water from fire hoses to disperse the crowd.

rambling [RAM bling] *adj.* seeming to be long and aimless
  The speaker's rambling introduction left her listeners bored and confused.

Word List B

conspicuous [kuhn SPIK yoo uhs] *adj.* very easy to notice; standing out
  The café's conspicuous neon light had become a local landmark.

delegation [del i GAY shuhn] *n.* a few who represent a bigger group
  The president sent a delegation to the conference on global warming.

depressing [di PRES sing] *adj.* making one feel sad
  It was depressing to read about the wasting illness of the novel's heroine.

deprived [di PRYVD] *adj.* having had something that was needed taken away
  The drought deprived us of all but the smallest bit of water for our garden.

inherently [in HAIR uhnt lee] *adv.* often essential part of something
  There was something inherently soothing about the lullaby.

migration [my GRAY shuhn] *n.* mass movement from one area to another
  There is a history of African American migration to northern cities.

partitions [par TISH uhnz] *n.* things that divide one area from another
  Curtains were used as partitions to separate the kitchen from the bedroom.

reverence [REV uhr uhns] *n.* respect and admiration
  The ancient ones showed their reverence for the moon with monthly rituals.

from Desert Exile: The Uprooting of a Japanese-American Family by Yoshiko Uchida
from The Way to Rainy Mountain by N. Scott Momaday
Vocabulary Warm-up Exercises

Exercise A *Fill in each blank in the paragraph with an appropriate word from Word List A. Use each word only once.*

Soon after non-native people settled in the rain forest, a somewhat shaky

[1] _____ grew between the indigenous people and the "outsiders." A new

[2] _____ of mutual support developed. Because the medicinal plants

were harvested by the natives and marketed by the outsiders, there was no issue of

[3] _____ over resources. Officials kept [4] _____ the

"outsiders" about the challenges of dealing with the natives anyway. To help reduce

conflict, they urged them to [5] _____ the forest dwellers' fears of losing

their lands. They described the natives' [6] _____ speaking style and

warned that elders should never be [7] _____ directly on delicate matters.

They noted that humor was best to [8] _____ tension.

Exercise B *Write a complete sentence to answer each question. Use a word from Word List B to replace each underlined word or group of words without changing its meaning.*

1. If you could put a <u>dividing wall</u> anywhere in your home, where would you put it?

    _____

2. What animals have you seen take part in a great <u>journey</u>?

    _____

3. Do you have any favorite books that could be described as <u>sad</u>?

    _____

4. If a song is <u>essentially</u> sad, do you think you could change its mood by playing it faster?

    _____

5. How would you expect people to act toward something they <u>respect and admire</u>?

    _____

6. What <u>obvious</u> landmark could help people find your street?

    _____

7. If you were part of a <u>commission</u> visiting a refugee camp, what might you do on your visit?

    _____

8. If you were <u>stopped from having</u> everything but one food item, what would you want that item to be?

    _____

from **Desert Exile: The Uprooting of a Japanese-American Family** by Yoshiko Uchida
from **The Way to Rainy Mountain** by N. Scott Momaday

Reading Warm-up A

Read the following passage. Pay special attention to the underlined words. Then, read it again, and complete the activities. Use a separate sheet of paper for your written answers.

When Koji was placed in the internment camp, he did not know what he would do. He had hoped that things would not be too uncomfortable, but every day, he was disappointed anew when <u>confronted</u> with the sparse furniture and awful food. His parents realized that he was suffering, and in order to <u>assuage</u> his boredom—and their own—they decided to organize games. Koji's favorites were the baseball games.

For ten years, Koji had grown up surrounded by American <u>culture</u>. He had never felt like an outsider, and he got along well with everybody. Now, however, he lived only with other families with Japanese ancestry because his country was at war with Japan. Japan, in <u>alliance</u> with Germany and Italy, was fighting the United States. Because Koji's parents were from Japan, it seemed that the United States government did not trust them. It was the same for all Japanese Americans.

Koji and his parents took some comfort from the baseball games. Koji's dad worked with him on his pitching, catching, and fielding. Koji became a pretty good pitcher; the more he played, the better he got. There was a fierce <u>competition</u> between the boys in his barracks and those in the next barracks over. Sometimes, the tensions between the groups grew. The parents were forever <u>cautioning</u> their sons against fighting. They did not really have to worry, though, because the boys really just wanted to prove themselves in baseball.

Later in his life, when Koji talked about the camp, he omitted the hardships. He did, however, tell long, <u>rambling</u> stories about his baseball team. Some of his teammates remained his lifelong friends. In one memorable game, the security guards came out to <u>disperse</u> the teams, forever ending the heated rivalry. The war had ended! Surely, their internment would end soon, too.

1. Underline the phrase that tells what Koji was <u>confronted</u> with. Then, explain what *confronted* means.

2. Circle the word that tells what Koji's parents were trying to <u>assuage</u>. Tell what *assuage* means.

3. Circle the word that tells which <u>culture</u> had surrounded Koji. Then, explain what *culture* is.

4. Underline the names of the countries that Japan was in <u>alliance</u> with. Then, explain what an *alliance* is.

5. Underline the phrase that tells who the fierce <u>competition</u> was between. Use *competition* in a sentence.

6. Circle the word that tells what the parents were <u>cautioning</u> their sons against. Then, tell what *cautioning* means.

7. Circle the other word used to describe the <u>rambling</u> stories. Then, explain what this sort of story would be like.

8. Circle the word that tells who the security guards came out to <u>disperse</u>. Then, write why they would *disperse* the teams on the day the war ended.

Name _____ Date _____

from Desert Exile: The Uprooting of a Japanese-American Family by Yoshiko Uchida
from The Way to Rainy Mountain by N. Scott Momaday
Reading Warm-up B

Read the following passage. Pay special attention to the underlined words. Then, read it again, and complete the activities. Use a separate sheet of paper for your written answers.

The Kiowas have a rich history. They believe that their ancestors lived in what is now Montana. They had always traveled from place to place, but after they got horses from the Spanish, they made a major <u>migration</u> to the southeast, to the southern plains.

There, the Kiowas had to interact with the Comanches and the Plains Apaches. At first, these groups did not get along, but in 1790, they made peace. These tribes lived by trade, hunting buffalo, and raiding other groups.

Once the United States government made treaties with these tribes in the 1860s, the Kiowas were <u>deprived</u> of almost all land except a small area in southwestern Oklahoma that became their reservation. For a nomadic people, there was something <u>inherently</u> sad about being limited to this small area. They also found it <u>depressing</u> when the government expected them to shift from being buffalo hunters to being farmers. Some say that the government intentionally killed off the buffalo, once such a <u>conspicuous</u> part of the landscape, so that the Plains Indians would lose their main source of food. In fact, the Kiowas also used the buffalo for clothing, tipis, and other necessities.

In 1901, the Kiowas lost more land rights when their reservation was opened to white settlers. <u>Partitions</u> divided the once-open land. A <u>delegation</u> of leaders went to Washington to protest the change in policy. They sued, and the case went as far as the Supreme Court. In the end, the Kiowas lost the case.

The Kiowas have always had a <u>reverence</u> for the sun, the moon, the stars, and the buffalo; their spiritual practices used to center on the sun. Today, many Kiowas are Christians, but they are very tolerant of other religions.

There are still thousands of Kiowas living in the United States, many of them in Oklahoma. Though they live like any other modern-day Americans, they share a special past.

1. Underline the word that tells the direction of the Kiowas' <u>migration</u>. Explain how a nomadic *migration* would be changed by horses.

2. Circle the name of the legal document that <u>deprived</u> the Kiowas of their lands. Write about when and by whom the Kiowas were *deprived* of their land.

3. Rewrite the sentence containing the word <u>inherently</u> using your own words.

4. Circle the word that is a synonym for <u>depressing</u>. Then, use *depressing* in a sentence.

5. Write about how the buffalo became a less <u>conspicuous</u> part of the landscape of the Great Plains.

6. Underline the words that tell what was divided by <u>partitions</u>. What would you use to make *partitions* on open land?

7. Circle the word that tells who was in the <u>delegation</u>. Explain what a *delegation* is.

8. Underline the phrase that tells what the Kiowas have had a <u>reverence</u> for. Write about something for which you feel *reverence*.

Name _____ Date _____

from **Desert Exile: The Uprooting of a Japanese-American Family** by Yoshiko Uchida
from **The Way to Rainy Mountain** by N. Scott Momaday

Writing About the Big Question

What kind of knowledge changes our lives?

Big Question Vocabulary

adapt	awareness	empathy	enlighten	evolve
growth	history	ignorance	influence	insight
modified	question	reflect	revise	understanding

A. *Use one or more words from the list above to complete each sentence.*

1. People are forced to _____ when world events cause unthinkable changes in everyday events.

2. If government leaders do not have _____ for all of their citizens, then injustice can flourish.

3. We will need to _____ our understanding of the history of native peoples and their struggles in America.

B. *Follow the directions in responding to each of the items below.*

1. List two different times that you were troubled by learning the truth about a historical event.

   _____

   _____

2. Write two sentences explaining one of the situations you listed, and describe the effect it had on your life. Use at least two of the Big Question vocabulary words.

   _____

   _____

C. *Complete the sentence below. Then, write a short paragraph in which you connect this experience to the Big Question.*

   You should learn about important historical events because _____

   _____

   _____

   _____

from **Desert Exile: The Uprooting of a Japanese-American Family** by Yoshiko Uchida
from **The Way to Rainy Mountain** by N. Scott Momaday

Literary Analysis: Author's Purpose

An **author's purpose** is his or her main reason for writing. Common purposes include the following:

- *to inform,* as in a newspaper report
- *to entertain,* as in a mystery story
- *to persuade,* as in an editorial
- *to pay tribute to,* or *commemorate,* as in an obituary

A writer may have more than a single purpose for writing. In these selections, for example, both Momaday and Uchida write to inform readers about a slice of history. However, each author has other, more personal, reasons for writing. These reasons may include to mourn what is gone, to heal old wounds, to expose an injustice, or to better understand themselves.

DIRECTIONS: *Identify Uchida's or Momaday's purpose for including the details in each of the following passages.*

from *Desert Exile*

1. It had rained the day before and the hundreds of people who had trampled on the track had turned it into a miserable mass of slippery mud. _____

_____

2. I wrote to my non-Japanese friends in Berkeley, shamelessly asking them to send us food, and they obliged with large cartons of cookies, nuts, dried fruit, and jams. _____

_____

3. The wonderful news had come like an unexpected gift, but even as we hugged each other in joy, we didn't quite dare believe it until we actually saw him. . . . _____

_____

from *The Way to Rainy Mountain*

4. I like to think of [my grandmother] as a child. When she was born, the Kiowas were living the last great moment of their history. For more than a hundred years they had controlled the open range. . . . _____

_____

5. At the top of the ridge I caught sight of Devil's Tower upthrust against the gray sky as if in the birth of time the core of the earth had broken through its crust and the motion of the world was begun. _____

_____

6. There, where it ought to be, at the end of a long and legendary way, was my grandmother's grave. . . . Looking back once, I saw the mountain and came away. _____

_____

Name _____   Date _____

from Desert Exile: The Uprooting of a Japanese-American Family by Yoshiko Uchida
from The Way to Rainy Mountain by N. Scott Momaday
Vocabulary Builder

Word List

adept   assuage   infirm   nomadic   tenuous   unwieldy

DIRECTIONS: *Find a synonym for each word in the Word List. Use each synonym in a sentence that makes the meaning of the word clear.*

Example: Word List word: *adept*   Synonym: *skilled*
Sentence: The Kiowa took pride in being *skilled* horsemen.

1. *unwieldy* Synonym: _____
   Sentence: _____

2. *assuage* Synonym: _____
   Sentence: _____

3. *infirm* Synonym: _____
   Sentence: _____

4. *nomadic* Synonym: _____
   Sentence: _____

5. *tenuous* Synonym: _____
   Sentence: _____

B. DIRECTIONS: *Circle the letter of the words that express a relationship most like the relationship of the pair of words in CAPITAL LETTERS.*

1. ADEPT : GYMNAST
   A. unappreciated : ignored
   B. physician : doctor
   C. entertain : audience
   D. knowledgeable : teacher

2. TENUOUS : STRONG
   A. certain : doubtful
   B. satisfied : contented
   C. quickly : hastily
   D. determined : purpose

3. UNWIELDY : UNMANAGEABLE
   A. confusion : chaos
   B. light : heavy
   C. teacher : student
   D. bright : color

4. ASSUAGE : GUILT
   A. bake : cook
   B. minimize : pain
   C. house : home
   D. sympathize : empathize

5. INFIRM : HEALTHY
   A. tall : immeasurable
   B. doctor : patient
   C. medication : pain
   D. fast : slow

6. NOMADIC : WORKERS
   A. cultivated : ploughed
   B. cattle : ranch
   C. permanent : farmers
   D. wandering : traveling

from **Desert Exile: The Uprooting of a Japanese-American Family** by Yoshiko Uchida
from **The Way to Rainy Mountain** by N. Scott Momaday
Support for Comparing Literary Works

An author's purpose is his or her main reason for writing. A reporter might write to inform people about a news event, while a short-story writer might write to entertain. Use the chart below to compare the authors' main and secondary reasons for writing these selections. Include details to support your ideas.

from *Desert Exile*	
Uchida's main purpose:	
Author's other purpose(s):	**Most powerful details in passage:**
1.	1.
2.	2.
3.	3.

from *The Way to Rainy Mountain*	
Momaday's main purpose:	
Author's other purpose(s):	**Most powerful details in passage:**
1.	1.
2.	2.
3.	3.

Now, use your notes to write a brief statement about the similarities and differences between the authors' purposes in these two selections.

from Desert Exile: The Uprooting of a Japanese-American Family by Yoshiko Uchida
from The Way to Rainy Mountain by N. Scott Momaday
Open-Book Test

Short Answer *Write your responses to the questions in this section on the lines provided.*

1. Read the following excerpt from *Desert Exile*: "A cook reached into a dishpan full of canned sausages and dropped two onto my plate with his fingers." What is Yoshiko Uchida's purpose in including this rather disgusting detail in her memoir?

   _____

   _____

2. In *Desert Exile*, the Uchidas come to think of dried prunes as a rare treat. What does their attitude toward prunes show about conditions in the camp?

   _____

   _____

   _____

3. If you were *adept* at shooting a basketball, would you have a good chance of making the team? Explain your answer, based on the meaning of *adept* in *Desert Exile*.

   _____

   _____

   _____

4. What is N. Scott Momaday's main purpose in writing *The Way to Rainy Mountain*?

   _____

   _____

5. In *The Way to Rainy Mountain*, Momaday blends some of his own childhood memories with an account of his grandmother's life and people. Why does he do this?

   _____

   _____

6. If your understanding of algebra were *tenuous*, would you do well on the final exam? Explain your answer, based on the meaning of *tenuous* in *The Way to Rainy Mountain*.

   _____

   _____

   _____

7. In *Desert Exile* and *The Way to Rainy Mountain*, both Uchida and Momaday convey a similar attitude toward the past of their people. What is that shared attitude?

_____

_____

8. What details about their people do Uchida and Momaday include in *Desert Exile* and *The Way to Rainy Mountain*? In the chart below, write two details for each selection. Then, on the lines below, write a sentence about what Uchida's and Momaday's people have in common in these two selections.

	Uchida	**Momaday**
Detail 1		
Detail 2		

_____

_____

9. In *Desert Exile*, Uchida provides a detailed description of her mother. In *The Way to Rainy Mountain*, Momaday provides an equally rich portrait of his grandmother. What major character traits do Uchida's mother and Momaday's grandmother share?

_____

_____

10. Uchida and Momaday take different approaches to recording their family experiences. How would you characterize the basic difference in the authors' approach in *Desert Exile* and *The Way to Rainy Mountain*?

_____

_____

Essay

Write an extended response to the question of your choice or to the question or questions your teacher assigns you.

11. An author's purpose is his or her main reason for writing—to inform, to entertain, to persuade, or to pay tribute to someone or something. In an essay, identify Uchida's main purpose in writing *Desert Exile* and Momaday's main purpose in writing *The Way to Rainy Mountain*. Support your answer with specific details from the selections.

12. Both *Desert Exile* and *The Way to Rainy Mountain* discuss the uprooting of a group of people of a certain ethnic background. In an essay, identify each group of people. Explain the reasons that they were uprooted. Then, discuss each author's attitude about these events.

13. *Desert Exile* and *The Way to Rainy Mountain* are about the difficult emotions people can suffer when they leave home and when they return home. In an essay, explain which selection focuses more on leaving home and which focuses more on returning home. Explain the reasons for the emotions surrounding these comings and goings. Support your answer with specific examples from both selections.

14. **Thinking About the Big Question: What kind of knowledge changes our lives?** In the selections from *Desert Exile* and *The Way to Rainy Mountain*, Uchida and Momaday provide readers with new knowledge about the treatment of two different ethnic groups in American history. How did reading these selections change your understanding of American history and culture? Support your response with specific examples from the selections.

Oral Response

15. Go back to question 2, 4, or 10 or to the question your teacher assigns you. Take a few minutes to expand your answer and prepare an oral response. Find additional details in *Desert Exile* and/or *The Way to Rainy Mountain* that support your points. If necessary, make notes to guide your oral response.

from Desert Exile: The Uprooting of a Japanese-American Family by Yoshiko Uchida
from The Way to Rainy Mountain by N. Scott Momaday
Selection Test A

Critical Reading *Identify the letter of the choice that best answers the question.*

____ 1. In *Desert Exile*, what is the "apartment" in which the Uchida family lives at Tanforan?
   A. a closet under the grandstand
   B. a former horse stall
   C. a black tar-papered shack
   D. a crowded mess hall

____ 2. What is Uchida's purpose for including the following detail in *Desert Exile*?
   When I reached the serving table and held out my plate, a cook reached into a dishpan full of canned sausages and dropped two onto my plate with his fingers.
   A. to point out the unsanitary conditions at the camp
   B. to entertain the reader with a comical detail
   C. to note that the food at the camp was healthy
   D. to inform the reader of standard cafeteria procedures

____ 3. In *Desert Exile*, why do the Uchidas come to think of dried prunes as a treat?
   A. They do not want to offend their neighbors.
   B. They always loved to eat prunes back at home.
   C. They remind the Uchidas of their father.
   D. They are almost always hungry.

____ 4. Why does Uchida conclude that the army was "ill-equipped to build living quarters for women and children"?
   A. The women did not have a place to do the laundry.
   B. There were no play areas for children.
   C. The men's bathrooms had hot water.
   D. Basic items, such as shower curtains, were missing.

____ 5. In *Desert Exile*, why does walking a mile for a hot shower boost the Uchida sisters' morale?
   A. It gets them away from their annoying neighbors.
   B. It is the only chance that they have to exercise.
   C. It is a small luxury that makes them feel good.
   D. They are only allowed to shower once a week.

_____ 6. What is one purpose Momaday has for writing *The Way to Rainy Mountain*?
   A. to pay tribute
   B. to amuse
   C. to persuade
   D. to make fun

_____ 7. Which of these statements about the grandmother in *The Way to Rainy Mountain* is true?
   A. She tells the story.
   B. She has died.
   C. She migrated from Montana.
   D. She did not have children.

_____ 8. In *The Way to Rainy Mountain*, why did the Kiowas migrate to the southeast?
   A. because they were instructed by the sun god to do so
   B. because the mountains provided them with more protection
   C. because the plains gave them a greater sense of freedom
   D. because they had heard legends about Devil's Tower

_____ 9. In *The Way to Rainy Mountain*, the author says that his grandmother had an "ancient awe." What does he mean by this?
   A. that she is respected because she is extremely old
   B. that she has been silent for most of her life
   C. that she worships her ancestors
   D. that she regards the world with wonder

_____ 10. In *The Way to Rainy Mountain*, Momaday includes some of his own childhood memories. What is his main reason for doing this?
   A. to connect his life with his grandmother's life
   B. to show that the Kiowas were unfairly treated
   C. to explain the role of women in Kiowa culture
   D. to suggest that he feels guilty about leaving home

_____ 11. Which purpose is shared by the authors of *Desert Exile* and *The Way to Rainy Mountain*?
   A. to honor a particular person
   B. to praise the U.S. government
   C. to record a piece of history
   D. to persuade readers to visit their families

____ **12.** The authors of *Desert Exile* and *The Way to Rainy Mountain* both express which idea?

    A. My people once fled their homes in search of new land.

    B. The importance of understanding the lessons of the past.

    C. Family is more important than country.

    D. Country is more important than family.

____ **13.** What do Uchida and Momaday feel toward their families?

    A. anger and resentment   **C.** impatience, but kindness

    B. detachment   **D.** a strong connection

Vocabulary

____ **14.** What does *unwieldy* mean in the following sentence from *Desert Exile*?

    "What ya got in here anyway?" they shouted good-naturedly as they struggled with the <u>unwieldy</u> bundle.

    A. awkward   **C.** tattered

    B. small   **D.** ancient

____ **15.** According to *The Way to Rainy Mountain*, the Kiowas were *adept* at horseback riding. What does this mean?

    A. that they were poor horseback riders

    B. that they rarely rode horses

    C. that they were skilled horsemen

    D. that they rode horses in rodeos

Essay

16. It could be said that *Desert Exile* is about leaving home and *The Way to Rainy Mountain* is about returning home. In a brief essay, explain who leaves home in *Desert Exile* and who comes home in *The Way to Rainy Mountain*. Then, give reasons for these comings and goings.

17. An author's purpose is his or her main reason for writing. For example, an author may write to inform readers about an event, to persuade readers to take action, to entertain readers, or to honor someone or something. In an essay, identify Momaday's main purpose in writing *The Way to Rainy Mountain* and Uchida's main purpose in writing *Desert Exile*. Support your ideas with examples from the works.

18. Thinking About the Big Question: What kind of knowledge changes our lives? In the selections from *Desert Exile* and *The Way to Rainy Mountain*, Uchida and Momaday provide readers with knowledge about two different cultural groups. How did these selections change your understanding of American history and culture? First, discuss how each selection provided you with new knowledge. Then, explain how this knowledge changed you. Support your response with specific examples from the selections.

from Desert Exile: The Uprooting of a Japanese-American Family by Yoshiko Uchida
from The Way to Rainy Mountain by N. Scott Momaday
Selection Test B

Critical Reading *Identify the letter of the choice that best completes the statement or answers the question.*

____ 1. In *Desert Exile*, why are the Uchidas taken to Tanforan?
A. because Uchida's father has committed a crime
B. because they have joined the military
C. because it is the only home they can find
D. because they are Japanese Americans

____ 2. Identify Uchida's purpose for including the following detail in *Desert Exile*.
> The space, while perhaps a good source of ventilation for horses, deprived us of all but visual privacy, and we couldn't even be sure of that because of the crevices and knotholes in the dividing walls.

A. to inform readers that the family was living in a stall
B. to emphasize the family's lack of privacy
C. to entertain readers by describing the family's absurd living conditions
D. to convey how hot and stuffy the family's living quarters were

____ 3. What does the following sentence from *Desert Exile* reveal about Uchida's attitude?
> I wondered how much the nation's security would have been threatened had the army permitted us to remain in our homes a few more days until the camps were adequately prepared for occupancy by families.

A. She resents not having had the time to pack more of her belongings.
B. She feels humiliated by being forced to live in such conditions.
C. She detects a certain irony in being treated as a national threat.
D. She is angry that the camp was not sufficiently prepared.

____ 4. In *Desert Exile*, why does Uchida include the anecdote about the neighbors' sleeping son?
A. to provide a bit of amusement in an otherwise serious account
B. to show that teenagers require a good deal of sleep
C. to demonstrate that in such close quarters, hostilities naturally arise
D. to give an example of the ways in which people can entertain themselves

____ 5. In *Desert Exile*, which phrase best describes how Uchida's family feels when they hear that their father will be "coming home"?
A. fearful, but happy
B. angry at him for being away
C. ambivalent and ashamed
D. cautiously joyful

____ 6. Which of the following statements about the grandmother in *The Way to Rainy Mountain* is true?
A. She died alone in her house near Rainy Mountain.
B. She migrated alone from western Montana.
C. She was the last remaining elder of the Kiowas.
D. She lived her long life in the shadow of Rainy Mountain.

____ 7. Which of the following best describes how the Kiowas felt when they entered the southern Plains in *The Way to Rainy Mountain*?
   A. confused
   B. liberated
   C. fearful
   D. contented

____ 8. According to *The Way to Rainy Mountain*, the Kiowas created a legend at the base of Devil's Tower in order to
   A. help them deal with their fear of the unknown.
   B. express their reverence for the sun.
   C. demonstrate their respect for Kiowa women.
   D. ask God to protect them on their journey.

____ 9. Why does Momaday describe what was happening with the Kiowas when his grandmother was a child?
   A. He wants to compare his grandmother's childhood with his own.
   B. He wants to give readers a complete sense of his grandmother's life.
   C. He wants to emphasize the Kiowas' former power.
   D. He wants to explain how the landscape near Rainy Mountain has changed.

____ 10. The author's main purpose in *The Way to Rainy Mountain* is to
   A. describe the world of his Kiowa ancestors.
   B. demonstrate the strength of Kiowa culture.
   C. explore the region near Rainy Mountain.
   D. expose the mistreatment of the Kiowas.

____ 11. Which purpose do the authors of *Desert Exile* and *The Way to Rainy Mountain* share?
   A. to inform readers about historical events
   B. to commemorate a person whom they hold in great esteem
   C. to celebrate joyful childhood memories
   D. to persuade readers to visit a particular location

____ 12. Which idea is expressed by the authors of both *Desert Exile* and *The Way to Rainy Mountain*?
   A. In the past, my people had a perfect life.
   B. In the past, my people have been treated unfairly.
   C. Today, I realize that family is more important than money.
   D. Today, I honor the greatness my people once achieved.

____ 13. Based on the selections, which word best describes both Momaday's grandmother and Uchida's mother?
   A. dignified
   B. afraid
   C. defeated
   D. soft-spoken

_____ **14.** Both *Desert Exile* and *The Way to Rainy Mountain* provide a reflection on
      A. happiness.
      B. freedom.
      C. displacement.
      D. religion.

_____ **15.** Which sentence best summarizes the difference between Momaday's and Uchida's essays?
      A. Momaday's has a broad scope, while Uchida's is tightly focused.
      B. Uchida's is more objective, while Momaday's is more personal.
      C. Momaday's is realistic, while Uchida's is fantastical.
      D. Uchida's is comical, while Momaday's is serious.

Vocabulary

_____ **16.** What does *nomadic* mean in the following sentence from *The Way to Rainy Mountain*?
      They acquired horses, and their ancient nomadic spirit was suddenly free of the ground.

      A. lonely
      B. oppressed
      C. old
      D. wandering

_____ **17.** The Uchidas' time at Tanforan makes them *adept* in new ways. This means that
      A. they grow increasingly angry.
      B. they develop new skills.
      C. they are treated like children.
      D. they become sullen and selfish.

_____ **18.** Before her death, Momaday's grandmother had become
      A. unwieldy.
      B. nomadic.
      C. infirm.
      D. tenuous.

Essay

19. Both *Desert Exile* and *The Way to Rainy Mountain* chronicle the uprooting of a certain group of people. In an essay, identify each group of people, explain how and why each group was uprooted, and describe each author's attitude toward these events.

20. The authors of *Desert Exile* and *The Way to Rainy Mountain* share some purposes for writing, but not others. In an essay, identify one or two purposes the authors have in common and one or two different purposes they have. In your opinion, which author is more successful in achieving his or her purposes? Why?

21. Thinking About the Big Question: What kind of knowledge changes our lives? In the selections from *Desert Exile* and *The Way to Rainy Mountain*, Uchida and Momaday provide readers with new knowledge about the treatment of two different ethnic groups in American history. How did reading these selections change your understanding of American history and culture? Support your response with specific examples from the selections.

Name _____ Date _____

Writing Workshop
Persuasion: Persuasive Essay

Prewriting: Gathering Details

Use the pro-and-con chart below to identify counter-arguments and to brainstorm for ideas that counter the opposing claims.

Your Supporting Arguments	Opposing Arguments

Drafting: Shaping Your Writing

Use the graphic organizer below to build your arguments to support your thesis.

Your Thesis Statement:

⬇

Your Least Persuasive Argument:

⬇

Another Persuasive Argument:

⬇

Your Most Persuasive Argument:

Writing Workshop
Persuasive Essay: Integrating Grammar Skills

Revising to Create Parallelism

Parallelism is the use of similar grammatical forms or patterns to express similar ideas. Effective use of parallelism adds rhythm and balance to your writing, strengthens the connections between your ideas, and makes what you say more powerful and memorable.

Parallel Construction	Nonparallel	Parallel
Nouns	The wildfire engulfed vehicles, businesses, and where people lived.	The wildfire engulfed vehicles, businesses, and homes.
Verbs	It burned down forests and ruined crops, and it also caused the destruction of several towns.	It burned down forests, ruined crops, and destroyed several towns.
Adjectives	The firefighters were strong and brave, and they also were skillful.	The firefighters were strong, brave, and skillful.
Adverbs	The fire blazed fiercely and in a relentless manner.	The fire blazed fiercely and relentlessly.
Prepositional Phrases	Victims survived atop roofs, in boats, and they were on high ground as well.	Victims survived atop roofs, in boats, and on high ground.
Gerunds	Schools were used for feeding, sheltering, and to counsel.	Schools were used for feeding, sheltering, and counseling.

A. DIRECTIONS: *For each sentence, circle the word or words you would change to create the parallel structures in parentheses.*

1. (gerunds) Brad likes to dance, acting, and singing.

2. (adverbs) He sings loudly, with exuberance, and tunefully.

3. (adjectives) Amelia is beautiful and talented, and she also has had luck.

B. DIRECTIONS: *On the lines below, rewrite these sentences using parallelism.*

1. My mom gardens to get exercise, to grow tasty food, and for the creation of beauty.

_____

2. Her garden contains vegetables, shade trees, and there are also plants that flower.

_____

3. In spring, she sows seeds and plants seedlings, plus there are plants that she moves.

_____

Name _____ Date _____

Unit 3 Vocabulary Workshop—1
Words With Multiple Meanings

Many words have **multiple meanings**. Sometimes words can be used as different parts of speech. To decide which meaning a writer is using in a sentence, look at context clues.

A. DIRECTIONS: *Use the dictionary to find and write two meanings for each word, including parts of speech. Then, write a sentence that clearly illustrates each meaning.*

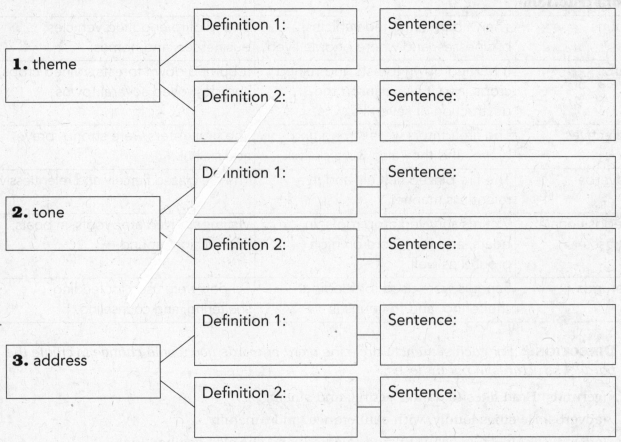

1. theme

Definition 1:

Sentence:

Definition 2:

Sentence:

2. tone

Definition 1:

Sentence:

Definition 2:

Sentence:

3. address

Definition 1:

Sentence:

Definition 2:

Sentence:

B. DIRECTIONS: *Circle context clues to the meaning of the underlined word in each sentence. Then, look up the word in a dictionary, and write a sentence that uses the word with a different meaning.*

1. Anyone who <u>objects</u> to the novel we chose for the book club does not have to read it.

_____

2. Each year, Earth makes one <u>revolution</u> around the sun.

_____

3. The settlers built a <u>rude</u> cabin out of rough logs to get them through the winter.

_____

Unit 3 Vocabulary Workshop—2
Words With Multiple Meanings

Many words have **multiple meanings**. Sometimes words can be used as different parts of speech. To decide which meaning a writer is using in a sentence, look at context clues.

A. DIRECTIONS: *Use the dictionary to find and write two meanings for each word, including parts of speech. Then, write a sentence that clearly illustrates each meaning.*

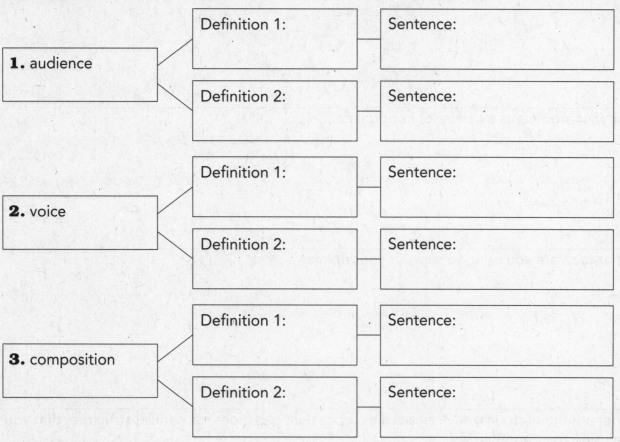

1. audience

Definition 1:

Sentence:

Definition 2:

Sentence:

2. voice

Definition 1:

Sentence:

Definition 2:

Sentence:

3. composition

Definition 1:

Sentence:

Definition 2:

Sentence:

B. DIRECTIONS: *Circle context clues to the meaning of the underlined word in each sentence. Then, look up the word in a dictionary, and write a sentence that uses the word with a different meaning.*

1. I like to sit by my window each evening and <u>reflect</u> on all that happened that day.

   _____

2. I will vote for him because his <u>values</u> are similar to the things I care about most.

   _____

3. She is an <u>articulate</u> speaker whose clarity never fails to persuade listeners.

   _____

Name _____ Date _____

Communications Workshop

Delivering a Persuasive Speech

After choosing a position on a current local or national issue, fill out the following chart. Use your notes to plan and organize your speech to the class.

Position on a current local or national issue: _____

What is your position on this issue?

List your arguments by order of importance.

What facts are you using to support your opinion?

What are the rhetorical devices, such as repetition, questions, or parallel structure, that you are using to strengthen your argument?

What are the memorable points that will form your conclusion?

Unit 3: Types of Nonfiction
Benchmark Test 6

MULTIPLE CHOICE

Reading Skills *Read the following selection. Then, answer the questions that follow.*

Our school's mission statement stresses community, cooperation, and personal and intellectual growth. But one of our school's practices—selecting a valedictorian and salutatorian each year—does not support our mission. This practice is divisive, it is unfair, it is archaic. So let's end it now!

For some students, jockeying for these positions begins when they start high school. They choose classes they can ace, as well as AP and IB courses that boost their grade point averages, rather than ones that excite their interest or challenge them. They pay plenty and spend hours in classes that promise to raise standardized test scores. Successful candidates are routinely accused of gaming the system. The formula for selecting the two "top" students is complex; selection can turn on several zeroes after a decimal point. At several schools around the country, students who lost out as valedictorian have sued. Is this the kind of situation we want to encourage at our school?

1. Which statement best summarizes the writer's argument?
   A. The positions of valedictorian and salutatorian are meaningless honors.
   B. The positions of valedictorian and salutatorian do not match our school's values.
   C. Students tend to cheat when they compete for valedictorian and salutatorian.
   D. The formula for determining which students are chosen valedictorian and salutatorian are too obscure.

2. Based on the writer's argument, which would be the best title for this selection?
   A. Save Our School's Reputation
   B. Let's Change Our Mission Statement
   C. Try a New Way to Choose Valedictorian and Salutatorian
   D. Valedictorian and Salutatorian Must Go!

3. What is the writer's appeal based upon?
   A. facts only
   B. opinions only
   C. facts and opinions
   D. neither facts nor opinions

4. What is the best question to ask yourself to evaluate a writer's argument?
   A. How does the writer's background affect his or her point of view?
   B. How closely do I agree with the writer's position?
   C. Does the writer support claims with evidence and reasoning?
   D. Does the writer's argument affect me emotionally?

5. What is the most important assumption the writer makes?
   A. that readers know what valedictorians and salutatorians are and how they are chosen
   B. that readers care about the system used to select valedictorians and salutatorians
   C. that readers know what AP and IB stand for
   D. that readers agree that the school's mission statement and practices should match

6. Which is a fact the writer uses to support his or her opinion?
   A. Selecting a valedictorian and salutatorian is divisive.
   B. Students who were not selected as valedictorian or salutatorian have sued.
   C. Students choose AP courses to boost their grade point averages.
   D. Students choose easy classes so they can get good grades.

7. Which of the following sentences most clearly expresses an opinion?
   A. Our school's mission statement stresses community, cooperation, and personal and intellectual growth.
   B. This practice is divisive, it is unfair, it is archaic.
   C. They pay plenty and spend hours in classes that promise to raise standardized test scores.
   D. The formula for selecting the two "top" students is complex; selection can turn on several zeroes after a decimal point.

Literary Analysis: Persuasive Writing

8. What is the main purpose of a persuasive composition?
   A. to provide facts and opinions
   B. to entertain readers or listeners
   C. to express the writer's or speaker's feelings
   D. to convince people to believe or do something

9. The sentence "This practice is divisive, it is unfair, it is archaic" is an example of which persuasive device?
   A. parallelism   C. slogan or saw
   B. repetition   D. rhetorical question

10. The sentence "Is this the kind of situation we want to encourage at our school?" is an example of which persuasive device?
    A. parallelism   C. slogan or saw
    B. repetition   D. rhetorical question

11. What is the rhetorical device in the following sentence?

    Our candidate is a fighter: he fights crime, he fights criminals, and he fights corruption

    A. parallelism   C. slogan or saw
    B. repetition   D. rhetorical question

12. Which rhetorical device is used in this sentence?

    Seize the moment!

    A. parallelism   C. slogan or saw
    B. repetition   D. rhetorical question

Unit 3 Resources: Types of Nonfiction
228

Literary Analysis: Analytic and Interpretive Essays *Read the following selection. Then, answer the questions.*

Picasso painted *Les Demoiselles d'Avignon*, which now hangs in the Museum of Modern Art in New York City, in 1907. The 8-foot by 7-foot-8-inch oil painting resulted from more than one hundred sketches and studies. According to most art historians, it is a key work in the early development of Cubism and, indeed, in all of modern art.

In the painting Picasso depicted each of the five angular figures grouped around an arrangement of fruit differently. The head of the woman on the far left is the most cubist. The figure at the right rear has an African mask. The figures at the center show the influence of Iberian sculptures.

13. Which is the most accurate description of the selection?
    A. descriptive
    B. interpretive
    C. partially descriptive and partially interpretive
    D. neither analytic nor interpretive

14. What kind of appeal does this selection include in its first paragraph?
    A. an appeal to authority
    B. an appeal to reason
    C. an appeal to emotion
    D. an appeal to shared values

15. What appeal does this sentence include?

    Given the facts of this case and my client's airtight alibi, there can be no other conclusion than that my client is innocent.

    A. an appeal to authority
    B. an appeal to reason
    C. an appeal to emotion
    D. an appeal to shared values

16. What appeal does this sentence use?

    This essay is for the children we love and who we want to inherit a less-polluted world than ours.

    A. an appeal to authority
    B. an appeal to reason
    C. an appeal to emotion
    D. an appeal to shared values

17. On what appeal is this sentence based?

    What better instance of honoring one's father and mother could we find?

    A. an appeal to authority
    B. an appeal to reason
    C. an appeal to emotion
    D. an appeal to shared values

18. What is true of both interpretive and analytic essays?
    A. They both always appeal to emotions and logic.
    B. They are both works of nonfiction.
    C. They are both short.
    D. They both break a subject into parts.

Literary Analysis

19. What is an author's purpose?
    A. the appeals the author uses
    B. the effect the author has on the reader
    C. the author's main reason for writing
    D. the author's ability to convince the reader

20. What was the author's purpose in writing the following statement?

    Shortly after I moved to California, there was an earthquake. Needless to say, it shook me up. Not only did I end up running into the street in my pajamas with kittens on them—in which any adult would be embarrassed to be seen—but I also forgot my keys inside the house when I locked the door.

    A. to inform   **B.** to entertain   **C.** to persuade   **D.** to memorialize

21. What is the purpose of a speech at the dedication of a war memorial?
    A. to inform   **B.** to entertain   **C.** to persuade   **D.** to commemorate

22. What is the primary purpose of most television commercials?
    A. to inform   **B.** to entertain   **C.** to persuade   **D.** to commemorate

Informational Texts: Analyze Text Structures

Read this selection from an encyclopedia entry. Then, answer the questions that follow.

NEW YORK CITY

DUTCH BEGINNINGS

In 1625, the Dutch founded the colony of New Amsterdam on the southern tip of an island that lay between two rivers. The colony became a center of trade, and began to grow.

ENGLISH TAKEOVER

In 1664, the English took control of New Amsterdam and renamed it New York. Over the next hundred years, the city's population rose dramatically. By 1776, it was one of the most important colonial cities.

THE UNITED STATES - 18th Century

After the colonies won independence from England, New York was briefly the new nation's capital. Though it lost this status, it has remained one of the country's most important cities.

23. Which statement is accurate?
    A. This article includes a lot of detail about each topic.
    B. This article gives the reader a very general idea of each topic.
    C. This article relies heavily on maps to communicate information.
    D. This article relies heavily on charts to communicate information.

24. How is the information in the article mainly presented?
    A. as a personal narrative   **C.** in chronological order
    B. through eyewitness statements   **D.** through charts and tables

25. Which of the following will most likely be the next section heading?
    A. 19th Century   **C.** Other Important Cities
    B. New York Today   **D.** Moving Toward the Future

Vocabulary: Word Roots and Prefixes

26. What is the definition of *transcends* in the following sentence?

Winning this prize transcends all of your past accomplishments.

A. lessens
B. ridicules
C. makes up for
D. goes beyond

27. What is the meaning of the root *-jur-* in the word *jurisdiction*?
A. law
B. place
C. speech
D. obedience

28. What does the prefix *im-* mean in the word *immaterial*?
A. human
B. ancient
C. not
D. bad

29. Which word has the same prefix as *embodied*?
A. emerald
B. embassy
C. emotion
D. empower

30. Which of the following sentences correctly uses the word *descend*?
A. The climbers had to go slowly on their descend of the mountain.
B. Having reached the top of the mountain, it was now time to descend.
C. The hikers took the longer trail to descend to the mountain's peak.
D. When climbing a peak, one should have a descend respect for the mountain.

31. Which word has the same root as *perjury*?
A. juror
B. jungle
C. intersperse
D. mercury

Grammar

32. Which degree of comparison is the word *choicest*?
A. positive
B. comparative
C. superlative
D. ablative

33. The following sentence contains what kind of adjective?

She was a brilliant scholar and teacher.

A. positive
B. comparative
C. superlative
D. predicate

34. The ending *-er* is associated with which degree?
A. positive
B. comparative
C. superlative
D. ablative

35. What form is the adverb *tediously*?
A. positive
B. comparative
C. superlative
D. ablative

36. In the following sentence, how many adverbs are in the comparative degree?

    Richard was fast, Seth was faster, but Robin was surely the fastest of all.

    A. one   C. three
    B. two   D. four

37. The word *most* is associated with which degree?
    A. positive   C. superlative
    B. comparative   D. ablative

38. What is the best way to fix this nonparallel sentence?

    Her job included teaching, writing papers, and to chair committees.

    A. Her job included teaching, writing papers, and chairing committees.
    B. Her job included to teach, to write papers, and to chair committees.
    C. Her job included teaching, to write papers, and to chair committees
    D. Her job included to teach, writing papers, and chairing committees.

39. In which sentence is the parallelism faulty?
    A. Who doesn't love parties, travel, and to eat at restaurants?
    B. Fighting evil, defending the helpless, and saving damsels in distress: that is my job.
    C. My ideal workout is running, biking, and swimming.
    D. The aim of the course is to instill curiosity, to teach research methods, and to encourage debate.

Spelling

40. What is the most compelling reason that computer spell-checkers are imperfect?
    A. They often provide incorrect spellings of commonly used words.
    B. They do not detect wrongly used words that are spelled correctly.
    C. They can be difficult to use.
    D. They often use the spelling rules of British English.

ESSAY

41. What public figure has done something recently that you thought was absolutely wonderful or extremely wrong-headed? Write a letter to that person. Explain your position clearly and briefly. If you disagree with what the person has done, try to persuade him or her to change perspective or to work to make the situation better. Use formal language and proper letter form in your communication.

42. Write a critique of a movie or performance you have seen recently. Be sure to support your opinions about the acting, the script, and the production with appropriate details.

43. Challenge your powers of persuasion by arguing against something that you believe. Take a position contrary to the one you actually hold about a much-debated current issue. Describe the issue and your position on it clearly. Support your position with facts, emotional appeals, and rhetorical devices.

Vocabulary in Context 3—Part 1

Identify the answer choice that best completes the statement.

1. The boxcars that had a destination farther west were _____ from the train.
   A. uncoupled
   B. overcome
   C. makeshift
   D. motionless

2. Wildflowers grew in riotous confusion throughout the _____ .
   A. avenues
   B. fertilizing
   C. meadow
   D. vacant

3. As the car sharply rounded the corner, the tires were _____ .
   A. squealing
   B. flitting
   C. throbbing
   D. hastened

4. The little girl's hair was curled into _____ .
   A. headlong
   B. panes
   C. chords
   D. ringlets

5. As the climber lost his hold and started to fall, he anxiously reached out to _____ a branch.
   A. seize
   B. survive
   C. vertical
   D. encounter

6. On the late-night television show, the audience enjoyed the stories told by the marvelous _____ .
   A. foe
   B. objector
   C. warrior
   D. raconteur

7. To get to the highway, this is the best _____ to take.
   A. lain
   B. route
   C. sojourn
   D. discourse

8. I saw so many fleas on my cat that I knew she was _____ with them.
   A. conjured
   B. menacing
   C. surged
   D. infested

9. Large sums of money are kept in the basement of the bank in the _____ .
   A. coves
   B. laboratories
   C. vaults
   D. chasm

10. Even though I really like those fancy shoes, I should buy something more _____ .
    A. practical
    B. divine
    C. application
    D. woebegone

11. The beachfront house is supported by a sturdy cement _____ .
    A. threshold
    B. foundation
    C. crevice
    D. backstage

12. I did not get much sleep last night, so I am a bit _____ today.
    A. stark
    B. drowsy
    C. conscientious
    D. droning

13. Throughout the canyon, the boom of the thunder _____ .
    A. echoed
    B. eased
    C. amid
    D. penetrate

14. That all students will do their homework assignments is every teacher's _____ .
    A. woe
    B. incredulity
    C. expectation
    D. inertia

15. We had to polish my grandmother's silver because it was so_____ .
    A. enthralled
    B. tremulous
    C. trodden
    D. tarnished

16. When a stringed instrument is played, sound is produced by the_____ of the string.
    A. mechanical
    B. independence
    C. vibration
    D. electrical

17. The baby cried every time she looked at me, wounding my_____ .
    A. humiliation
    B. moral
    C. pep
    D. ego

18. Ramps were constructed at the entrance to the town hall to make it wheelchair_____ .
    A. barricade
    B. accessible
    C. unaccustomed
    D. characterized

19. To provide meat for the winter, Dad brought two cows to the market to be_____ .
    A. diverted
    B. impaled
    C. slaughtered
    D. regenerated

20. By asking me so many unanswerable questions, my little brother_____ me.
    A. renounced
    B. provoked
    C. illuminated
    D. discriminated

Diagnostic Tests and Vocabulary in Context
Use and Interpretation

The Diagnostic Tests and Vocabulary in Context were developed to assist teachers in making the most appropriate assignment of *Prentice Hall Literature* program selections to students. The purpose of these assessments is to indicate the degree of difficulty that students are likely to have in reading/comprehending the selections presented in the *following* unit of instruction. Tests are provided at six separate times in each grade level—a *Diagnostic Test* (to be used prior to beginning the year's instruction) and a *Vocabulary in Context*, the final segment of the Benchmark Test appearing at the end of each of the first five units of instruction. Note that the tests are intended for use not as summative assessments for the prior unit, but as guidance for assigning literature selections in the upcoming unit of instruction.

The structure of all Diagnostic Tests and Vocabulary in Context in this series is the same. All test items are four-option, multiple-choice items. The format is established to assess a student's ability to construct sufficient meaning from the context sentence to choose the only provided word that fits both the semantics (meaning) and syntax (structure) of the context sentence. All words in the context sentences are chosen to be "below-level" words that students reading at this grade level should know. All answer choices fit *either* the meaning or structure of the context sentence, but only the correct choice fits *both* semantics and syntax. All answer choices—both correct answers and incorrect options—are key words chosen from specifically taught words that will occur in the subsequent unit of program instruction. This careful restriction of the assessed words permits a sound diagnosis of students' current reading achievement and prediction of the most appropriate level of readings to assign in the upcoming unit of instruction.

The assessment of vocabulary in context skill has consistently been shown in reading research studies to correlate very highly with "reading comprehension." This is not surprising as the format essentially assesses comprehension, albeit in sentence-length "chunks." Decades of research demonstrate that vocabulary assessment provides a strong, reliable prediction of comprehension achievement—the purpose of these tests. Further, because this format demands very little testing time, these diagnoses can be made efficiently, permitting teachers to move forward with critical instructional tasks rather than devoting excessive time to assessment.

It is important to stress that while the Diagnostic and Vocabulary in Context were carefully developed and will yield sound assignment decisions, they were designed to *reinforce*, not supplant, teacher judgment as to the most appropriate instructional placement for individual students. Teacher judgment should always prevail in making placement—or indeed other important instructional—decisions concerning students.

Name _____ Date _____

Diagnostic Tests and Vocabulary in Context
Branching Suggestions

These tests are designed to provide maximum flexibility for teachers. Your *Unit Resources* books contain the 40-question **Diagnostic Test** and 20-question **Vocabulary in Context** tests. At *PHLitOnline,* you can access the Diagnostic Test and complete 40-question Vocabulary in Context tests. Procedures for administering the tests are described below. Choose the procedure based on the time you wish to devote to the activity and your comfort with the assignment decisions relative to the individual students. Remember that your judgment of a student's reading level should always take precedence over the results of a single written test.

Feel free to use different procedures at different times of the year. For example, for early units, you may wish to be more confident in the assignments you make—thus, using the "two-stage" process below. Later, you may choose the quicker diagnosis, confirming the results with your observations of the students' performance built up throughout the year.

The **Diagnostic Test** is composed of a single 40-item assessment. Based on the results of this assessment, make the following assignment of students to the reading selections in Unit 1:

Diagnostic Test Score	Selection to Use
If the student's score is 0–25	more accessible
If the student's score is 26–40	more challenging

Outlined below are the three basic options for administering **Vocabulary in Context** and basing selection assignments on the results of these assessments.

1. For a one-stage, quicker diagnosis using the *20-item* test in the *Unit Resources:*

Vocabulary in Context Test Score	Selection to Use
If the student's score is 0–13	more accessible
If the student's score is 14–20	more challenging

2. If you wish to confirm your assignment decisions with a *two-stage* diagnosis:

Stage 1: Administer the 20-item test in the *Unit Resources*	
Vocabulary in Context Test Score	Selection to Use
If the student's score is 0–9	more accessible
If the student's score is 10–15	(Go to Stage 2.)
If the student's score is 16–20	more challenging

Stage 2: Administer items 21–40 from *PHLitOnline*	
Vocabulary in Context Test Score	Selection to Use
If the student's score is 0–12	more accessible
If the student's score is 13–20	more challenging

3. If you base your assignment decisions on the full 40-item **Vocabulary in Context** from *PHLitOnline:*

Vocabulary in Context Test Score	Selection to Use
If the student's score is 0–25	more accessible
If the student's score is 26–40	more challenging

Grade 10—Benchmark Test 5
Interpretation Guide

For remediation of specific skills, you may assign students the relevant Reading Kit Practice and Assess pages indicated in the far-right column of this chart. You will find rubrics for evaluating writing samples in the last section of your Professional Development Guidebook.

Skill Objective	Test Items	Number Correct	Reading Kit
Literary Analysis			
Reflective Essay	1, 2		pp. 104, 105
Expository essay	3, 4		pp. 102, 103
Humorous Essay	5, 6, 7, 8		pp. 106, 107
Reading Skill			
Main Idea and Supporting Details	9, 10, 11, 12, 13, 14, 15, 16		pp. 108, 109
Follow and Critique Technical Directions	17, 18, 19		pp. 110, 111
Vocabulary			
Word Roots and Prefixes -tact-, -fig-, suc-, para-	20, 21, 22, 23, 24, 25		pp. 112, 113
Grammar			
Direct and Indirect Objects	26, 27, 32		pp. 114, 115
Predicate Nominative and Predicate Adjectives	28, 29, 33		pp. 116, 117
Combine Short Sentences	30, 31, 34		pp. 118, 119
Writing			
Business Letter	35	Use rubric	pp. 120, 121
Brief Memoir	36	Use rubric	pp. 122, 123
Letter to the Editor	37	Use rubric	pp. 124, 125

Unit 3 Resources: Types of Nonfiction

Name _____ Date _____

Grade 10—Benchmark Test 6
Interpretation Guide

For remediation of specific skills, you may assign students the relevant Reading Kit Practice and Assess pages indicated in the far-right column of this chart. You will find rubrics for evaluating writing samples in the last section of your Professional Development Guidebook.

Skill Objective	Test Items	Number Correct	Reading Kit
Literary Analysis			
Persuasive Writing	8, 9, 10, 11, 12		pp. 130, 131
Analytic and Interpretive Essays	13, 14, 15, 16, 17, 18		pp. 132, 133
Author's Purpose	19, 20, 21, 22		pp. 134, 135
Reading Skill			
Evaluating Persuasive Texts	1, 2, 3, 4, 5, 6, 7		pp. 126, 127
Analyze Text Structure	23, 24, 25		pp. 128, 129
Vocabulary			
Word Roots and Prefixes -scend-, -jur-, im-, em-	26, 27, 28, 29, 30, 31		pp. 136, 137
Grammar			
Degrees of Adjectives	32, 33, 34		pp. 140, 141
Degrees of Adverbs	35, 36, 37		pp. 138, 139
Parallelism	38, 39		pp. 142, 143
Spelling			
Tools for Checking Spelling	40		pp. 144, 145
Writing			
Persuasive Letter	41	Use rubric	pp. 146, 147
Critique	42	Use rubric	pp. 148, 149
Persuasive Essay	43	Use rubric	pp. 150, 151

ANSWERS

Big Question Vocabulary—1, p. 1

Sample Answers

1. A person might adapt by making new friends, learning about the town and the school, and adjusting his or her attitudes and behavior to suit expectations in the new environment.

2. The audience shows its awareness by alertly reacting to developments in the game. For example, they might cheer for a point earned or boo for a foul play.

3. My sister did not do well on a test, and I could imagine how she felt since it has happened to me. I made her some hot cocoa to let her know I understood.

4. A teacher might enlighten, or give knowledge to, her students by leading a discussion about the selection.

5. A person might form one opinion, such as believing that a local company is polluting the environment, and then change that opinion over time as new information becomes available. For example, if the company has been taking aggressive steps to reduce pollution, the person's opinion of the company might not be as bad as it was before.

Big Question Vocabulary—2, p. 2

Sample Answers

1. Children's intellectual growth can be increased if they read every night.

   The growth of the Internet has changed the nation's economy.

2. Tomas and I have a history of arguing about politics.

   I love to read about history because learning about life in the past fascinates me.

3. She displayed her ignorance of cooking skills when she burned the macaroni.

   My mother expects us to know how to behave and does not tolerate ignorance of the rules.

4. Knowing these facts might influence his opinion on the matter.

   I will try not to influence your decision since you are supposed to be impartial.

5. Reading Kari's poetry gave me some insight about why she seems so happy all the time.

   The character's insight about his father's past changed the tone of the entire story.

Big Question Vocabulary—3, p. 3

Sample response

Last year, I did a research paper about the British Romantic poets. I thought I had a pretty good understanding of these poets and their writing, but I ended up having to revise my opinion. The information I found caused me to reflect on their poetry again and question the conclusions I had drawn. I modified my thesis statement and wrote a new draft.

"Everest" *from* Touch the Top of the World
by Erik Weihenmayer

Vocabulary Warm-up Exercises, p. 8

A.
1. destiny
2. confirmed
3. spectacular
4. horrendous
5. barriers
6. despite
7. accomplished
8. descent

B. Sample Answers

1. The money from the fund drive will be benefiting public television.

2. Looking back, I see that getting lost was inevitable without a map.

3. The basketball team is looking for corporate sponsorship.

4. I think that stereotypes lead to prejudice.

5. We make periodic visits to the dentist.

6. Her perfect score on the biology test was unprecedented.

7. Our mayor implemented a new school safety program.

Reading Warm-up A, p. 9

Sample Answers

1. view from the top of the world; I saw a *spectacular* sunset at the beach.

2. (Mt. Everest); Mt. Everest was one of the *barriers* separating Norgay from his goal or his destiny—to make it to the top of the world.

3. The pull of Everest was stronger for me than any force on Earth; *Destiny* means "a sense that something is fated to happen or an inevitable part of your life or future."

4. (he reached the highest point on Earth); Last year, I *accomplished* my goal of joining the debate team.

5. The icy winds shift unpredictably. The air becomes thinner, holding less and less essential oxygen. A *horrendous* trip might be a journey across a desert without water.

6. (managed to reach the summit); I would like to become a doctor *despite* the fact that the training is long and difficult.

7. (climbing up the mountain); The *descent* is "climbing down."

8. they were included on *Time* magazine's list of the "most important people of the century"; My opinion that physics is fascinating was *confirmed* when I read the article about waves.

Reading Warm-up B, p. 10

1. <u>Today, it is the largest organization for the blind in the United States.</u> *Unprecedented* means "not having happened before."

2. <u>many of the 1.1 million blind people living in the United States today</u>; New parking rules are *benefiting* our school by preventing traffic jams.

3. <u>whenever new research is available</u>; *Periodic* means "appearing from time to time."

4. (positive); Someone with a *negative* point of view always looks at the dark or unpleasant side of things.

5. <u>Some sighted people think that blind people need constant assistance and cannot lead independent lives.</u> *Stereotypes* are overly simple and broad ideas about groups of people.

6. (the latest findings); A virtual frog dissection program via computer has been *implemented* by the science department.

7. I think it is *inevitable* that the sun will rise tomorrow morning.

8. A science club might seek *sponsorship* in order to gain money to buy supplies or equipment.

Erik Weihenmayer

Listening and Viewing, p. 11

Sample Answers

Segment 1. Students should note that Weihenmayer believes that writing can go in many directions and has no limits, whereas mountain climbing is somewhat predictable. They are likely to say that Weihenmayer's statement surprises them because mountain climbing can be extremely dangerous. Alternatively, they may say that they are not surprised because his remarks are logical and he does not compare the dangerousness of the two activities.

Segment 2. Weihenmayer believes that honesty helps readers connect to an author and allows them to relate to an author's writing on a personal level. Students may say that it is important to be honest to win the audience's trust.

Segment 3. Before beginning to write, Weihenmayer records his thoughts on a tape recorder and then organizes them. Students should describe their writing process. They may state, for example, that they can generate their ideas by brainstorming and organize them by outlining.

Segment 4. Students may suggest that Weihenmayer's attitude has made them realize that sharing experiences through writing can inspire and motivate others to achieve their goals.

Learning About Nonfiction, p. 12

A. 1. persuasive essay
   2. narrative essay
   3. address

4. descriptive essay
5. expository essay
6. lecture

B. This is a speech. The use of "Hi" suggests that it is spoken, and phrases like "just wanted to" indicate that the style is informal and the tone is conversational.

"Everest" *from* Touch the Top of the World
by Erik Weihenmayer

Model Selection: Nonfiction, p. 13

Sample Answers

A. *Style:* The style is relatively formal. Weihenmayer does not use slang or many contractions, and he uses sophisticated words and phrases ("four distinct changes," "terrain," "intermingled," "internal balance"). He uses sensory details and simile ("It was like moving through a bizarre atmosphere of syrup mixed with a narcotic" and "the infinite sound of space around me"). He organizes the material chronologically, in the order in which events occurred ("As we got higher"), with an occasional flashback ("A few weeks earlier").

Tone: The tone is matter-of-fact and somewhat modest (he waits to reveal the fact that he is blind). He gives the audience the impression that he knows a lot about his subject ("the terrain above the South Col consisted of steep forty-five-degree snow faces a hundred yards wide, intermingled with ten-to-fifty-foot crumbly rock steps) and feels confident ("I could breathe, scan my ice axe, and count on the next step").

Perspective: Weihenmayer expresses his opinion of the people who belittled his achievement ("those cynics") and his own opinion about his climbing ("I don't climb mountains to prove to anyone that blind people can do this or that"). He also expresses his pride in his achievement and his hope that it will help other people realize that they do not have to be limited by "barriers."

B. 1. It explains the process of climbing a mountain like Everest.

2. It conveys Weihenmayer's thoughts about climbing Everest and about being the first blind person to do so.

3. It describes Weihenmayer's sensory impressions of his experience.

4. It attempts to inspire readers to think about the possibilities that exist when one is not restricted by the barriers of negative stereotyping.

Open-Book Test, p. 14

Short Answer

1. She should write a narrative essay because it tells the story of her personal experiences.

   Difficulty: *Easy*   **Objective:** *Literary Analysis*

2. He or she wants to inform or instruct the audience.
   Difficulty: *Average*   **Objective:** *Literary Analysis*
3. Examples of Tone: formal, ironic, amused, mournful, respectful, angry, suspicious. A formal, respectful tone best suits an expository essay.
   Difficulty: *Average*   **Objective:** *Literary Analysis*
4. It would probably be a descriptive essay with the goal of creating an impression about a person, object, or experience.
   Difficulty: *Average*   **Objective:** *Literary Analysis*
5. It is a narrative essay because it tells the story of real events that a person experienced.
   Difficulty: *Average*   **Objective:** *Literary Analysis*
6. The climbers face both external and internal obstacles. The external obstacles are hazardous terrain, harsh weather conditions, and difficulty communicating. The internal obstacles are exhaustion, fear, and finding the willpower needed to get to the top.
   Difficulty: *Challenging*   **Objective:** *Interpretation*
7. It is surprising because earlier, Jeff announces that he is "wasted" and will not continue to the very top of the mountain.
   Difficulty: *Easy*   **Objective:** *Interpretation*
8. Weihenmayer views the criticism as cynical, unfair, and misinformed.
   Difficulty: *Average*   **Objective:** *Interpretation*
9. The main emotion is pride in what he has accomplished.
   Difficulty: *Challenging*   **Objective:** *Interpretation*
10. I would more likely feel *apprehension* before my first bungee jump because the possible danger would make me nervous.
    Difficulty: *Average*   **Objective:** *Vocabulary*

Essay

11. Students should focus on one aspect of the essay—a description of climbing or nature, a specific event, or an expression of emotion. They should support their choice with at least two concrete examples from the essay.
    Difficulty: *Easy*   **Objective:** *Essay*
12. Students should note some of the advantages of blindness that Weihenmayer mentions: He is not concerned about snow blindness, frozen corneas, frozen goggles, or darkness. They should also point out that Weihenmayer's other senses are more sensitive than those of a sighted person. Some students might argue, however, that having sight and a balanced set of senses would have made the task of climbing Everest easier.
    Difficulty: *Average*   **Objective:** *Essay*
13. Students should identify the tone as respectful, filled with awe, excited, or another supportable characteristic. They should support their choice with several examples from "Everest."
    Difficulty: *Challenging*   **Objective:** *Essay*

14. Students should note that the climbers gained important weather information from satellite reports on the Internet. Their speedy access to this knowledge allowed them to make life-saving decisions about whether or not to proceed in certain areas and under certain conditions. This knowledge increased the climbers' confidence and, therefore, increased their chances of achieving their goal.
    Difficulty: *Average*   **Objective:** *Essay*

Oral Response

15. Oral responses should be clear, well organized, and well supported by appropriate examples from the selection.
    Difficulty: *Average*   **Objective:** *Oral Interpretation*

Selection Test A, p. 17

Learning About Nonfiction

1. ANS: C	DIF: Easy	OBJ: Literary Analysis
2. ANS: D	DIF: Easy	OBJ: Literary Analysis
3. ANS: A	DIF: Easy	OBJ: Literary Analysis
4. ANS: A	DIF: Easy	OBJ: Literary Analysis
5. ANS: C	DIF: Easy	OBJ: Literary Analysis

Critical Reading

6. ANS: B	DIF: Easy	OBJ: Literary Analysis
7. ANS: B	DIF: Easy	OBJ: Comprehension
8. ANS: D	DIF: Easy	OBJ: Comprehension
9. ANS: B	DIF: Easy	OBJ: Comprehension
10. ANS: A	DIF: Easy	OBJ: Comprehension
11. ANS: B	DIF: Easy	OBJ: Literary Analysis
12. ANS: C	DIF: Easy	OBJ: Comprehension
13. ANS: B	DIF: Easy	OBJ: Interpretation
14. ANS: A	DIF: Easy	OBJ: Comprehension
15. ANS: C	DIF: Easy	OBJ: Interpretation

Essay

16. Students should write about one moment that Weihenmayer describes. For example, students might mention the scene in which the author realizes that his friend Jeff has reached the summit, too. Students should cite two details to support their explanation of why the moment that they have chosen affected them more than any other in the essay.
    Difficulty: *Easy*   **Objective:** *Essay*
17. Students should recognize that Weihenmayer is proud of his accomplishment and knows that he climbed the mountain on his own. They should point to Weihenmayer's stated reason for climbing mountains: the experience gives him "great joy"; they should mention one of the goals he hopes his achievement will accomplish: forcing some people to have high expectations of what

they might achieve or contributing to the act of making more opportunities available to more people. They should mention at least one of the criticisms: that Weihenmayer's achievement will encourage unskilled people to attempt dangerous climbs, thereby causing them to get hurt, and that Weihenmayer's achievement was not noteworthy because he did not do the skilled climbing unaided. They should identify those statements as biased because they suggest that blind people are or should be limited in their aspirations and achievements.

Difficulty: *Easy* **Objective:** *Essay*

18. Students should note that the weather report allowed them to make life-saving decisions about whether or not to continue at certain points along their climb (students should provide examples of when and how this happened). The report also increased the climbers' confidence. Their change in attitude, as well as their knowledge about what the weather would be like, helped the climbers reach the top of Everest.

Difficulty: *Average* **Objective:** *Essay*

Selection Test B, p. 20

Learning About Nonfiction

1. ANS: B	DIF: Challenging	OBJ: Literary Analysis
2. ANS: B	DIF: Challenging	OBJ: Literary Analysis
3. ANS: A	DIF: Average	OBJ: Literary Analysis
4. ANS: B	DIF: Average	OBJ: Literary Analysis
5. ANS: B	DIF: Average	OBJ: Literary Analysis
6. ANS: C	DIF: Average	OBJ: Literary Analysis

Critical Reading

7. ANS: B	DIF: Average	OBJ: Comprehension
8. ANS: C	DIF: Challenging	OBJ: Interpretation
9. ANS: A	DIF: Average	OBJ: Comprehension
10. ANS: A	DIF: Average	OBJ: Comprehension
11. ANS: C	DIF: Average	OBJ: Comprehension
12. ANS: C	DIF: Average	OBJ: Interpretation
13. ANS: A	DIF: Average	OBJ: Comprehension
14. ANS: B	DIF: Average	OBJ: Interpretation
15. ANS: B	DIF: Challenging	OBJ: Interpretation
16. ANS: B	DIF: Challenging	OBJ: Literary Analysis
17. ANS: B	DIF: Average	OBJ: Literary Analysis

Essay

18. Students should note the advantages that Weihenmayer mentions: He is not concerned with snow blindness, frozen corneas, frozen goggles, or darkness. They should also comment on the overall effect of his lack of vision. They might say, for example, that because his senses of hearing and touch are better developed than those of a sighted person, Weihenmayer is better equipped to deal

with the climb, or they may say that his lack of vision outweighs the advantages.

Difficulty: *Average* **Objective:** *Essay*

19. Students should demonstrate that they understand that the tone of a work is the author's attitude toward the subject and the audience. Their choice of supporting details should clearly relate to the tone they name.

Difficulty: *Average* **Objective:** *Essay*

20. Students should recognize that the quotation refers to the "detractors," the people who suggest that Weihenmayer's achievement is not a "big deal" because anyone can be helped to climb Everest and to those who suggest that because of Weihenmayer's achievement, unskilled climbers will get hurt attempting to climb Everest. Students should identify the stereotypes as having to do with limitations that characterize anyone who has some physical disadvantage. They might also recognize that Weihenmayer believes his ascent of Everest completely negates that stereotype. He feels satisfaction because he believes that he has proved that blindness is not a limitation.

Difficulty: *Challenging* **Objective:** *Essay*

21. Students should note that the climbers gained important weather information from satellite reports on the Internet. Their speedy access to this knowledge allowed them to make life-saving decisions about whether or not to proceed in certain areas and under certain conditions. This knowledge increased their confidence and therefore increased their chances of achieving their goal.

Difficulty: *Average* **Objective:** *Essay*

"The Spider and the Wasp"
by Alexander Petrunkevitch

Vocabulary Warm-up Exercises, p. 24

A. 1. tarantula
2. maneuvering
3. instinctive
4. aggressive
5. hostile
6. persistent
7. solitude
8. efficient

B. Sample Answers

1. I can make tuna fish and noodles *adequately*.
2. I have had *insufficient* funds to buy a new digital camera.
3. I would not let a toddler watch a *ghastly* movie because it might give him or her nightmares.
4. I might *inflict* harm by gossiping and telling stories.
5. I have shown *initiative* by improving my diet and exercise plans.

6. I can determine the *dimensions* of my room by measuring it.

7. It is *ruthless* to cheat to get ahead because it is unfair to others.

Reading Warm-up A, p. 25

Sample Answers

1. (spider); The *tarantula* ate the beetles in our backyard.
2. (hurt small animals); *Hostile* means "very unfriendly."
3. its bite will not do us much harm; *Aggressive* means "behaving in a violent way."
4. (a female); *Maneuvering* means "skillfully moving."
5. It is amazing that a male tarantula *tries repeatedly* to find a female.
6. (Female tarantulas); I enjoy being with other people too much to enjoy *solitude*.
7. (buy crickets at the pet store); It is more *efficient* to buy crickets because it might take a long time to hunt insects.
8. (to retreat); Two other examples of animals' *instinctive* needs are the mole's need to burrow and the duck's need to fly south for the winter.

Reading Warm-up B, p. 26

Sample Answers

1. the book's appeal; *Adequately* means "done well enough for a particular purpose."
2. harm on his animals; *Inflict* means "to make someone suffer something bad."
3. A character with multiple *dimensions* is more lifelike, whereas a one-dimensional character is more obviously a fictional creation.
4. My persuasive powers were *insufficient* to change my friend's mind about joining the soccer team.
5. (forcefully); Nan *vigorously* scrubbed the bathroom floor.
6. prevent this outcome; *Initiative* means "the ability to make decisions and take action."
7. If Wilbur were slaughtered, the word *ghastly* would be appropriate because it means "extremely bad or upsetting."
8. The pirate was *ruthless* when he marooned the mutineers on the island.

Writing About the Big Question, p. 27

A. 1. adapt
2. awareness
3. empathy
4. growth

B. Sample Answers

1. I learned information about global warming. I learned that the national soccer team is playing in Germany.
2. The information I learned about global warming did change my life, because it raised my **awareness** about the earth's climate. My new knowledge might

influence my behavior as I try to be more responsible toward the environment.

C. Sample Answer

Concrete information can be overruled by a gut reaction when you sense danger. I knew that the rollercoaster was safe, but my instinct told me it was going too fast. I decided not to ride and later in the day, it was closed for repairs.

Literary Analysis: Inductive and Deductive Reasoning in an Expository Essay, p. 28

Sample Answers

Spider: rules/evidence—instinctive behavior cannot be changed; spider has three types of reactions to touch but does not react to wasp's investigation; spider always dies in conflict with wasp; conclusion—instinctive

Wasp: rules/evidence—wasp behaves with purpose and clear method; wasp carefully inspects spider to determine species; wasp changes behavior to suit each situation; conclusion—intelligent

Reading: Analyze Main Ideas and Supporting Details by Summarizing, p. 29

Sample Answers

A. Main idea—The spider dies because it acts on instinct alone, while the wasp succeeds because it behaves intelligently. Supporting details—the spider has three types of instinctive reactions; the spider's reactions fail it against the wasp; spiders die in conflicts with wasps; wasps need spiders to lay eggs on; wasp inspects spider to determine correct species; wasp changes behavior to suit needs of each situation

B. Students' summaries should clearly state the main idea of the essay and explain how important details support the main idea. Sample response: The spider dies because it acts on instinct alone, while the wasp succeeds because it behaves intelligently. A digger wasp takes advantage of a tarantula's instincts. It does this by not triggering the spider's instinctive reactions. The spider does not defend itself until it is too late. The wasp seems to be acting intelligently because it is able to modify its actions to fit the situation.

Vocabulary Builder, p. 30

A. Sample Answers

1. The principal customarily presents the awards at our annual assembly. It is her custom to present the Principal's Award for Excellence last.
2. There are three distinct types of students at our school. The athletes are distinctively fit and confident.
3. Young children generally enjoy the tactile sensation of hugging a stuffed animal. Tactile sensitivity is important for a surgeon.
4. The wasp is smaller but is a *formidable* foe. The wasp's technique for killing the spider is *formidable*.

5. The spider's odd behavior has been *evoking* curiosity in scientists.
   The behavior is *evocative* because it seems to contradict the spider's nature.

B. 1. A *tactless* person would probably tease or be rude to someone who fell in a mud puddle.

2. You could *contact* a friend by sending a letter or a note through e-mail or by calling the person on the telephone.

3. A dropped glass that remained *intact* did not break, which would make you happy.

Enrichment: Planning a Nature Documentary, p. 31

Evaluate students' documentary plans based on the following criteria: factual accuracy, neatness and quality of writing and artwork, effective presentation of main idea and supporting details, and individual and group effort.

Open-Book Test, p. 32

Short Answer

1. Spiders seem to operate by instinct, while wasps seem to use something more like reason or intelligence.
   Difficulty: *Easy*   **Objective:** *Literary Analysis*

2. You would rarely find them in shallow triangular holes because that is not their usual habitat.
   Difficulty: *Average*   **Objective:** *Vocabulary*

3. It would not cause a *tactile* response because it relates to the spider's sense of sight, not touch.
   Difficulty: *Average*   **Objective:** *Vocabulary*

4. Tarantula's responses to touch should include three of the following: move off slowly for short distance, immediate attack, shake leg, vibrate hairs, jerk four front legs, sudden jump.
   The tarantula's failure to respond suggests that the digger wasp avoided triggering the tarantula's defenses.
   Difficulty: *Average*   **Objective:** *Literary Analysis*

5. The wasp does not approach the spider from above.
   Difficulty: *Easy*   **Objective:** *Literary Analysis*

6. Tarantulas have many more young than wasps do.
   Difficulty: *Easy*   **Objective:** *Reading*

7. He concludes that the wasp's behavior is intelligent, not just instinctive.
   Difficulty: *Challenging*   **Objective:** *Literary Anaysis*

8. This description shows that the spider has no idea how much danger it is in until the last minute.
   Difficulty: *Average*   **Objective:** *Interpretation*

9. The wasp's superior intelligence allows it to take advantage of the tarantula's confusion.
   Difficulty: *Average*   **Objective:** *Reading*

10. The spider always builds its web in three dimensions and cannot change this technique to adapt to new circumstances.
    Difficulty: *Challenging*   **Objective:** *Reading*

Essay

11. The most important main idea is that the spider operates on instinct alone, while the wasp uses intelligence. Students should provide other main ideas to lead up to this final one. For example, the wasp's intelligent behavior gives it an advantage over the spider. A digger wasp is "smart" enough to avoid triggering the spider's instinctive responses. The spider does not defend itself becauses it does not realize it is in danger until it is too late. Students should provide additional examples from the essay to support their points.
    Difficulty: *Easy*   **Objective:** *Essay*

12. Students should note that instinctive behavior is fixed and unchangeable, while intelligent behavior adapts to new situations. They should note that tarantulas operate mainly by instinct, while wasps are intelligent because they can change their behavior to suit a given situation. Students should provide examples from the essay to support their points.
    Difficulty: *Average*   **Objective:** *Essay*

13. Students should examine one of Petrunkevitch's theories or try to come up with their own explanation. For example, some students might suggest that the tarantula does not react because it does not feel cornered until the last minute. Other students might think that the wasp has some method of moving that avoids the tarantula's instinctive defenses. Students might also suppose that the spider is not hungry and so is not interested in attacking the wasp.
    Difficulty: *Challenging*   **Objective:** *Essay*

14. The wasp seems to respond much more effectively to new knowledge, and thus seems to rely on a kind of reasoning. The spider dies because it acts on instinct alone and does not seem to learn from the new information presented to it. Students should provide examples from the essay to support their points.
    Difficulty: *Average*   **Objective:** *Essay*

Oral Response

15. Oral responses should be clear, well organized, and well supported by appropriate examples from the selection.
    Difficulty: *Average*   **Objective:** *Oral Interpretation*

Selection Test A, p. 35

Critical Reading

1. ANS: A	DIF: Easy	OBJ: Literary Analysis
2. ANS: B	DIF: Easy	OBJ: Comprehension
3. ANS: C	DIF: Easy	OBJ: Literary Analysis
4. ANS: B	DIF: Easy	OBJ: Literary Analysis
5. ANS: C	DIF: Easy	OBJ: Comprehension
6. ANS: D	DIF: Easy	OBJ: Interpretation
7. ANS: B	DIF: Easy	OBJ: Literary Analysis
8. ANS: A	DIF: Easy	OBJ: Reading
9. ANS: C	DIF: Easy	OBJ: Reading

Vocabulary and Grammar

10. ANS: B	DIF: Easy	OBJ: Vocabulary
11. ANS: A	DIF: Easy	OBJ: Vocabulary
12. ANS: C	DIF: Easy	OBJ: Grammar
13. ANS: C	DIF: Easy	OBJ: Grammar

Essay

14. Students should summarize "The Spider and the Wasp." They should point out the main idea, which is that the spider dies because it acts on instinct alone, while the wasp succeeds because it behaves intelligently. Supporting details might include the following: A digger wasp takes advantage of a tarantula's instincts. It does this by not triggering the spider's instinctive reactions. The spider does not defend itself because it does not seem to realize it is in danger until it is too late. The wasp seems to be acting intelligently because it can change its behavior to suit the situation.
    Difficulty: *Easy*   Objective: *Essay*

15. Students should define instinctive behaviors as those that a creature cannot change and intelligent behaviors as those that a creature can change to fit a situation. Petrunkevitch classifies tarantulas as having instinctive behaviors. He states that wasps behave in what seems to be an intelligent way because they can change their behaviors to suit a situation. Petrunkevitch implies that it is because of this that wasps win against the spiders they choose. Students should give examples from the passage to support these classifications.
    Difficulty: *Easy*   Objective: *Essay*

16. The wasp seems to respond to new information by using reasoning, while the spider responds by using instinct. The wasp responds to new situations much better because it changes its behavior. On the other hand, the spider dies in new situations because it does not seem to learn from earlier situations. Students should provide examples from the essay to support their points.
    Difficulty: *Average*   Objective: *Essay*

Selection Test B, p. 38

Critical Reading

1. ANS: A	DIF: Average	OBJ: Literary Analysis
2. ANS: B	DIF: Average	OBJ: Comprehension
3. ANS: C	DIF: Average	OBJ: Literary Analysis
4. ANS: A	DIF: Average	OBJ: Reading
5. ANS: D	DIF: Average	OBJ: Reading
6. ANS: A	DIF: Average	OBJ: Comprehension
7. ANS: A	DIF: Average	OBJ: Comprehension
8. ANS: D	DIF: Average	OBJ: Comprehension
9. ANS: D	DIF: Challenging	OBJ: Literary Analysis
10. ANS: D	DIF: Challenging	OBJ: Literary Analysis
11. ANS: B	DIF: Challenging	OBJ: Reading

Vocabulary and Grammar

12. ANS: B	DIF: Average	OBJ: Vocabulary
13. ANS: D	DIF: Average	OBJ: Vocabulary
14. ANS: C	DIF: Average	OBJ: Grammar
15. ANS: B	DIF: Average	OBJ: Grammar

Essay

16. Students should define instinct as an inherited pattern of behavior and intelligence as reasoning or modifying a behavior to fit a situation. Petrunkevitch classifies tarantulas as having instinctive behaviors that lead to their doom in encounters with digger wasps. He classifies wasps as behaving in an intelligent way because they can change their behaviors to suit situations. Students should give examples from the passage to support these classifications. They should also agree or disagree with these classifications and explain why.
    Difficulty: *Average*   Objective: *Essay*

17. Students should summarize the passage. They should point out the main idea, which is that the spider dies because it acts on instinct alone, while the wasp succeeds because it behaves intelligently. Supporting details might include the following: The wasp seems to be acting intelligently because it can change its behavior to suit the situation. It will only attack the right species of tarantula. A digger wasp is able to avoid triggering the spider's instinctive reactions. The spider does not defend itself until it is too late. Based on this example, students might make the generalization that intelligence is more likely to win against instinct.
    Difficulty: *Average*   Objective: *Essay*

18. Students might choose one of Petrunkevitch's theories or come up with their own ideas. For example, a student might theorize that the tarantula does not react to the wasp because the wasp does not corner the spider until the very end. Because the spider does not feel cornered, it does not feel threatened enough to fight. Another theory is that the wasp must have some way of avoiding the spider's instinctive reactions. She apparently does not approach from above or fan air on the spider's hairs with her wings, or the spider would react defensively. They may also theorize that the spider must not be hungry, or it would attack and eat the wasp at its first touch.
    Difficulty: *Challenging*   Objective: *Essay*

19. The wasp seems to respond much more effectively to new knowledge, and thus seems to rely on a kind of reasoning. The spider dies because it acts on instinct alone and does not seem to learn from the new information presented to it. Students should provide examples from the essay to support their points.
    Difficulty: *Average*   Objective: *Essay*

from Longitude by Dava Sobel

Vocabulary Warm-up Exercises, p. 42

A.
1. astronomer
2. devised
3. fervor
4. whereabouts
5. accuracy
6. virtually
7. triumphed
8. era

B. Sample Answers

1. T; A *notable* fact is worth mentioning, so it could help support an opinion.
2. F; A *crisscrossing* path is crooked, so it is not short. A straight line would be shorter.
3. F; You should not make an important decision *arbitrarily*, but through careful thought and consideration.
4. T; An *orb* is a sphere, like the shape of a baseball, an orange, or a pea.
5. T; *Variations* usually resemble the original in some ways.
6. F; A *deformity* probably decreases the quality and value of a diamond.
7. F; You might look slightly different after making *modifications* to your hairstyle.
8. F; If you *ultimately* achieve your goal, you accomplish your goal.

Reading Warm-up A, p. 43

Sample Answers

1. there has been so much to do that I have fallen behind; It is *virtually* impossible for people to visit Mars.
2. (an amazing timepiece); *Devised* means "figured out a way to build."
3. (his fourth design); A microscope can measure very small objects with great *accuracy*.
4. for nearly three years; every day from dusk until past sunset; *Fervor* means "a strong interest, enthusiasm, or emotion."
5. In the thick morning fog, I often felt lost in a huge emptiness. *Whereabouts* means "the place where a person or thing is located."
6. Each night, we stand on deck and gaze at the stars. I think every *astronomer* needs patience and curiosity.
7. (our mission); I *triumphed* over my aunt when we played chess last night.
8. when so many great things are being done; We live in an *era* that is dominated by television and the media.

Reading Warm-up B, p. 44

Sample Answers

1. (sphere) (globe); A basketball and a melon have the shape of an *orb*.
2. some distortion, a bending or twisting of the true shape or size; *Deformity* means "a state of having a bad or changed form."
3. longitude and latitude lines. This grid of imaginary lines; *Crisscrossing* means "making a pattern of crossed lines."
4. Noise pollution has been a *notable* problem in our community since the airport was built two years ago.
5. Instead of using the equator as the place where size is most accurate, he selected 38 degrees south and 38 degrees north as the standard parallels. *Modifications* means "slight changes."
6. based on many calculations and observations; Every morning, I *arbitrarily* decide what socks to wear.
7. *Ultimately*, I think that hybrid cars will reduce pollution in our cities.
8. yield more and more truthful views of the world; These *variations* will not be completely different because they will still show the same land masses and oceans.

Writing About the Big Question, p. 45

A.
1. history
2. evolve
3. empathy
4. question

B. Sample Answers

1. mathematics; science, such as physics or chemistry; literature
2. Knowledge gained through literature can **enlighten** your perspective of the world and change your life. You can develop **empathy** for other people and cultures, which can change your relationship to the world.

C. Sample Answer

Information that changes the world often deals with problems. People look for solutions, which can sometimes take years to find. Sometimes accidents can lead to understanding, and often people argue about whether new information is valid.

Literary Analysis: Inductive and Deductive Reasoning in an Expository Essay, p. 46

Sample Answers

Importance of clocks: rules/evidence—accurate timekeeping necessary to determine longitude; early clocks slowed down, sped up, or stopped on board ships; captains got lost and countless sailors died; conclusion—lack of accurate clocks was dangerous to sailors Harrison's clock:

rules/evidence—made of materials that did not rust or create friction; compensated for changes in motion and temperature; kept accurate time on board ships; conclusion—solved the problem of measuring longitude

Reading: Analyze Main Ideas and Supporting Details by Summarizing, p. 47

Sample Answers

A. Main idea—Ocean voyages were very dangerous until John Harrison invented a clock that could help sailors measure longitude at sea. Supporting details—longitude is determined by comparing time on a ship to time at some fixed point; early clocks could not keep accurate time on board ships; many sailors got lost or died due to inability to measure longitude; many great minds struggled to find a solution; Harrison invented an accurate shipboard clock and solved longitude problem

B. Students' summaries should clearly state the main idea of the essay and explain how important details support the main idea. Sample response: Navigation was very dangerous until Harrison invented a clock that could help sailors measure longitude at sea. Captains got lost, and many sailors died because of poor navigation. Measuring latitude was easy, but measuring longitude required comparing accurate times aboard ships to times at known locations. Early clocks could not keep accurate time on ships. John Harrison invented an accurate clock and solved the problem of longitude.

Vocabulary Builder, p. 48

A. Sample Answers

1. My English teacher regularly changes the configuration of the desks in her classroom. She likes to configure them in groups or rows.

2. The detective derived a theory about who committed the crime based on the evidence. However, his partner might derive a completely different theory.

3. The safety seal is underline{impervious} to tampering. Despite her attempts to appear underline{impervious} to people's unkind comments, I could tell she was hurting inside.

4. Lines of longitude all *converge* at ends of the Earth. The *convergence* of longitude lines means they meet at the poles.

5. John Harrison's enemies *contested* his solution to the problem of longitude.
   When Harrison invented a special clock for ships, he won a *contest* by beating many other scientists.

B. 1. A child might present a fabricated story, a *figment*, from her imagination because she does not want to admit to breaking the rule.

2. A *figurine* is a small carved or molded figure or statuette, which would be too hard to be a baby's toy, while a rag doll would be soft and more appropriate.

3. A classroom would need more seating if parents were coming to visit, so a teacher might *reconfigure* the chairs to make more room.

Enrichment: Planning a Documentary, p. 49

Evaluate students' documentary plans based on the following criteria: factual accuracy, neatness and quality of writing and artwork, effective presentation of main idea and supporting details, and individual and group effort.

"The Spider and the Wasp"
by Alexander Petrunkevitch
from Longitude by Dava Sobel

Integrated Language Skills: Grammar, p. 50

A. 1. DO: tarantula
2. DO: spider
3. IO: spider; DO: grave, it
4. DO: latitude
5. IO: sailors; DO: problem
6. DO: time

B. Students' responses will vary. Check to be sure that direct objects are underlined and indirect objects are circled in students' paragraphs.

Open-Book Test, p. 53

Short Answer

1. The author explains the difference between latitude and longitude.
   Difficulty: *Easy*   **Objective:** *Literary Analysis*

2. The map would not be reliable because it would be disorganized and unplanned.
   Difficulty: *Average*   **Objective:** *Vocabulary*

3. "An armchair appreciation" means an understanding that is gained from reading rather than from direct experience. The reader can deduce this meaning based on the fact that Ptolemy used traveler's reports, not his own observations.
   Difficulty: *Challenging*   **Objective:** *Literary Analysis*

4. Mapmakers have moved the prime meridian to several different cities over the centuries. This means its placement only depends on who gets to make the decision.
   Difficulty: *Easy*   **Objective:** *Reading*

5. Because of mechanical problems and inaccurate clocks, it was impossible to know the exact time on board ships and to compare it with the time in the home port.
   Difficulty: *Challenging*   **Objective:** *Literary Analysis*

6. The navigators reset the ship's clock to local noon when the sun reached the highest point in the sky. Then, they compared that time to the time at the ship's starting point.
   Difficulty: *Challenging*   **Objective:** *Reading*

7. Possible reasons: movement of ship caused clocks to speed or slow; lubricating oil too thick or too thin; changes in barometric pressure changed time.

Possible changes to make clocks more accurate: find a lubricating oil that doesn't respond to temperature; create a clock that floats so it doesn't move with the ship. Accept any reasonable answer.

Difficulty: *Average*   **Objective:** *Reading*

8. The court scientists wanted a purely astronomical solution from a recognized scientist and did not want the prize to go to a watchmaker with little formal training.

Difficulty: *Average*   **Objective:** *Interpretation*

9. They were losing ships, men, and trade because they couldn't navigate accurately.

Difficulty: *Average*   **Objective:** *Interpretation*

10. You would be insulting him because you would be saying that reason has no effect on him—he is unreasonable.

Difficulty: *Average*   **Objective:** *Vocabulary*

Essay

11. Students should identify the following main idea: Ocean voyages were very dangerous until John Harrison invented a clock that could help sailors measure longitude at sea. Supporting details are as follows: Longitude is determined by comparing time on a ship to time at some fixed point. Early clocks could not keep accurate time on board ships. Many sailors got lost or died because of their inability to measure longitude. Harrison invented an accurate clock and solved the longitude problem.

Difficulty: *Easy*   **Objective:** *Essay*

12. Students should explain that latitude lines are parallels that circle the globe from the Equator to the poles. They should explain that lines of longitude, or meridians, go the other way: they extend from the North Pole to the South Pole in circles of the same size, and they are farther apart at the Equator and closer together at the poles. The zero-degree line of longitude—the prime meridian—is placed for political reasons and can be anywhere. One must know the exact time at the home port and on board a ship to determine longitude. Longitude is more difficult to determine because it is not set by the laws of nature and because it requires a precise timekeeping device.

Difficulty: *Average*   **Objective:** *Essay*

13. Students might argue that Harrison's clock was a major invention because it opened up the world to exploration, mapping, and trade. Without it, such developments might have taken much longer to happen. Students might point out that the clock made long ocean voyages much safer and more reliable.

Difficulty: *Challenging*   **Objective:** *Essay*

14. The invention of an accurate maritime clock in the eighteenth century completely transformed and advanced seafaring trade, travel, and exploration. Prior to the invention of an accurate clock, captains and navigators could only estimate their locations and often ended up in the wrong places or ran into unanticipated dangers. With

the invention of the clock—and the navigational knowledge it provided—travel by sea made huge strides in efficiency, safety, and reliability. The clock also led to new inventions and the creation of yet more knowledge.

Difficulty: *Average*   **Objective:** *Essay*

Oral Response

15. Oral responses should be clear, well organized, and well supported by appropriate examples from the selection.

Difficulty: *Average*   **Objective:** *Oral Interpretation*

Selection Test A, p. 56

Critical Reading

1. ANS: A	DIF: Easy	OBJ: Literary Analysis
2. ANS: A	DIF: Easy	OBJ: Interpretation
3. ANS: D	DIF: Easy	OBJ: Comprehension
4. ANS: C	DIF: Easy	OBJ: Comprehension
5. ANS: B	DIF: Easy	OBJ: Literary Analysis
6. ANS: A	DIF: Easy	OBJ: Literary Analysis
7. ANS: D	DIF: Easy	OBJ: Interpretation
8. ANS: C	DIF: Easy	OBJ: Comprehension
9. ANS: C	DIF: Easy	OBJ: Reading
10. ANS: D	DIF: Easy	OBJ: Reading

Vocabulary and Grammar

11. ANS: C	DIF: Easy	OBJ: Vocabulary
12. ANS: C	DIF: Easy	OBJ: Vocabulary
13. ANS: C	DIF: Easy	OBJ: Grammar

Essay

14. Students' summaries should include the main idea of the passage and a few key supporting details. For example, navigation was very dangerous until John Harrison invented a clock that could help sailors measure longitude at sea. Captains got lost, and many sailors died because of poor navigation. Measuring latitude was easy, but measuring longitude required comparing accurate times aboard ship to times at known locations. Early clocks could not keep accurate time on ships. John Harrison invented an accurate clock and solved the problem of measuring longitude.

Difficulty: *Easy*   **Objective:** *Essay*

15. Students should explain that determining latitude is easy because lines of latitude are set by the movement of the sun. Longitude is much more difficult because one must know the exact time aboard a ship as well as at the home port to determine longitude. Students should explain that during the Age of Exploration, sailors did not have accurate clocks, so they frequently got lost. They needed a way to determine longitude so they could safely navigate to new lands and find their way home again.

Difficulty: *Easy*   **Objective:** *Essay*

16. The invention of an accurate maritime clock greatly improved trade, travel, and exploration. Prior to the invention of an accurate clock, captains and navigators could only guess at their locations, and they often ended up in the wrong places or ran into danger. With the invention of the clock, travel by sea became safer and more reliable. The clock also led to new inventions and the creation of even more knowledge. Accept any response that students back up with examples from the text and/or logical reasoning.

Difficulty: *Average*   Objective: *Essay*

Selection Test B, p. 59

Critical Reading

1. ANS: C	DIF: Average	OBJ: Literary Analysis
2. ANS: C	DIF: Challenging	OBJ: Interpretation
3. ANS: D	DIF: Average	OBJ: Comprehension
4. ANS: A	DIF: Average	OBJ: Literary Analysis
5. ANS: A	DIF: Average	OBJ: Comprehension
6. ANS: C	DIF: Average	OBJ: Interpretation
7. ANS: B	DIF: Average	OBJ: Comprehension
8. ANS: A	DIF: Average	OBJ: Literary Analysis
9. ANS: C	DIF: Average	OBJ: Reading
10. ANS: A	DIF: Challenging	OBJ: Reading
11. ANS: D	DIF: Challenging	OBJ: Reading

Vocabulary and Grammar

12. ANS: A	DIF: Average	OBJ: Vocabulary
13. ANS: D	DIF: Average	OBJ: Vocabulary
14. ANS: C	DIF: Average	OBJ: Grammar
15. ANS: C	DIF: Challenging	OBJ: Grammar

Essay

16. Students should explain that lines of latitude run parallel to each other; they are always an equal distance apart from each other; and their placement is determined by the sun's movement. Longitude lines run from pole to pole, so they are farther apart at the equator and closer together at the poles. The zero-degree line of longitude, the prime meridian, is placed for political reasons and can be anywhere. One must know the exact time at the home port and onboard a ship to determine longitude. Longitude is more difficult to determine because it is not set by the laws of nature and because it requires a precise timekeeping device.

Difficulty: *Average*   Objective: *Essay*

17. Students' summaries should include the main idea of the passage, main ideas of its major sections, and key supporting details. For example, navigation was very dangerous until John Harrison invented a clock that could help sailors measure longitude at sea. Captains got lost and many sailors died because of poor navigation. Measuring latitude was easy, but measuring longitude required comparing accurate times aboard ship to

times at known locations. Early clocks could not keep accurate time on ships. John Harrison invented an accurate clock and solved the problem of measuring longitude. Students should also state an opinion on these events' importance in the course of history.

Difficulty: *Average*   Objective: *Essay*

18. Students might say that Harrison's clock was extremely important because it helped to open the world to explorers and traders. It also saved many sailors' lives. Without it, it might have been several hundred more years before world exploration became safe enough for colonization. Students might speculate about the impact this would have had on the birth of the United States. In their essays, students should mention at least one other historic invention and compare its importance to Harrison's clock.

Difficulty: *Challenging*   Objective: *Essay*

19. The invention of an accurate maritime clock in the eighteenth century completely transformed and advanced seafaring trade, travel, and exploration. Prior to the invention of an accurate clock, captains and navigators could only estimate their locations and often ended up in the wrong places or ran into unanticipated dangers. With the invention of the clock--and the navigational knowledge it provided--travel by sea made huge strides in efficiency, safety, and reliability. The clock also led to new inventions and the creation of yet more knowledge.

Difficulty: *Average*   Objective: *Essay*

"The Sun Parlor" by Dorothy West

Vocabulary Warm-up Exercises, p. 63

A. 1. appointed
2. energy
3. premises
4. mingling
5. sentiments
6. referred
7. smudges
8. separation

B. Sample Answers

1. I spent time *cajoling* my parents about going on an out-of-state trip.
2. I imagine dreams come from the *subconscious,* as the imagery can seem surprising.
3. I have worked with special *diligence* on a speech for the student assembly.
4. An allergic reaction I had to seafood was *abnormal* for me.
5. It is important to feed babies *pap* because they cannot swallow solid food.
6. My piano teacher made my progress seem *subordinate* to her own career needs.
7. I had a *babysitter* named Debbie who knew how to entertain small children.

Reading Warm-up A, p. 64

Sample Answers

1. <u>family and friends</u>; *Separation* means "being apart."
2. (vitality); The city seemed full of *energy* as construction workers built a new museum.
3. <u>They believed that the arts were important for African Americans</u>; *Sentiments* are "beliefs and opinions."
4. (jazzy sounds), (popular music of the day); As I get ready for school, I hear the sounds of pop music *mingling* with the roar of traffic outside.
5. (the party); *Appointed* means "agreed upon."
6. *Smudges* would come with rent money as crowds of people marked up the floors and walls with their shoes, boots, and, possibly, dirty hands.
7. (a piano player); *Premises* means "building or section of a building."
8. <u>They thought that rent parties, and the dire economic straits that prompted them, reflected poorly on the black community.</u> *Referred* means "spoke about" or "wrote about."

Reading Warm-up B, p. 65

Sample Answers

1. <u>out of the ordinary</u>; In our family, it is *abnormal* for a person to leave the dinner table without finishing the food on his or her plate.
2. My friend began *cajoling* and then begging to get me to help her with her paper.
3. <u>I could sense my mother's fears</u>; *Subconscious* is "a deep, hidden part of the mind."
4. My mother has spent *uncounted* hours organizing our photos into albums.
5. An adult who approached play with *diligence* might plan activities well and strive to make play meaningful.
6. <u>disinterested</u>; Our favorite *babysitter* is Chantee, who gently rocks the baby to sleep.
7. If the children were *subordinate* to the babysitter's friends and homework, he or she probably talked on the phone and read books instead of spending time with the children.
8. (a real meal), (chicken and potatoes); Two foods that could be served as *pap* are applesauce and mashed peas.

Writing About the Big Question, p. 66

A. 1. insight
2. influence
3. reflect

B. Sample Answers

1. I learned that I am not patient. I learned that I really value friendship.
2. I learned that I value friendship, because I treated a friend selfishly and lost her friendship. This experience changed my life because I learned that **empathy** is very important in friendships and that I need to **adapt** to the needs of others.

C. Sample Answer

When you gain insight through your mistreatment of others, you often feel ashamed that you have behaved badly but grateful that you have learned from your behavior. This insight can lead to deep self-understanding, which can change how you treat others and change your life in the process.

Literary Analysis: Reflective Essay, p. 67

Sample Answers

1. The lesson is that children are more important than rooms or houses.
2. She regrets not allowing Sis to play in the sun parlor. She probably worried that Sis thought the room was more important to her than Sis was and that this harmed her relationship with the girl.
3. She tells the story over a period of decades, which shows that she has thought about these events and the lesson she learned for most of her life.
4. Students' responses will vary. They might say that West wants Sis to know that she regrets not letting her play in the sun parlor. Perhaps she feels it is no longer important whether her mother let the girl play in the room. Many students will probably say that they would have wanted to know the answer to the question or that they would not have waited so long to talk to Sis about it. Others might say they would feel the same way as West did.

Reading: Ask Questions to Analyze Main Ideas and Supporting Details, p. 68

A. Sample Answers

1. the author's memories of her sun parlor
2. that no room is worth as much as a child
3. West's memories of how her mother taught her that a house belongs to the children, not the children to the house; the author's regret about not allowing Sis to play in the sun parlor; West's mother's comment that a little girl had wanted to love the room

B. West reflects on the sun parlor and the summer when she put her pride in the room ahead of her respect for a child. She remembers how her mother taught her that a house belongs to the children who live there, not the other way around. Then she expresses regret that she did not allow Sis, a young relative of hers, to play in the sun parlor. Too late, she remembers her mother's lesson about respecting children over belongings.

Vocabulary Builder, p. 69

A. Sample Answers

1. The performance went well, which one can tell because the director gave the cast and crew extremely generous praise.
2. No, a coach is not subordinate to his team; rather, the team is below the coach in rank.

3. No, an argument with my best friend would not bring a sense of feeling renewed and energetic. Instead, it would probably make me feel depressed and angry.

4. An actress would be more likely to experience being coaxed with flattery.

5. She had a severe case of the flu, because she needed a long time to *convalesce*, or regain good health.

6. You said just a few words to give a *succinct*, or briefly stated, response.

B. 1. *Succor* means to give aid, so someone who was hurt would need help.

2. When you *succumb* to temptation, you give in, so you will be eating the chocolate cake.

3. The *successor* to the team captain is the person who is the next captain, and she might be unsure of herself because she is new to the job.

Enrichment: Connecting to Culture by Studying Families, p. 70

Assess students' oral reports based on how well they gather, organize, and deliver information relevant to the study of families.

Open-Book Test, p. 71

Short Answer

1. There should be check marks in the second column next to the following: Scene, Place, Idea. Students should identify two of the following: the scene is the family house, the place is the sun parlor, and the idea is the relationship between a place and the people who occupy it.

   Difficulty: *Average*   **Objective:** *Literary Analysis*

2. Some students may say that the main moral is that respect for children is more important than pride in one's home or belongings. Others might make a more general point about the way houses and rooms come to reflect the spirit of the people who occupy them.

   Difficulty: *Challenging*   **Objective:** *Literary Analysis*

3. All of her mother's friends think the house is beautiful and bring their other friends to see it.

   Difficulty: *Easy*   **Objective:** *Interpretation*

4. West is so proud of her painting job in the sun parlor that she does not want Sis to play in the room.

   Difficulty: *Average*   **Objective:** *Interpretation*

5. West is worried that Sis will come to believe that rooms are more important than children.

   Difficulty: *Average*   **Objective:** *Reading*

6. The aunt is recovering from a heart attack, and so she cannot climb the stairs to get to the bedrooms.

   Difficulty: *Easy*   **Objective:** *Interpretation*

7. A room becomes a reflection of the people in it. In this case, because the sun parlor becomes a sick room, it makes the aunt feel afraid and unlike herself.

   Difficulty: *Challenging*   **Objective:** *Reading*

8. West is afraid to find out that she might have hurt Sis's feelings by barring her from the sun parlor during that long-ago summer.

   Difficulty: *Challenging*   **Objective:** *Interpretation*

9. Houses are *subordinate* to children because they are less important.

   Difficulty: *Average*   **Objective:** *Vocabulary*

10. I am reluctant to do it because I need coaxing.

    Difficulty: *Easy*   **Objective:** *Vocabulary*

Essay

11. Students might summarize the author's memories of her childhood home; the sun parlor and Sis (main idea: a child is more important than a room); the aunt's illness and death (main idea: the aunt and her relatives are adjusting to old age, sickness, and death); or the conversation with Sis many years later (main idea: people learn lessons about life far after the actual event, and they can heal and forgive each other). Students should cite the details that support the main idea of the section they chose.

    Difficulty: *Easy*   **Objective:** *Essay*

12. Students should explain that the moral or lesson West wishes to teach is that people make a house what it is. It is not the other way around; a house or a room does not make people what they are. For example, the sun parlor is usually a cheerful place, but it becomes a sad place when West bars Sis from entering it, and again when it becomes a sick room for West's ailing aunt. Another possible moral is that people should never become less important than their house or their belongings. West probably chose to write a reflective essay because sometimes it is better to teach a lesson through your own experience rather than lecturing or preaching to readers.

    Difficulty: *Average*   **Objective:** *Essay*

13. Students should speculate that Sis is crushed when West bars her from the sun parlor. They should provide details to support the probability that Sis would have answered yes to West's question at the end of the essay. For example, Sis smiles rather than responding verbally; if the answer were no, Sis might have blurted out the answer anyway. She kindly spares West's feelings by keeping silent while still suggesting the answer.

    Difficulty: *Challenging*   **Objective:** *Essay*

14. When West sees how disappointed Sis is at being barred from the sun parlor, she begins to realize that a child is more important than a room or a house. As her mother later tells her, "We learn so many lessons as we go through life." West responds, "I know that now. I wish I had known it then." Students should observe that this central event—and the knowledge it provides—makes West a better person in the long run.

    Difficulty: *Average*   **Objective:** *Essay*

Oral Response

15. Oral responses should be clear, well organized, and well supported by appropriate examples from the selection.
    Difficulty: *Average* **Objective:** *Oral Interpretation*

Selection Test A, p. 74

Critical Reading

1. ANS: B	DIF: Easy	OBJ: Literary Analysis
2. ANS: D	DIF: Easy	OBJ: Literary Analysis
3. ANS: B	DIF: Easy	OBJ: Comprehension
4. ANS: B	DIF: Easy	OBJ: Reading
5. ANS: C	DIF: Easy	OBJ: Comprehension
6. ANS: C	DIF: Easy	OBJ: Comprehension
7. ANS: A	DIF: Easy	OBJ: Comprehension
8. ANS: C	DIF: Easy	OBJ: Interpretation
9. ANS: A	DIF: Easy	OBJ: Interpretation
10. ANS: D	DIF: Easy	OBJ: Interpretation
11. ANS: B	DIF: Easy	OBJ: Reading
12. ANS: C	DIF: Easy	OBJ: Literary Analysis

Vocabulary and Grammar

13. ANS: A	DIF: Easy	OBJ: Vocabulary
14. ANS: D	DIF: Easy	OBJ: Vocabulary
15. ANS: B	DIF: Easy	OBJ: Grammar

Essay

16. Students might say that they relate to the feeling of wanting to protect a room or belonging that they treasure. Based on their own experiences or feelings about belongings, they may agree or disagree with West's original desire to keep Sis out of her sun parlor. Either way, students should explain their feelings, how they would have reacted in West's place, and why.
    Difficulty: *Easy* **Objective:** *Essay*

17. Students might summarize the author's memories of her childhood home; the sun parlor and Sis; the aunt's illness and death; or the conversation with Sis many years later. They should explain what general truth about families the event illustrates. For example, the author's memories of her childhood home show how mothers generally love their children more than anything else in the world. The aunt's illness and death show how rooms in a family's home are affected by the people who live there and the events that take place in them. It also shows how families take care of one another.
    Difficulty: *Easy* **Objective:** *Essay*

18. When West sees how disappointed Sis is at being banned from the sun parlor, she begins to realize that a child is more important than a room or a house. By the time West is an adult, she has learned the lesson completely. Students should observe that this central event—and the knowledge it provides—makes West a better person in the long run.
    Difficulty: *Average* **Objective:** *Essay*

Selection Test B, p. 77

Critical Reading

1. ANS: C	DIF: Average	OBJ: Literary Analysis
2. ANS: B	DIF: Average	OBJ: Comprehension
3. ANS: D	DIF: Average	OBJ: Comprehension
4. ANS: A	DIF: Average	OBJ: Interpretation
5. ANS: C	DIF: Challenging	OBJ: Interpretation
6. ANS: C	DIF: Average	OBJ: Comprehension
7. ANS: B	DIF: Challenging	OBJ: Literary Analysis
8. ANS: D	DIF: Average	OBJ: Interpretation
9. ANS: D	DIF: Challenging	OBJ: Interpretation
10. ANS: D	DIF: Average	OBJ: Reading
11. ANS: C	DIF: Challenging	OBJ: Reading
12. ANS: D	DIF: Average	OBJ: Literary Analysis

Vocabulary and Grammar

13. ANS: A	DIF: Average	OBJ: Vocabulary
14. ANS: B	DIF: Average	OBJ: Vocabulary
15. ANS: A	DIF: Average	OBJ: Grammar
16. ANS: B	DIF: Average	OBJ: Grammar

Essay

17. Students should explain that the moral or lesson West wishes to convey is that children are more important than one's home or belongings. Students might suggest that West chose to write a reflective essay because this is a lesson she learned through her own life experiences. Therefore, since a reflective essay is about the author's life experiences, it is an appropriate way for her to teach her lesson about life. West might also have chosen to write a fiction story or even a persuasive essay.
    Difficulty: *Average* **Objective:** *Essay*

18. Students might say that West feels guilty about not really listening to Sis when the girl said that the sun parlor was the most beautiful room she had ever seen. The moment was very important to the child, but West did not realize it until it was too late. West worries that she may have caused Sis to think that the room was more important than Sis was. At the end of the essay, West does not really want to know the answer to her question. She just wants to know that Sis really heard her and understood West's regret about the incident.
    Difficulty: *Average* **Objective:** *Essay*

19. Students should state whether they think Sis was affected by West's actions. They might write about how excited Sis was when she first saw the sun parlor and how disappointed she felt when West told her not to go in. They might indicate that Sis remained upset about the incident for years or that she forgot about it immediately. Students should also decide whether they believe West's mother ever allowed Sis to play in the sun parlor when West was absent.
    Difficulty: *Challenging* **Objective:** *Essay*

Unit 3 Resources: Types of Nonfiction

20. When West sees how disappointed Sis is at being barred from the sun parlor, she begins to realize that a child is more important than a room or a house. As her mother later tells her, "We learn so many lessons as we go through life." West responds, "I know that now. I wish I had known it then." Students should observe that this central event—and the knowledge it provides—makes West a better person in the long run.

Difficulty: *Average*   **Objective:** *Essay*

from In Commemoration: One Million Volumes
by Rudolfo Anaya

Vocabulary Warm-up Exercises, p. 81

A.
1. budding
2. aimlessly
3. discourse
4. participate
5. volumes
6. tattered
7. doze
8. enroll

B. Sample Answers
1. F; A *haven* is a safe place, so people probably would not feel nervous or frightened there.
2. F; A *storehouse* is a place where things are kept, so a furniture storehouse would be much larger than one kitchen table.
3. T; Being *idealistic* means believing in the possibility of perfection; being pessimistic means looking at the negative side of things.
4. T; Feeling *exhilaration* would be a typical response to meeting a hero.
5. T; The *inspiration* for a painting could come from many different sources.
6. F; If the city has *ample* food, it is possible that everyone will have enough to eat.
7. F; An office that feels like a *labyrinth* is like a maze, with many walls, passages, and confusing corners and turns.
8. F; Sometimes deleting unnecessary or confusing words can *clarify* writing more than adding words would.

Reading Warm-up A, p. 82

Sample Answers
1. drifting from room to room; Paula was talking *aimlessly*, just going on and on without really thinking about what she was saying.
2. (Grandfather); *Doze* means "sleep lightly."
3. (worn); My red T-shirt is very *tattered*.
4. (poetry); You might find *volumes* on a bookshelf or in a library.
5. interest in Mexican literature; *Budding* means "beginning to appear."

6. (a class about Latin American culture); I would like to *enroll* in a jewelry-making class.
7. They shared information and ideas in long, serious discussions. A *discourse* is a serious discussion about ideas.
8. (an exchange program); Our class could *participate* in a pen pal program through the Internet.

Reading Warm-up B, p. 83

Sample Answers
1. holding the wisdom of the ages on every topic; A *storehouse* could also hold office equipment or imported foods.
2. (a safe place); The attic in our house is a *haven* because it has a nice window and is very quiet.
3. discovering the perfect book; *Exhilaration* is a feeling of extreme happiness or excitement.
4. (maze); A *labyrinth* probably has lots of confusing passageways or hallways.
5. the process of finding a book; I would *clarify* a recipe by offering tips on how to complete the complicated parts of the process.
6. hoped to create a perfect system for organizing books; Someone is *idealistic* if he or she believes that a perfect world is possible.
7. (alphabet); My baby sister has been an *inspiration* to me in many ways.
8. (plenty); I usually have *ample* time to finish my homework.

Writing About the Big Question, p. 84

A.
1. evolve
2. enlighten
3. understanding
4. ignorance

B. Sample Answers
1. I read a book about how oceans were formed. I read an excellent novel.
2. Reading the novel changed my life. I learned that writers could create worlds that seemed real, had fascinating characters, and raised important issues. I had never thought of writing and reading as life-changing activities, but they are.

C. Sample Answer

For the author, acquiring information means that you are connected to the world of ideas, but also to the world of your own history and people. Reading, for the author, is the key that opens the door to the past and to the future.

Literary Analysis: Reflective Essay, p. 85

Sample Answers
1. The lesson is that books and libraries provide a wealth of knowledge and imagination.
2. He feels that libraries are havens, gathering places, and storehouses of knowledge.

3. He tells the story in terms of his experiences with stories, books, and especially libraries. He shows how he grew as a reader and a writer through his memories of these things.

4. Anaya believes the information in libraries represents the history of the world, which must be kept free of censorship. To Anaya, access to this knowledge represents freedom.

Reading: Ask Questions to Analyze Main Ideas and Supporting Details, p. 86

A. Sample Answers

1. the author's love of words, books, and libraries
2. that books and libraries contain a wealth of knowledge and imagination, preserve cultures and freedom, and house the collective memory of humanity
3. Anaya's memories of his people's oral tradition; his recollection of his visits to several libraries, including the small library in his home village, his high school library in Albuquerque, and the large library at the University of New Mexico; his memories of idealistic discussions with his university friends

B. Anaya reflects on his love of words, books, and libraries. He writes about how the older members of his family would tell stories, which gave him his love of words. He then describes his visits to libraries, ranging from the tiny one-room library in his home village to the massive University of New Mexico Library. Anaya summarizes his feelings about books and libraries by stating that books and libraries contain the collective memory of humanity. They preserve cultures and freedom by providing information and by stimulating readers' imaginations.

Vocabulary Builder, p. 87

A. Sample Answers

1. No, the knowledge of history is something that must be learned; it is not inborn.
2. A dilapidated courthouse would be more in need of repair than one that is not shabby.
3. Yes, a movie that enthralls its audience is likely to make money because it is extremely interesting to viewers.
4. Graduating from high school would be more poignant because it is a very emotional turning point in most people's lives.
5. No, a library cannot have an endless supply of books, because a building can only physically hold a certain number of books.
6. No, a *paradox* is a statement that seems contradictory, so the answer would probably be confusing or require serious thought.

B. 1. No, a *parasite* must live beside or on something else to survive.
2. No, to *paraphrase* something is to put it in your own words.
3. You would follow a *paradigm*, or model, of the experiment.

Enrichment: Improving a Library, p. 88

Students should cite specific wishes and improvements for a local library. Proposals should reflect a workable plan for implementation, including suggestions about funding.

"The Sun Parlor" by Dorothy West
from In Commemoration: One Million Volumes by Rudolfo A. Anaya

Integrated Language Skills: Grammar, p. 89

A. 1. girl (PN); 2. sad, regretful (PA, PA); 3. children (PN); 4. refuge (PN); 5. exciting, uplifting (PA, PA); 6. man (PN)

B. Students' responses will vary. Check to be sure that predicate nominatives are underlined once and predicate adjectives are underlined twice. There should be at least five subject complements in the paragraph.

Open-Book Test, p. 92

Short Answer

1. Possible key experiences: his grandfather's storytelling and love of words, spending time in the library as a boy, and his devotion to books and learning as a student and teacher.
   Several experiences throughout Anaya's life inspired his love for books and learning.
   Difficulty: *Average*   **Objective:** *Literary Analysis*

2. The idea of a million stars—or coins—in the night sky expanded Anaya's young imagination and filled him with a spirit of magic and wonder.
   Difficulty: *Challenging*   **Objective:** *Reading*

3. Anaya points out that the winter snow destroys sheep and cattle, while the green grass nourishes them.
   Difficulty: *Easy*   **Objective:** *Reading*

4. Anaya spoke Spanish at home, but he had to speak English in school. English was new and awkward for him.
   Difficulty: *Easy*   **Objective:** *Interpretation*

5. Anaya read at the library while his friends played. This shows that Anaya was more interested in words and books than in the activities that attracted most boys his age.
   Difficulty: *Average*   **Objective:** *Interpretation*

6. For any library to serve its purpose, ideas must be free and unlimited. Anaya's experiences apply to all libraries.
   Difficulty: *Challenging*   **Objective:** *Literary Analysis*

7. Anaya worked his way through high school by writing love poems for other students in the library. Many of the girls who read the poems fell in love with him.
   Difficulty: *Easy*   **Objective:** *Reading*

8. This is a paradox because books both satisfy the hunger for knowledge and create a hunger for more knowledge.
   Difficulty: *Challenging*   **Objective:** *Interpretation*

9. He associates the memories with happiness and contentment.
   Difficulty: *Average*   **Objective:** *Vocabulary*

10. I would want to return because the place would captivate and fascinate me.

    Difficulty: *Easy*   Objective: *Vocabulary*

Essay

11. Students should name a book, story, article, essay, or other text that has stimulated or excited them. They should use specific examples to explain what inspired them. Students should then compare their reading experience with one or more of the reading experiences Anaya discusses in "In Commemoration: One Million Volumes."

    Difficulty: *Easy*   Objective: *Essay*

12. Students should discuss Anaya's belief in the power of words to expand the mind and the imagination. Books and stories also help to preserve cultures by passing on ideas and traditions to the next generation. Stories and books encourage people to talk and to think about different and exciting ideas. Students should support their points with details from the text.

    Difficulty: *Average*   Objective: *Essay*

13. Students should identify clear differences between online and print reading, and they should outline the consequences of the trend toward reading online. They should support their points with examples from "In Commemoration: One Million Volumes" and from their own experiences.

    Difficulty: *Challenging*   Objective: *Essay*

14. Anaya's devotion to words and books totally transformed his life. When he was a child, his grandfather's stories expanded his imagination. When he was a boy, the local library drew him away from other boys' games and into the worlds of literature and knowledge. As he grew older, his love of books guided him into a career as a writer and teacher. Students should support their points with specific examples of the types of information that influenced Anaya.

    Difficulty: *Average*   Objective: *Essay*

Oral Response

15. Oral responses should be clear, well organized, and well supported by appropriate examples from the selection.

    Difficulty: *Average*   Objective: *Oral Interpretation*

Selection Test A, p. 95

Critical Reading

1. ANS: B	DIF: Easy	OBJ: Literary Analysis
2. ANS: C	DIF: Easy	OBJ: Comprehension
3. ANS: C	DIF: Easy	OBJ: Comprehension
4. ANS: A	DIF: Easy	OBJ: Interpretation
5. ANS: C	DIF: Easy	OBJ: Reading
6. ANS: A	DIF: Easy	OBJ: Comprehension
7. ANS: D	DIF: Easy	OBJ: Interpretation
8. ANS: B	DIF: Easy	OBJ: Interpretation
9. ANS: C	DIF: Easy	OBJ: Comprehension

10. ANS: C	DIF: Easy	OBJ: Reading
11. ANS: D	DIF: Easy	OBJ: Literary Analysis

Vocabulary and Grammar

12. ANS: B	DIF: Easy	OBJ: Vocabulary
13. ANS: D	DIF: Easy	OBJ: Vocabulary
14. ANS: A	DIF: Easy	OBJ: Grammar
15. ANS: B	DIF: Easy	OBJ: Grammar

Essay

16. Students should list some of the points Anaya makes about libraries. For example, he states that the library is a place to discover other worlds and spark one's imagination; it preserves cultures; it represents freedom from censorship; it is a place to gather and discuss issues and ideas. Anaya believes a library should be the heart of a city and should be a warm place that reflects the needs and aspirations of the people.

    Difficulty: *Easy*   Objective: *Essay*

17. Students should explain that Anaya believes there is power in words. Both the stories of "the old ones" and the stories in books contain the power to inspire listeners' or readers' imaginations. They also both help to preserve cultures by passing those stories on to the children. They are ways to get people to talk together or think about one another's ideas.

    Difficulty: *Easy*   Objective: *Essay*

18. Anaya's love of books totally changed his life. When he was a child, his grandfather's stories expanded his imagination. When he was a boy, the library drew him away from other boys' games and got him interested in the worlds of literature and knowledge. As he grew older, his love of books guided him into a career as a writer and teacher. Students should support their points with specific examples of the types of knowledge that changed Anaya.

    Difficulty: *Average*   Objective: *Essay*

Selection Test B, p. 98

Critical Reading

1. ANS: A	DIF: Average	OBJ: Literary Analysis
2. ANS: C	DIF: Average	OBJ: Comprehension
3. ANS: C	DIF: Average	OBJ: Comprehension
4. ANS: D	DIF: Challenging	OBJ: Comprehension
5. ANS: B	DIF: Average	OBJ: Interpretation
6. ANS: D	DIF: Average	OBJ: Interpretation
7. ANS: A	DIF: Average	OBJ: Interpretation
8. ANS: A	DIF: Average	OBJ: Interpretation
9. ANS: C	DIF: Challenging	OBJ: Interpretation
10. ANS: C	DIF: Average	OBJ: Reading
11. ANS: A	DIF: Average	OBJ: Reading
12. ANS: D	DIF: Challenging	OBJ: Reading
13. ANS: C	DIF: Average	OBJ: Literary Analysis

Unit 3 Resources: Types of Nonfiction

Vocabulary and Grammar

14. ANS: B   DIF: Challenging   OBJ: Vocabulary
15. ANS: A   DIF: Average   OBJ: Vocabulary
16. ANS: A   DIF: Average   OBJ: Grammar
17. ANS: B   DIF: Average   OBJ: Grammar

Essay

18. Students should name a book, poem, story, or other writing that has inspired or excited them in some way and explain exactly what it is about this work that exhilarated them. They might name anything from a novel that they could not put down to children's literature they remember fondly. Students should then compare their experience with reading to the experiences Anaya describes in his essay.

    Difficulty: *Average*   **Objective:** *Essay*

19. Students may make a wide range of predictions about the library's role in the future. Some students may speculate that libraries will eventually be replaced by electronic media. Others may reason that libraries will not become extinct because it is more difficult to determine the reliability of information obtained on the Internet. They may also state that many people still prefer hard-copy books for their research and enjoyment. Regardless of their position, students' essays should indicate that they have considered Anaya's stance on the primary functions of the library: the library as an archive of "the collective memory of all mankind" and a place where issues should be "discussed and debated and researched."

    Difficulty: *Average*   **Objective:** *Essay*

20. Students should indicate in their essays that Anaya's references to his native culture provide sensory images that allow Spanish history to come alive. The many references to Spanish and Anaya's uses of the language both provide authenticity to Anaya's reminiscences and make his childhood more vivid. They also suggest a model of multicultural pluralism and harmony. They preserve his cultural heritage and the diversity he hopes to see preserved in the library.

    Difficulty: *Challenging*   **Objective:** *Essay*

21. Anaya's devotion to words and books totally transformed his life. When he was a child, his grandfather's stories expanded his imagination. When he was a boy, the local library drew him away from other boys' games and into the worlds of literature and knowledge. As he grew older, his love of books guided him into a career as a writer and teacher. Students should support their points with specific examples of the types of information that influenced Anaya.

    Difficulty: *Average*   **Objective:** *Essay*

"A Toast to the Oldest Inhabitant: The Weather of New England" by Mark Twain
"The Dog That Bit People" by James Thurber

Vocabulary Warm-up Exercises, p. 102

A.
1. specimens
2. residents
3. municipal
4. varying
5. climax
6. foliage
7. favorable
8. compels

B.
1. You might write a *postscript* to add something you forgot to mention.
2. The decorations in my room create a *harmonious* atmosphere.
3. You might need *burly* workers for jobs that require heavy lifting.
4. When spring *commences*, flowers begin to grow and there is more daylight.
5. You might feel *incredulity* after seeing a movie that is either amazingly good or astonishingly bad.
6. No, not every *prophecy* is equally accurate. Some come true, but others do not.
7. A crack or chip could cause a diamond to be *blemished*.

Reading Warm-up A, p. 103

Sample Answers

1. (leaves); The *foliage* of the banana tree is very large and green.
2. The most spectacular foliage follows a wet spring, a warm summer, and a fall with sunny days and cool nights. *Favorable* means "acting in a helpful or beneficial way."
3. (visitors); *Residents* are people who live in a place.
4. local populations increase dramatically; At the *climax* of the film, the hero rescues the kidnapped child.
5. (fall parades, carnivals, and festivals); *Municipal* means "relating to city government."
6. I could collect *specimens* of fall leaves by choosing one leaf from each tree in our area.
7. from deep reds to hot oranges and yellows; *Varying* means "ranging from one thing to another."
8. (the autumn landscape); The desire to go to college *compels* me to study.

Reading Warm-up B, p. 104

Sample Answers

1. (begins); The school week *commences* on Monday.

2. noisy and chaotic; A rowing team working together looks very *harmonious*.

3. It is *inconceivable* that every sophomore will join the Math Club.

4. (our spotless reputation); *Blemished* means "stained."

5. weighing in at over ninety pounds; I might feel afraid if I saw a *burly* dog in a dark alley.

6. he or she cannot believe I am so clumsy; *Incredulity* means "state of disbelief or doubt."

7. You might find a *postscript* at the bottom of a letter.

8. A self-fulfilling *prophecy* is a prediction that comes true because you have predicted it will happen.

Writing About the Big Question, p. 105

A. 1. modified
2. empathy
3. revise
4. evolve

B. Sample Answers

1. My dog pulled me into a mud puddle. I got soaking wet in a rain shower.

2. At first I was serious when my dog dragged me into the puddle, because I was embarrassed and wanted my dog to have **awareness** of his misdeed. But I looked so funny covered in mud, that I had to **adapt** and see the **humor** in the situation.

C. Sample Answer

To change your attitude toward a bad situation, you should think about whether you can use humor to make things less bad. If the situation is serious and likely to affect many people, humor may be inappropriate; however, humor can sometimes put even a serious situation into perspective.

Literary Analysis: Humorous Writing, p. 106

1. hyperbole, because one hundred and thirty-six different kinds of weather could not occur within the space of a day

2. understatement, because drowning and getting struck by lightning are tragedies rather than mere "disappointments"

3. understatement, because it would be a great (rather than slight) advantage to be bitten as little as possible

4. hyperbole, because such a dramatic and dangerous incident would not typically occur between a household pet and a member of that household

Vocabulary Builder, p. 107

Sample Answers

A. 1. Her perfect day was blemished by a single criticism.

2. Once the presentation commences, please hold your questions.

3. The vagaries of the weather prevent us from planning our outdoor activities in advance.

4. Jack's mother showed incredulity when he claimed to have cleaned his room in ten minutes.

5. The choleric old woman scolded the children in her front yard.

6. Getting less than seven hours' sleep makes me irascible in the morning.

7. Mia felt indignant when she was not given a part in the play.

B. 1. B; 2. C; 3. D 4. B; 5. C

Open Book Test, p. 109

Short Answer

1. The main quality he discusses is the weather's unpredictability.

   Difficulty: *Easy*   **Objective:** *Interpretation*

2. Possible examples of hyperbole: more than 100 types of weather in 1 day; hundreds of kinds of weather unheard of before; killing poets for writing about "Beautiful Spring"

   Accept any answer supported by a reason.

   Difficulty: *Average*   **Objective:** *Literary Analysis*

3. If you were dining in *sumptuous* surroundings, you would most likely find yourself in a fancy restaurant, because a fancy restaurant is more lavish than a coffee shop.

   Difficulty: *Easy*   **Objective:** *Vocabulary*

4. It illustrates understatement because Mother tries to minimize the effect of the bite.

   Difficulty: *Average*   **Objective:** *Literary Analysis*

5. It is satire because it points out the foolishness of Mother's attempts to make up for the dog's constant biting.

   Difficulty: *Average*   **Objective:** *Literary Analysis*

6. A teacher with a *choleric* temperament would most likely not show much patience with students because he or she would have a quick temper.

   Difficulty: *Average*   **Objective:** *Vocabulary*

7. Both writers use hyperbole. They exaggerate ordinary events to make them funny.

   Difficulty: *Easy*   **Objective:** *Literary Analysis*

8. Both selections explore the ways in which humans react to nonhuman forces—the weather (Twain) and a dog (Thurber).

   Difficulty: *Average*   **Objective:** *Interpretation*

9. "A Toast to the Oldest Inhabitant" relies more heavily on hyperbole, with its wild exaggerations of the types of New England weather. Although "The Dog That Bit People" contains examples of hyperbole, it relies more heavily on understatement. For example, Mother constantly minimizes the dog's biting.

   Difficulty: *Challenging*   **Objective:** *Literary Analysis*

10. They seem to share an understated admiration for their subjects, even though they find them a bit annoying.

   Difficulty: *Challenging*   **Objective:** *Interpretation*

Essay

11. Students should select one passage from either selection. They should explain why they found the passage amusing by citing specific examples and explaining the techniques that make them humorous—i.e., hyperbole, understatement, or satire.

    Difficulty: *Easy* Objective: *Essay*

12. Students should clearly state which essay they found more amusing. They should explain their preference and support it with specific examples from both selections.

    Difficulty: *Average* Objective: *Essay*

13. Students should note that Twain satirizes weather forecasters by pointing out that their forecasts are so general that they can never be wrong—or right. They should note that Thurber satirizes pet owners through Mother, who spoils Muggs and makes excuses for him every time he creates problems. Students should state which portrait is more effective—or state that they are equally effective—and explain why.

    Difficulty: *Challenging* Objective: *Essay*

14. Students should note that in both selections, the authors use humor to convey insights about human behavior, and insights are a form of knowledge. From Twain, a reader might change by developing a greater appreciation of the variety of weather, how people adapt to it, and how beautiful it can be. They also might try to be more specific when reporting or discussing topics in their writing or speaking. From Thurber, a reader might come away with a renewed appreciation for people's affection for pets, despite—or even because of—their faults. They might stop being overly protective of their pets.

    Difficulty: *Average* Objective: *Essay*

Oral Response

15. Oral responses should be clear, well organized, and well supported by appropriate examples from the selection(s).

    Difficulty: *Average* Objective: *Oral Interpretation*

Selection Test A, p. 112

Critical Reading

1. ANS: C	DIF: Easy	OBJ: Comprehension
2. ANS: A	DIF: Easy	OBJ: Literary Analysis
3. ANS: D	DIF: Easy	OBJ: Interpretation
4. ANS: D	DIF: Easy	OBJ: Comprehension
5. ANS: B	DIF: Easy	OBJ: Interpretation
6. ANS: C	DIF: Easy	OBJ: Comprehension
7. ANS: B	DIF: Easy	OBJ: Comprehension
8. ANS: C	DIF: Easy	OBJ: Literary Analysis
9. ANS: D	DIF: Easy	OBJ: Interpretation
10. ANS: A	DIF: Easy	OBJ: Literary Analysis
11. ANS: B	DIF: Easy	OBJ: Interpretation

12. ANS: A	DIF: Easy	OBJ: Literary Analysis
13. ANS: B	DIF: Easy	OBJ: Interpretation

Vocabulary

14. ANS: D	DIF: Easy	OBJ: Vocabulary
15. ANS: C	DIF: Easy	OBJ: Vocabulary

Essay

16. Students should identify one humorous passage in each essay (for example, the sample forecast Twain provides in "A Toast to the Oldest Inhabitant" or the episode in which Thurber swings Muggs around by the tail in "The Dog That Bit People"). Students should logically explain why the passage is humorous—for example, because it is unexpected, because it is an understatement, or because it is an exaggeration. They should also identify which essay they found funnier and explain why.

    Difficulty: *Easy* Objective: *Essay*

17. Students should note that Twain satirizes weather forecasters by giving a sample forecast in which all kinds of weather are included just to cover all the bases, and Thurber satirizes pet owners through the character of his mother, who spoils Muggs and defends him even when he is guilty. Students are likely to agree that these portrayals contain kernels of truth—that weather forecasters do tend to give overly general forecasts for the sake of being at least partially right and that pet owners do tend to coddle their pets.

    Difficulty: *Easy* Objective: *Essay*

18. Students should explain that from Twain a reader might change by developing a greater appreciation of the weather, how people adapt to it, and how beautiful it can be. They also might try to be more specific when writing or speaking. From Thurber a reader might gain a better understanding for people's love of pets. They might stop being overly protective of their pets. Students should back up their points with examples from both selections.

    Difficulty: *Average* Objective: *Essay*

Selection Test B, p. 115

Critical Reading

1. ANS: C	DIF: Average	OBJ: Comprehension
2. ANS: A	DIF: Average	OBJ: Literary Analysis
3. ANS: D	DIF: Average	OBJ: Comprehension
4. ANS: B	DIF: Average	OBJ: Interpretation
5. ANS: C	DIF: Average	OBJ: Comprehension
6. ANS: B	DIF: Challenging	OBJ: Literary Analysis
7. ANS: A	DIF: Average	OBJ: Interpretation
8. ANS: D	DIF: Challenging	OBJ: Literary Analysis
9. ANS: C	DIF: Challenging	OBJ: Comprehension
10. ANS: C	DIF: Average	OBJ: Literary Analysis

11. ANS: A	DIF: Average	OBJ: Interpretation
12. ANS: A	DIF: Challenging	OBJ: Literary Analysis
13. ANS: D	DIF: Average	OBJ: Literary Analysis
14. ANS: B	DIF: Challenging	OBJ: Literary Analysis
15. ANS: C	DIF: Challenging	OBJ: Interpretation

Vocabulary

16. ANS: D	DIF: Average	OBJ: Vocabulary
17. ANS: D	DIF: Average	OBJ: Vocabulary
18. ANS: B	DIF: Challenging	OBJ: Vocabulary

Essay

19. Students should define hyperbole as exaggeration, or speaking of a person, a thing, or an event as if it were much greater than it is. Understatement is speaking of a person, a thing, or an event as if it were much less than it is. They should note that Twain uses a good deal of hyperbole to cast the weather as a hugely unpredictable and varied force. He also uses understatement, but to a lesser extent. For example, he describes weather-related tragedies as "great disappointments." Students should note that Thurber uses hyperbole to exaggerate the dog's behavior and understatement to emphasize mother's inability to see Muggs for what he is. Students' examples of these techniques will vary.

    Difficulty: *Average*   **Objective:** *Essay*

20. Students should identify the basic conflict in "A Toast to the Oldest Inhabitant" as one between humans and nature, or the weather. The basic conflict in "The Dog That Bit People" is one between either Muggs and Thurber or between dogs and humans. Students should note that in both conflicts, human beings are portrayed as the underdog and that both authors identify with the underdog. This allows them to render their subjects humorously as larger-than-life aggressors. Students should use examples from the essays to support their claims.

    Difficulty: *Challenging*   **Objective:** *Essay*

21. Students should note that in both selections, the authors use humor to convey insights about human behavior, and insights are a form of knowledge. From Twain a reader might change by developing a greater appreciation of the variety of weather, how people adapt to it, and how beautiful it can be. They also might try to be more specific when reporting or discussing topics in their writing or speaking. From Thurber a reader might come away with a renewed appreciation for people's affection for pets, despite—or even because of—their faults. They might stop being overly protective of their pets.

    Difficulty: *Average*   **Objective:** *Essay*

Writing Workshop

Letter to the Editor: Integrating Grammar Skills, p. 119

A. 1. compound subject; 2. compound object of a preposition; 3. compound direct object; 4. compound indirect object

B. 1. Neither Joel nor Delphine is in the school play this year.
2. We rehearse on Mondays and Thursdays.
3. We may rehearse in the school auditorium or at Luisa's house.
4. The rehearsal usually begins at three and ends at five.
5. The play is long but interesting.

Benchmark Test 5, p. 120

MULTIPLE CHOICE

1. ANS: C
2. ANS: D
3. ANS: B
4. ANS: C
5. ANS: C
6. ANS: A
7. ANS: C
8. ANS: B
9. ANS: B
10. ANS: A
11. ANS: C
12. ANS: D
13. ANS: B
14. ANS: D
15. ANS: C
16. ANS: B
17. ANS: C
18. ANS: D
19. ANS: A
20. ANS: C
21. ANS: A
22. ANS: D
23. ANS: D
24. ANS: D
25. ANS: A
26. ANS: B
27. ANS: A
28. ANS: D

29. ANS: C
30. ANS: A
31. ANS: B
32. ANS: B
33. ANS: D
34. ANS: D

ESSAY

35. Students should use correct letter form, appropriate tone and diction, and logical and persuasive appeals. Essays should also include information a prospective donor would want to know.

36. Students' memoirs should include appropriate details and precise language.

37. Students' letters to the editor should use appropriate language and appropriate formatting. Their opinions should be clearly stated and supported by evidence.

"Keep Memory Alive" by Elie Wiesel

Vocabulary Warm-up Exercises, p. 128

A. 1. perished
2. ghetto
3. bewilderment
4. guilty
5. identified
6. endure
7. behalf
8. mankind

B. Sample Answers

1. Because the people faced *deportation*, they knew they would have to start over in a new country.
2. *Multitudes* of people live in the city, so it is very crowded.
3. Evidence showed he had *committed* the crime, so we found him guilty.
4. When Eve became a painter, she fulfilled her *destiny* to be a great artist.
5. After working so hard for the prize, he felt great *anguish* when he did not win it.
6. The *naïve* boy had a simple, innocent sense of humor.
7. Nell had a *profound* desire to help people, so she always put others first.

Reading Warm-up A, p. 129

Sample Answers

1. (in the Polish city of Warsaw); *Ghetto* means "an impoverished part of the city."
2. (starvation and disease); *Endure* means "to suffer pain or deal with a hard situation for a long time."
3. As a mother herself; As someone who has asthma, I *identified* with others who had lung problems.
4. (confusion); Tara felt *bewilderment* when her boyfriend broke up with her for no apparent reason.

5. a terrible crime; *Guilty* means "having broken a law or rule."
6. (concentration camps); Some animals *perished* when the barn caught fire.
7. They were among the millions killed by the Nazis in one of the darkest chapters in the history of mankind. They were among the millions killed by the Nazis in one of the darkest chapters in the history of *humanity*.
8. the others who had sacrificed their own safety to save people's lives; *Behalf* means "in the interest of" or "for."

Reading Warm-up B, p. 130

Sample Answers

1. (unsophisticated); It was *naïve* of me to trust the smooth-talking saleswoman.
2. people in the world; It is easier to make peace among a smaller group because when *multitudes* of people are involved, there is more opportunity for violence and disagreement.
3. (the powerful); *Committed* means "having done something wrong or illegal."
4. (shame); She felt *humiliation* when she was screamed at in front of the class.
5. (suffering); When my friend was very ill, I felt great *anguish*.
6. If I were faced with *deportation*, I would insist on consulting with an attorney.
7. I have a *profound* desire to make peace with my enemies.
8. suffering peoples; *Destiny* means "the thing that will happen to someone in the future."

Writing About the Big Question, p. 131

A. 1. history
2. insight
3. ignorance
4. influence

B. Sample Answers

1. I learned about racial segregation in South Africa. I saw people ridiculed in my city because they did not speak English.
2. I felt angry when I learned about racial segregation in South Africa, because the people who enforced those laws did not want to develop **empathy** for the people they were oppressing. The rest of the world finally made the leaders **adapt** their policies.

C. Sample Answer

When you learn that people are capable of brutality against others, you can choose to ignore their cruelty and hope they stop tormenting others, or you can speak out and try to help those who are being hurt. It is scary and dangerous to speak out, but the world would be much scarier and much more dangerous if people did *not* speak out against brutality. How to you know that you will not be the next to suffer?

Literary Analysis: Persuasive Writing, p. 132

Sample Answers

1. Students might choose the following: "And that is why I swore never to be silent whenever and wherever human beings endure suffering and humiliation" or "We must always take sides."

2. Wiesel repeats the statement, "I remember." This is the rhetorical device of repetition, used to emphasize the main message of keeping memory alive. Wiesel also often uses introductory statements set off by colons; this is parallelism. There is also parallelism in the final two sentences: "Neutrality helps the oppressor, never the victim. Silence encourages the tormentor, never the tormented." "How could the world remain silent?" is a rhetorical question.

3. The message is more powerful coming from Wiesel than from someone else because Wiesel is a Holocaust survivor. He personally experienced the events of which he speaks.

4. He says that forgetting makes others guilty as well because it makes it possible for such crimes to happen again. He believes that ignoring, forgetting, or keeping silent about terrible events only helps the oppressors, not the victims.

Reading: Test the Writer's Logic to Evaluate Persuasive Appeals, p. 133

Sample Answers

1. We cannot be silent or neutral when others are being oppressed and tormented; we must take sides and fight injustice.

2. A. There are many appeals in "Keep Memory Alive." Wiesel states that he is humbled because he does not feel that he has the right to represent those who have died. This is an emotional appeal, but he supports it with the argument that no one may speak for the dead.
   B. He then makes another emotional appeal by telling the story of his experiences as a young boy. He supports his appeal by mentioning specific events, but not really with logic.
   C. Wiesel makes another appeal when he refers to the "fiery altar upon which the history of our people and the future of mankind were meant to be sacrificed." With this, he makes a logical connection between the Jewish people and all of mankind.
   D. He also makes an appeal about silence and forgetting. He says that silence makes others into "accomplices" who help the oppressors by not speaking out against them. Students might say that it is not logical to say that those who were silent were just as guilty as those who operated gas chambers. However, Wiesel supports his point by saying that silence does not help victims, only the tormentors.

Vocabulary Builder, p. 134

A. 1. A snowstorm in Miami in July might cause *bewilderment*.
   2. A group of friends who plan a surprise event for another friend *could be accomplices*.

3. Someone who is *naïve* is trusting, innocent, or easily swayed.

4. A person who is wise, such as a religious leader, or someone who has lived through extraordinary experiences might make a *profound* statement.

5. A person might feel elation, joy, or pride in excelling at a task.

B. 1. We knew that to *ascend* the mountain, we would have to climb up carefully.
   2. The mountaineer's *descent* took her down into the valley below.
   3. The ballerina's dance was *transcendent*, and the audience gasped at her display of talent.

Enrichment: Connecting to Art, p. 135

Assess students' stamps based on the following criteria: relevance to subject matter, neatness, creativity, and presence of explanatory text.

Open-Book Test, p. 136

Short Answer

1. Question 1: Do I have the right to represent the people who died in the Holocaust?
   Question 2: Do I have the right to accept this honor?
   From Wiesel's point of view, the answer to both questions is no.
   Difficulty: *Average* **Objective:** *Literary Analysis*

2. No, it would not be *presumptuous*. It would be appropriate because a lawyer is an expert on legal matters.
   Difficulty: *Average* **Objective:** *Vocabulary*

3. He uses a series of short sentence fragments that parallel each other and make it seem like events are passing quickly.
   Difficulty: *Challenging* **Objective:** *Literary Analysis*

4. The honor is really dedicated to all the survivors of the Holocaust.
   Difficulty: *Average* **Objective:** *Interpretation*

5. He is using repetition.
   Difficulty: *Easy* **Objective:** *Literary Analysis*

6. Wiesel expresses shock about the world's indifference to the horrors of the Holocaust.
   Difficulty: *Average* **Objective:** *Interpretation*

7. He means that although the Holocaust happened several decades ago, it is as alive in his memory as though it were yesterday.
   Difficulty: *Challenging* **Objective:** *Interpretation*

8. People must never forget crimes against humanity and must always speak out against oppression and injustice.
   Difficulty: *Average* **Objective:** *Reading*

9. He bases this appeal on the argument that if we forget or ignore the horrors of the Holocaust, we become part of its crimes.
   Difficulty: *Challenging* **Objective:** *Reading*

10. I probably would have done poorly because I was confused while taking it.
Difficulty: *Easy* **Objective:** *Vocabulary*

Essay

11. Students should explain Wiesel's belief that forgetting about the Holocaust makes people accomplices in its crimes. Remembering helps us to avoid repeating such terrible events and honors the victims—both those who died and those who survived. Students should provide details from the speech to support their points.
Difficulty: *Easy* **Objective:** *Essay*

12. Students should point out that Wiesel supports his claims about the importance of memory with his own vivid memories of the Holocaust. He claims that keeping these events in the public memory makes it less likely that the events will happen again. He uses the techniques of parallelism, repetition, and rhetorical questions. Students should support their opinions about the persuasiveness of the speech with at least two examples from the text.
Difficulty: *Average* **Objective:** *Essay*

13. Wiesel is claiming that individuals have a strong moral obligation to the community, and they must speak out against injustice whenever they see it. Students should cite examples from the text to support their opinion about whether or not people have that responsibility. They might point out that it is not always safe to speak out against injustice because someone might hurt you for expressing your opinion. On the other hand, if you do not speak out, someone might act the same way against you someday.
Difficulty: *Challenging* **Objective:** *Essay*

14. Wiesel's life and work have had a major impact on people all over the world. Thanks to his devotion to exposing the truths and horrors of the Holocaust, people are more aware of the need for tolerance among people of different backgrounds and religions. People and governments all over the world are now much less likely to stand by in silence when terrible acts are occurring. Wiesel claims that people become less likely to commit terrible acts themselves when they know how destructive the Holocaust was.
Difficulty: *Average* **Objective:** *Essay*

Oral Response

15. Oral responses should be clear, well organized, and well supported by appropriate examples from the selection.
Difficulty: *Average* **Objective:** *Oral Interpretation*

5. ANS: A	DIF: Easy	OBJ: Literary Analysis
6. ANS: C	DIF: Easy	OBJ: Interpretation
7. ANS: A	DIF: Easy	OBJ: Interpretation
8. ANS: C	DIF: Easy	OBJ: Reading Strategy
9. ANS: B	DIF: Easy	OBJ: Comprehension
10. ANS: B	DIF: Easy	OBJ: Literary Analysis
11. ANS: D	DIF: Easy	OBJ: Literary Analysis
12. ANS: C	DIF: Easy	OBJ: Reading Strategy

Vocabulary and Grammar

13. ANS: C	DIF: Easy	OBJ: Vocabulary
14. ANS: C	DIF: Easy	OBJ: Vocabulary
15. ANS: D	DIF: Easy	OBJ: Grammar

Essay

16. Students should explain Wiesel's belief that forgetting makes the rest of the world accomplices to the Holocaust. Remembering helps us to avoid repeating such horrible events. Remembering helps honor those who died and those who survived. It also helps to fight future oppressors by making people more likely to take sides and speak out against injustice when it occurs.
Difficulty: *Easy* **Objective:** *Essay*

17. Students should identify Wiesel's desire for listeners to speak out against injustice in the world. He also wants his audience to remember the Holocaust. Most students will probably feel that Wiesel supported his arguments well. For example, he uses his own experiences during the Holocaust to back up his claim that it was a horrifying event that we must not repeat. He supports his claim that neutrality and silence help oppressors by pointing out that neutrality and silence helped the Nazis and not the Jewish people during the Holocaust. Some students might feel that Wiesel did not effectively support his arguments. They might say that it is not logical to claim that people who did not participate in the Holocaust could be considered accomplices because they remained neutral.
Difficulty: *Easy* **Objective:** *Essay*

18. Thanks to Wiesel's devotion to teaching people about the Holocaust, people are more aware of the need for accepting people of all backgrounds and religions. People and governments all over the world are now less likely to stand by in silence when violence is happening. If we forget about the Holocaust, we might repeat it—or even do something worse.
Difficulty: *Average* **Objective:** *Essay*

Selection Test A, p. 139

Critical Reading

1. ANS: A	DIF: Easy	OBJ: Comprehension
2. ANS: D	DIF: Easy	OBJ: Comprehension
3. ANS: D	DIF: Easy	OBJ: Literary Analysis
4. ANS: B	DIF: Easy	OBJ: Comprehension

Selection Test B, p. 142

Critical Reading

1. ANS: D	DIF: Average	OBJ: Comprehension
2. ANS: D	DIF: Average	OBJ: Interpretation
3. ANS: D	DIF: Average	OBJ: Interpretation

4. ANS: A	DIF: Average	OBJ: Reading Strategy
5. ANS: C	DIF: Average	OBJ: Comprehension
6. ANS: A	DIF: Average	OBJ: Comprehension
7. ANS: C	DIF: Challenging	OBJ: Reading Strategy
8. ANS: C	DIF: Average	OBJ: Interpretation
9. ANS: D	DIF: Challenging	OBJ: Literary Analysis
10. ANS: B	DIF: Average	OBJ: Literary Analysis
11. ANS: A	DIF: Challenging	OBJ: Interpretation
12. ANS: B	DIF: Challenging	OBJ: Literary Analysis
13. ANS: A	DIF: Challenging	OBJ: Literary Analysis
14. ANS: D	DIF: Challenging	OBJ: Literary Analysis
15. ANS: D	DIF: Average	OBJ: Reading Strategy

Vocabulary and Grammar

16. ANS: A	DIF: Average	OBJ: Vocabulary
17. ANS: A	DIF: Average	OBJ: Vocabulary
18. ANS: D	DIF: Average	OBJ: Grammar
19. ANS: B	DIF: Average	OBJ: Grammar

Essay

20. Students should mention Wiesel's belief that forgetting makes the rest of the world accomplices to the Holocaust. Remembering helps us to avoid repeating such horrible events. Remembering helps honor those who died and those who survived. It also helps to fight would-be oppressors by making people more likely to take sides and speak out against injustice.
    Difficulty: *Average*   Objective: *Essay*

21. Students should mention a current situation, issue, or event that involves injustice toward a group of people. They might mention genocides, ethnic and religious persecutions, governments expelling people, terrorism, and so on. Students might say that people can write letters to national leaders or boycott goods to encourage change to occur.
    Difficulty: *Average*   Objective: *Essay*

22. Students should identify Wiesel's central argument as his call for listeners to speak out against injustice in the world. He also wants his audience to remember the Holocaust. Most students will probably feel that Wiesel effectively supports his arguments with logic. For example, he uses the facts of his own experience to back up his claim that the Holocaust was a horrifying event that we must avoid repeating. He supports his claim that neutrality and silence help oppressors by pointing out that neutrality and silence helped the Nazis. Some students might feel that Wiesel did not effectively support his arguments. They might say that it is illogical to claim that nonparticipants could be considered accomplices because they remained neutral.
    Difficulty: *Challenging*   Objective: *Essay*

23. Wiesel's life and work have had a major impact on people all over the world. Thanks to his devotion to exposing the truths and horrors of the Holocaust, people are more aware of the need for tolerance

among people of different backgrounds and religions. People and goverments all over the world are now much less likely to stand by in silence when terrible acts are occurring. Wiesel claims that people become less likely to commit terrible acts themselves when they know how destructive the Holocaust was.
    Difficulty: *Average*   Objective: *Essay*

from "Nobel Lecture" by Alexander Solzhenitsyn

Vocabulary Warm-up Exercises, p. 146

A. 1. acute
   2. organizations
   3. analysis
   4. expelled
   5. internal
   6. violence
   7. unity
   8. essentially

B. 1. If a group expresses *unanimous* support for an idea, no one has disagreed.
   2. Because *persecution* is cruel treatment, no one who has experienced it is likely to want to experience it again.
   3. If an author complains of bad *translations* of her work, she is not talking about the artwork, but about the versions of the book's text that exist in other languages.
   4. If a political party *advocated* an action, its members would be happy when the action took place.
   5. If Mary is a *literary* agent, she represents writers.
   6. If Ted has been *nominated* for a prize, he has been chosen as a possible winner, but he has not necessarily won.
   7. If an actor is famous <u>exclusively</u> for comedy, he is famous only for comedies and not dramatic roles.
   8. If Barb is meeting her *colleagues* for lunch, she is meeting people whom she knows from work.

Reading Warm-up A, p. 147

Sample Answers

1. (a dreamer); *Essentially* means "relating to the basic or most important qualities of something."
2. (brutality); Lisa was horrified by the *violence* of the battle scenes in the movie.
3. <u>the inequality between the rich and the poor</u>; *Acute* means "very powerful perception."
4. (playwrights'); *Organizations* are "groups or clubs that have formed for a particular purpose."
5. <u>most outsiders would not understand</u>; *Internal* means "within a particular company or organization."
6. (school); *Expelled* means "to officially make someone leave a school, an organization, or a country."

7. "Remember that theater exists not only to teach, but also to entertain. Your lessons are sound, but your theater is not." When I read my teacher's *analysis* of my work, I was struck by her insights.

8. (artists and dreamers); The students felt *unity* when working together to clean up the school grounds.

Reading Warm-up B, p. 148

Sample Answers

1. PEN; Members of a *literary* organization might share interests in writing, editing, and/or reading books.

2. The members believed that the *only way* to achieve world peace was by building understanding among people, which writers do through their work. *Exclusively* means "only."

3. other writers who faced lack of freedom, discrimination, or harassment from their governments; He enjoyed meeting new *colleagues* at the professional conference.

4. If they were *unanimous* in agreement, no one objected to the goals.

5. (selected); I hope to be *nominated* for the Good Citizen's Award.

6. PEN makes sure that *translations* are available so that people who speak different languages can still share writers' works.

7. (campaigned); The action *advocated* by extremists was unpopular with the mainstream.

8. Rapid Response program; An outspoken journalist in another country might face *persecution* such as imprisonment, harassment, or worse.

Writing About the Big Question, p. 149

A. 1. history

2. question

3. enlighten

4. ignorance

B. Sample Answers

1. I had to tell the truth when I saw a friend bully someone at lunch. I had to tell my parents the truth when they suspected that I went somewhere I was not supposed to go.

2. I felt angry and scared when I had to tell my teacher I saw my friend bully a new student at lunch. I had to **revise** my opinion of my friend after seeing her behavior, because I had no **understanding** of how she could act the way she did.

C. Sample Answer

Writers who present the truth about society help people learn from the past and prepare for the future. Sometimes it is difficult and even dangerous to speak the truth, and it can difficult to hear and accept information about the cruelty some people display toward others. If the truth goes unspoken, however, injustice will be allowed to continue and hurt others.

Literary Analysis: Persuasive Writing, p. 150

Sample Answers

A. 1. Several sentences from the excerpt sum up the author's point, including "I think that world literature has the power in these frightening times to help mankind see itself accurately despite what is advocated by partisans and by parties" and "Writers and artists can do more: they can VANQUISH LIES!"

2. Solzhenitsyn repeats the words "lies" and "truth" many times in the last few paragraphs of his lecture. The rhetorical device of repetition emphasizes the main message of art's ability to end lies and violence. Solzhenitsyn also uses a slogan-like statement, a Russian proverb, to reinforce his point: "One Word of Truth Outweighs the World." "Who, if not writers, are to condemn their own unsuccessful governments . . . ?" is a rhetorical question.

3. The message is more powerful coming from Solzhenitsyn than from someone else because Solzhenitsyn's writings were banned in his own country. He speaks about being part of world literature and about how a writer's truth can overcome lies and violence, but his work was not read by his own people until many years later.

4. He wants to make his listeners feel that literature is a unifying force in the world. It helps him make the point that literature, wherever it originates, is a powerful weapon against violence and injustice.

B. Students might say that they were persuaded by the fact that Solzhenitsyn speaks from personal experience and genuine emotions. Since his writing was banned in his own country, he found his audience elsewhere. He believes passionately in the unifying power of art and literature against injustice and violence. Students might also mention particular words, phrases, or rhetorical devices that stood out for them. On the other hand, students might say that they were not persuaded because they could not relate to Solzhenitsyn's opinions and experiences or because they did not understand the imagery and symbolism he used.

Reading: Test the Writer's Logic to Evaluate Persuasive Appeals, p. 151

Sample Answers

1. Writers have the power and responsibility to use truth to challenge lies, corruption, injustice, and violence in the world.

2. A. There are many appeals in the excerpt from Solzhenitsyn's "Nobel Lecture." Here are some examples: Solzhenitsyn makes the claim that there is a world literature that goes beyond national boundaries. He supports this claim by giving the example of how his work is read around the world, even though it is banned in his own country.

B. He goes on to state that, once lies are dispelled, violence will collapse. He supports this claim with the argument that violence can only continue if it is shielded by lies, so without the lies it cannot continue to exist. He does not, however, back it up with examples.

C. He goes on to make the claim that a courageous person is one who refuses to support lies. Again, he supports this appeal by implying a connection to his own courage in writing against his government.

D. Finally, he states that lies cannot stand against art. He does not offer logical arguments to support this claim.

Vocabulary Builder, p. 152

Sample Answers

A. 1. The changing of the seasons happens *inexorably*.
2. The *aggregate* of plastic milk cartons we collected was the largest at the school.
3. Our principal's *jurisdiction* extends only to this school and not to the elementary school across the street.
4. The students will surely *condemn* the vandals who damaged the sports fields.
5. My sister's *oratory* was remarkable, and her speech drew cheers from all the students.

B. 1. No, a *jury* is a group of people chosen to decide if someone accused of a crime is guilty, so a jury enforces, not breaks, the law.
2. You would not play a football game because an *injury* means that your leg is hurt, so you would go to a doctor.
3. A *juror* would report to a courtroom because a juror is a member of a jury, a group of people who listen to trials in a court of law.

Enrichment: Current Events, p. 153

Sample Answers

1. patriotic essays and speeches leading up to the American Revolution; political cartoons before the Civil War
2. A. genocide or exile of ethnic groups; cruel dictatorships; government-approved prejudice or persecution of ethnic or religious groups
   B. write essays, letters, newspaper articles, or fliers to educate the public and to call for action; create artwork that shows people what injustices are taking place and/or showing people how they can take action
3. A. racial injustice, mistreatment or neglect of the rights of disabled individuals, or lack of adequate health care for the poor
   B. Students' responses will vary. Evaluate responses based on appropriateness to the subject, neatness, creativity, and effective writing or artwork.

"Keep Memory Alive" by Elie Wiesel
from "Nobel Lecture" by Alexander Solzhenitsyn

Integrated Language Skills: Grammar, p. 154

A. 1. Superlative
2. Positive
3. Positive
4. Comparative

B. Students' responses will vary. Check to be sure that positive adverbs are underlined once, comparative adverbs are underlined twice, and superlative adverbs are underlined three times. There should be at least six adverbs showing degrees of comparison in the paragraph.

Open-Book Test, p. 157

Short Answer

1. Students should paraphrase two of the following questions: Who has been the uniting force in a country? Who but writers should condemn harmful acts in society? What can literature do to end violence?

   The questions cue us to answer the question in the way Solzhenitsyn wants us to.
   Difficulty: *Average* **Objective:** *Literary Analysis*

2. Solzhenitsyn wants his audience to read the great literature of the world and to think about their own roles in ending lies and violence.
   Difficulty: *Average* **Objective:** *Reading*

3. He uses the image of a heart beating for the world.
   Difficulty: *Easy* **Objective:** *Literary Analysis*

4. Communication is so fast now that people can discover overseas writers and their work much more quickly than they could before.
   Difficulty: *Easy* **Objective:** *Reading*

5. He uses repetition. The repeated phrase is "anything but indifferent."
   Difficulty: *Average* **Objective:** *Literary Analysis*

6. He argues that violence and lying are closely connected.
   Difficulty: *Average* **Objective:** *Interpretation*

7. He says that the job of all true artists and writers is to expose lies and to tell the great truths about human life.
   Difficulty: *Challenging* **Objective:** *Reading*

8. He likes this development because it suggests a world in which people of all countries are concerned about justice and the well-being of all other people.
   Difficulty: *Challenging* **Objective:** *Interpretation*

9. He is using parallelism. He is also using repetition.
   Difficulty: *Challenging* **Objective:** *Literary Analysis*

10. You would most likely be in a concert hall because *oratory* is delivered in a public setting, not a private one.
   Difficulty: *Average* **Objective:** *Vocabulary*

Essay

11. Students should state that Solzhenitsyn sees writers as people who want to tell the truth. This is why they are the best people to get rid of injustice and violence. Some students might agree that writers tend to be more dedicated to truth than most people. Others might argue that writers do not have knowledge of the truth just because they have a strong desire to tell it. Students should back up their points with examples from the speech.
Difficulty: *Easy* **Objective:** *Essay*

12. Students should discuss an example of an issue they feel strongly about. They should back up their opinions with examples and reasons from "Nobel Lecture."
Difficulty: *Average* **Objective:** *Essay*

13. Students should recognize that Solzhenitsyn's main claim is that if writers use their power to fight against unjust policies, world literature can be a great healing and unifying force for humankind. They should give examples from the text, such as the statement that Solzhenitsyn's work was being read around the world even when it was banned in his own country.
Difficulty: *Challenging* **Objective:** *Essay*

14. Solzhenitsyn argues that violence always thrives in an atmosphere of lies. If people understand the truth about each other's lives, they are more likely to recognize each other's common humanity and less likely to hurt each other. If literature is devoted to telling the major truths about human life, it can play an important role in spreading a sense of common humanity. This knowledge will reduce the likelihood of war and violence.
Difficulty: *Average* **Objective:** *Essay*

Oral Response

15. Oral responses should be clear, well organized, and well supported by appropriate examples from the selection.
Difficulty: *Average* **Objective:** *Oral Interpretation*

Selection Test A, p. 160

Critical Reading

1. ANS: B	DIF: Easy	OBJ: Literary Analysis
2. ANS: C	DIF: Easy	OBJ: Comprehension
3. ANS: B	DIF: Easy	OBJ: Comprehension
4. ANS: D	DIF: Easy	OBJ: Interpretation
5. ANS: D	DIF: Easy	OBJ: Reading Strategy
6. ANS: D	DIF: Easy	OBJ: Comprehension
7. ANS: A	DIF: Easy	OBJ: Comprehension
8. ANS: D	DIF: Easy	OBJ: Literary Analysis
9. ANS: D	DIF: Easy	OBJ: Reading Strategy
10. ANS: C	DIF: Easy	OBJ: Interpretation
11. ANS: A	DIF: Easy	OBJ: Reading Strategy
12. ANS: C	DIF: Easy	OBJ: Literary Analysis

Vocabulary and Grammar

13. ANS: D	DIF: Easy	OBJ: Vocabulary
14. ANS: A	DIF: Easy	OBJ: Vocabulary
15. ANS: B	DIF: Easy	OBJ: Grammar

Essay

16. Students should agree or disagree with Solzhenitsyn's claim about truth and art and explain their positions. Students might say that Solzhenitsyn's reasoning convinced them that the statement is true. If so, they should give specific examples of Solzhenitsyn's arguments that convinced them. For example, he says that art and writing can cross international boundaries despite governments' attempts to ban them. Students might also say that they do not agree with Solzhenitsyn or were not convinced by his reasoning. They may feel that art is not necessarily always truthful or well-intentioned, so it might in fact help to uphold lies.
Difficulty: *Easy* **Objective:** *Essay*

17. Students may agree with Solzhenitsyn that writers and artists should use their abilities to try to make the world a better place. Or, they might say that artists and writers should simply entertain people and bring beauty into the world. Some might say that artists and writers should simply create things that make them happy and not worry about what the rest of the world thinks. Responses should be supported by examples from Solzhenitsyn's writing.
Difficulty: *Easy* **Objective:** *Essay*

18. Solzhenitsyn argues that violence always happens in an atmosphere of lies. If people understand the truth about each other's lives, they are more likely to recognize what they have in common. This will make them less likely to hurt each other. Solzhenitsyn writes that literature's job is to tell the major truths about human life. This gives literature an important role in spreading a sense of common humanity. This knowledge will help prevent war and violence.
Difficulty: *Average* **Objective:** *Essay*

Selection Test B, p. 163

Critical Reading

1. ANS: A	DIF: Average	OBJ: Interpretation
2. ANS: D	DIF: Challenging	OBJ: Comprehension
3. ANS: B	DIF: Average	OBJ: Comprehension
4. ANS: A	DIF: Challenging	OBJ: Reading Strategy
5. ANS: A	DIF: Average	OBJ: Interpretation
6. ANS: C	DIF: Average	OBJ: Literary Analysis
7. ANS: D	DIF: Challenging	OBJ: Interpretation
8. ANS: D	DIF: Challenging	OBJ: Interpretation
9. ANS: B	DIF: Average	OBJ: Reading Strategy
10. ANS: B	DIF: Challenging	OBJ: Literary Analysis

11. ANS: C   DIF: Challenging   OBJ: Interpretation
12. ANS: D   DIF: Challenging   OBJ: Literary Analysis
13. ANS: D   DIF: Average   OBJ: Literary Analysis
14. ANS: D   DIF: Average   OBJ: Reading Strategy

Vocabulary and Grammar

15. ANS: B   DIF: Challenging   OBJ: Vocabulary
16. ANS: A   DIF: Average   OBJ: Vocabulary
17. ANS: B   DIF: Average   OBJ: Grammar
18. ANS: D   DIF: Average   OBJ: Grammar

Essay

19. Students should acknowledge that Solzhenitsyn's experience under a repressive government is the source for this speech. He emphasizes the relationship between violence and lying. He feels that neither is necessary because we can, and should, live by the truth. Writers, claims Solzhenitsyn, are the ones who can best tell the truth to a wide audience and therefore keep governments accountable to their people and to the world. Solzhenitsyn believes writers and artists have the duty to stand up against violence and lies and speak out against injustice. Also, he feels that people cannot ignore bad things happening in other parts of the world.
Difficulty: *Average*   Objective: *Essay*

20. Students should identify the central claim as Solzhenitsyn's statement that writers must use their power to fight against unjust governments. Some students may believe that Solzhenitsyn adequately supported his claim with logic. They might give examples of logical arguments such as his statement that his work was being read around the world even when his writing was being banned in his own country. Other students might say that Solzhenitsyn does not adequately prove the ideas that violence would end without lies and that writers have the unique power to vanquish lies.
Difficulty: *Average*   Objective: *Essay*

21. Students should write a persuasive essay about an issue that is currently relevant. They might write about a political or an international issue, an issue of social injustice, an issue that has to do with human or animal rights, or any other issue about which they feel strongly. Students should inform readers about the issue, take a position, and support their claims with logical reasoning.
Difficulty: *Challenging*   Objective: *Essay*

22. Solzhenitsyn argues that violence always thrives in an atmosphere of lies. If people understand the truth about each other's lives, they are more likely to recognize each other's common humanity and less likely to hurt each other. If literature is devoted to telling the major truths about human life, it can play an important role in spreading a sense of common humanity. This knowledge will reduce the likelihood of war and violence.
Difficulty: *Average*   Objective: *Essay*

"The American Idea" by Theodore H. White

Vocabulary Warm-up Exercises, p. 167

A. 1. continental
2. correspondence
3. rivalry
4. pursuit
5. relentlessly
6. traditional
7. couriers
8. anniversary

B. 1. She *embodied* grace as she seemed to glide down the stairs.
2. Because clean water is a *universal* right, every country should enjoy it.
3. The *emigrants* traveled to a new country to find a home.
4. The writer *edited* the draft after she wrote it.
5. They believed their ruler's *divine* power was granted by a heavenly Creator.
6. The two *administrations* governed for a total of eight years.
7. He was *endowed* with natural intelligence, so learning was easy for him.

Reading Warm-up A, p. 168

Sample Answers

1. (Congress); *Continental* means "relating to a continent."
2. (two hundredth); *Anniversary* means "a date on which something special happened."
3. *1776* has long sections with no singing or dancing; *Traditional* means "following old or established ways."
4. friendship; The *rivalry* between the two schools made for healthy competition.
5. (badgered); If Adams badgered his colleagues *relentlessly,* he tried repeatedly to convince them with his arguments.
6. his lovely wife; *Pursuit* means "the act of trying to achieve something in a determined way."
7. (his wife, Abigail); I treasure the letters from my *correspondence* with Maria.
8. (brings news of the war); *Couriers* deliver messages, letters, and packages.

Reading Warm-up B, p. 169

Sample Answers

1. the American dream; *Embodied* means "was the best example of an idea or a quality."
2. If you believe in *divine* power, you believe that God has caused the storm.
3. (amazing intelligence); My mother is *endowed* with a gift for storytelling.
4. Hamilton found success there. An *emigrant* whom I admire is Albert Einstein.

5. As one of the *revolutionaries*, Hamilton did not believe the colonies should be governed by Great Britain.

6. Three rights that should be *universal* are the right to vote, the right to a free press, and the right to protest. *Universal* means "appropriate or true in any situation."

7. Presidential *administrations* that have existed in my lifetime are those of Bill Clinton and George W. Bush.

8. When Hamilton's son *edited The Federalist,* he probably chose what to include in that edition and fixed errors in the text.

Writing About the Big Question, p. 170

A. 1. growth

2. history

3. modified

4. evolve

B. Sample Answers

1. I compromised with my sister about what to eat for lunch. I wanted our class project to help our own school, but I compromised and we helped a less fortunate school.

2. Compromising and helping a school that was not our own was a great experience for my class and me. I gained so much **insight** into the problems other students struggle with, and I feel my knowledge will help me have valuable **empathy** for others.

C. Sample Answer

People who left their countries to live in the United States developed an awareness of how important individual liberty is in this country. These emigrants were willing to fight for the freedoms the new country promised. The Declaration of Independence reflects the desire of these men and women to govern themselves.

Literary Analysis: Analytic and Interpretive Essays, p. 171

Sample Answers

A. Authority: White uses the words of Thomas Jefferson, John Adams, and other founding fathers to establish and support the "American Idea" that is the topic of this essay.

Reason: The author argues that the United States is unique because it is a nation born of an idea. He supports this claim with examples of other, older countries in which a sense of nationhood comes from generations of people living there. He also states that the "American Idea" has changed and stretched. He supports this idea with examples of how the idea began, how it was debated, and how it continues to mean different things to different people.

Emotion: The author attempts to make his American readers feel pride and optimism by using words and phrases such as "rang the call," "great statue," "freedoms," "something worth dying for," "tough men fighting for a very tough idea," "the story we celebrate," and "young nation flourished."

Values: The author makes the assumption that his readers value freedom, pride in their country, and appreciation for the sacrifices of the founding fathers.

B. Students should realize that this essay is both analytic and interpretive. The author first presents his own interpretation of the meaning and significance of the American idea. The last part of the essay is analytic because White analyzes Jefferson's and Adams's contrasting points of view about "America's call."

Reading: Distinguish Between Fact and Opinion to Evaluate Writers' Appeals, p. 172

Sample Answers

Facts: Examples include the reasons why the first European Americans came to the new continent, the date of the meeting of the First Continental Congress, how long Jefferson worked on his first draft of the Declaration of Independence, the existence of a debate between Jefferson and Adams, and the dates of Jefferson's and Adams's deaths.

Opinions: The freedom of the wilderness made the first European settlers want more freedom. The new Americans were tough men fighting for a tough idea. The story of the American idea is the most important story. We all celebrate the story of how the American idea worked out. There was glory enough for Jefferson and Adams to share, so their rivalry faded.

Support for Opinions: White calls upon the shared value of freedom to support the idea that the first settlers wanted more freedom. He proves that American fighters were tough because they successfully fought against the best-trained troops in the world. He supports the claim that the American idea is the most important story and that we all celebrate it by giving many examples of how it grew and changed. He supports the idea that Jefferson and Adams had enough glory to share by telling the story of how their rivalry faded and their respect for each other grew.

Vocabulary Builder, p. 173

A. 1. Yes, because your thoughts would be represented, or *embodied*, by the physical object of the soft dog toy.

2. *Emigrants* would be packed and leaving their home country to settle elsewhere.

3. No, there would be no stillness, because the wind would be blowing without a pause, *relentlessly*.

4. Yes, everyone would wear a hat, because *universal* means of or for the whole, for all people.

5. No, she had three gray cats in a row, owning one at a time.

6. No, the dictator was worried about people who wanted to make a radical change in the government, so he did not trust the citizens.

B. 1. An *emperor* is in power. The prefix *em-* means "in" and the root word refers to setting things in order, so an emperor has the power to create order or to rule.

2. Someone with *empathy* has the capacity to be in the emotions of another, so that person would care about, not disregard, others' feelings.

3. You are putting your arms around a person in an *embrace*, which means "in the arms of."

Enrichment: Current Events, p. 174

Evaluate students' political cartoons based on the following criteria: relevance to the topic, clarity of thought, appropriate use of symbolism, neatness, and creativity.

Open-Book Test, p. 175

Short Answer

1. Possible fact: Congress passed the Declaration of Independence.
   Possible opinion: The new Americans were tough men fighting for a tough idea.
   A fact can be proved to be true, while an opinion cannot.
   Difficulty: *Average* **Objective:** *Reading*
2. All men are created equal and have the right to life, liberty, and the pursuit of happiness.
   Difficulty: *Average* **Objective:** *Interpretation*
3. He is using an appeal to shared values.
   Difficulty: *Challenging* **Objective:** *Reading*
4. He is using an emotional appeal.
   Difficulty: *Easy* **Objective:** *Reading*
5. It caused them to want more freedoms.
   Difficulty: *Easy* **Objective:** *Interpretation*
6. The United States has inspired movements for freedom all over the world.
   Difficulty: *Average* **Objective:** *Literary Analysis*
7. The American people came from all over the world.
   Difficulty: *Average* **Objective:** *Reading*
8. He is using an appeal to authority.
   Difficulty: *Average* **Objective:** *Reading*
9. Adams respected Jefferson and knew he would keep the American idea alive. Adams did not want American ideals to die along with him.
   Difficulty: *Challenging* **Objective:** *Interpretation*
10. I would probably not be enjoying the lecture because the lecturer would be repeating herself without stopping.
    Difficulty: *Average* **Objective:** *Vocabulary*

Essay

11. Students should note that the American idea is based on the values of freedom and equality. Students should support their interpretation of the American idea with at least two examples from White's essay.
    Difficulty: *Easy* **Objective:** *Essay*
12. Students should note that the story about Adams and Jefferson is meant to show that the American idea can mean different things to different people. It also shows that the American idea can change yet remain true to its

original values. Students should cite specific examples from White's essay to support their response. They will most likely claim that White thinks Adams's and Jefferson's ideas are equally important.
   Difficulty: *Average* **Objective:** *Essay*
13. Students should note that the American idea spread to many other nations and inspired them to change their government, identity, and culture. Students should cite details from the essay to support their opinion about the role of the American idea in the world.
   Difficulty: *Challenging* **Objective:** *Essay*
14. White believes that the American idea—equality, liberty, and the pursuit of happiness—has had an explosive effect because at the time that the American founders came up with these ideals, they were new to the world. When the word of the American Revolution reached other lands, it sparked a hunger for the same freedoms in other peoples, first in France and later throughout the globe. Most students will agree that the American idea has changed people, mostly for the better, throughout the world. Other students might argue that the American idea did (or does) not necessarily work well for other cultures and nations.
   Difficulty: *Average* **Objective:** *Essay*

Oral Response

15. Oral responses should be clear, well organized, and well supported by appropriate examples from the selection.
    Difficulty: *Average* **Objective:** *Oral Interpretation*

Selection Test A, p. 178

Critical Reading

1. ANS: A	DIF: Easy	OBJ: Literary Analysis
2. ANS: A	DIF: Easy	OBJ: Comprehension
3. ANS: C	DIF: Easy	OBJ: Comprehension
4. ANS: A	DIF: Easy	OBJ: Comprehension
5. ANS: C	DIF: Easy	OBJ: Literary Analysis
6. ANS: D	DIF: Easy	OBJ: Interpretation
7. ANS: A	DIF: Easy	OBJ: Reading Strategy
8. ANS: A	DIF: Easy	OBJ: Interpretation
9. ANS: B	DIF: Easy	OBJ: Comprehension
10. ANS: B	DIF: Easy	OBJ: Reading Strategy
11. ANS: A	DIF: Easy	OBJ: Interpretation
12. ANS: C	DIF: Easy	OBJ: Literary Analysis

Vocabulary and Grammar

13. ANS: D	DIF: Easy	OBJ: Vocabulary
14. ANS: C	DIF: Easy	OBJ: Vocabulary
15. ANS: B	DIF: Easy	OBJ: Grammar

Essay

16. Students might say that the American idea means democracy, or personal freedom, or "life, liberty and the pursuit of happiness." Whatever their interpretation, they should support it with examples of how the American idea affects them and others. For example, students might point out that they are allowed to speak freely or practice the religion of their choice without fear of punishment. They might say that their families emigrated to the United States and found opportunities they could not have found in their old countries. They might also mention how the United States and its allies try to encourage other countries to become democracies.

Difficulty: *Easy* **Objective:** *Essay*

17. Students should explain that the story about Adams and Jefferson is meant to show that the American idea means different things to different people. It is also meant to show that the American idea can grow and change and still have meaning for people around the world. Students will probably say that White does not favor one side over the other. He seems to be presenting both points of view as part of the American idea. However, an argument could be made that White seems to slightly favor Jefferson. He includes an inspiring quotation about Jefferson's hopes for freedom around the world in the future; he does not include such a quotation to support Adams's point of view.

Difficulty: *Challenging* **Objective:** *Essay*

18. Students should provide three examples of how the new American ideals changed the world. For example, when the word of the American Revolution reached other lands, it sparked a hunger for the same freedoms, first in France and later throughout the world. Accept any response that students support with details from the text.

Difficulty: *Average* **Objective:** *Essay*

Selection Test B, p. 181

Critical Reading

1. ANS: D	DIF: Average	OBJ: Literary Analysis
2. ANS: B	DIF: Average	OBJ: Comprehension
3. ANS: D	DIF: Challenging	OBJ: Reading Strategy
4. ANS: D	DIF: Average	OBJ: Comprehension
5. ANS: B	DIF: Average	OBJ: Comprehension
6. ANS: D	DIF: Average	OBJ: Interpretation
7. ANS: B	DIF: Challenging	OBJ: Reading Strategy
8. ANS: C	DIF: Average	OBJ: Interpretation
9. ANS: D	DIF: Average	OBJ: Reading Strategy
10. ANS: A	DIF: Challenging	OBJ: Literary Analysis
11. ANS: C	DIF: Challenging	OBJ: Literary Analysis
12. ANS: A	DIF: Average	OBJ: Literary Analysis
13. ANS: C	DIF: Average	OBJ: Reading Strategy

Vocabulary and Grammar

14. ANS: C	DIF: Average	OBJ: Vocabulary
15. ANS: A	DIF: Average	OBJ: Vocabulary
16. ANS: B	DIF: Average	OBJ: Grammar
17. ANS: C	DIF: Average	OBJ: Grammar

Essay

18. Students should take a position on the great debate between Jefferson and Adams and justify their choice. Some will agree with Jefferson because they believe the American call to freedom should spread throughout the world. Others will agree with Adams because they believe the American idea should not be forced on other peoples and nations.

Difficulty: *Average* **Objective:** *Essay*

19. Students might say that the American idea means democracy, personal freedom, or "life, liberty and the pursuit of happiness." Whatever their interpretation, they should support it with persuasive appeals such as appeals to authority, appeals to reason, appeals to emotion, and appeals to shared values. An example would be an emotional appeal that makes readers feel proud or patriotic.

Difficulty: *Average* **Objective:** *Essay*

20. Students might mention the ongoing debate among Americans and people around the world about the global role of the United States. Many people feel that it is the responsibility of the United States to spread freedom around the world. Others feel that it is not appropriate for the United States to pressure other countries to become democracies. Students should take a side and explain their thinking on the issue, using White's essay as a basis for their writing.

Difficulty: *Challenging* **Objective:** *Essay*

21. White believes that the American idea—equality, liberty, and the pursuit of happiness—has had an explosive effect because at the time that the American founders came up with these ideals, they were new to the world. When the word of the American Revolution reached other lands, it sparked a hunger for the same freedoms in other peoples, first in France and later throughout the globe. Most students will agree that the American idea has changed people, mostly for the better, throughout the world. Other students might argue that the American idea did (or does) not necessarily work well for other cultures and nations.

Difficulty: *Average* **Objective:** *Essay*

"What Makes a Degas a Degas?"
by Richard Mühlberger

Vocabulary Warm-up Exercises, p. 185

A. 1. enthusiastic
2. lifelong
3. ballerina
4. silhouette
5. sheen
6. backstage

7. dimpled
8. conveyed

B. Sample Answers

1. No, an *intimate* secret would be too private to share with a stranger.

2. I would like to have a black *lacquered* dresser decorated with stenciled flowers.

3. A grandmother might read a story to her grandchild to share a moment of *intimacy*.

4. I would recommend the following *masterpieces* to a friend: the novel *The Great Gatsby* by F. Scott Fitzgerald and the painting *Guernica* by Pablo Picasso.

5. A *backdrop* for a play set in a big city might include a skyline lit up by lights at night.

6. Yes, it is a good idea that each tile on a roof *overlaps* the ones near it because this is one way to prevent leaks.

7. No, a photograph of a person's *profile* would show only one eye, and that would be seen from the side.

8. My tenth-grade English teacher is an *inspiration* to me because she obviously enjoys her work and does a wonderful job at it.

Reading Warm-up A, p. 186

Sample Answers

1. (ballet lovers); *Enthusiastic* means "having or showing intense or eager interest."

2. Clara; The knuckles of the baby's chubby hands were *dimpled*.

3. (another guest); No, a person in the audience cannot see what is happening *backstage* because that section is hidden by curtains.

4. that he has unusual powers; *Conveyed* means "communicated by words, actions, or appearance."

5. (shadowy); A *silhouette* is any dark shape seen against a light background.

6. protector; Another way of saying *lifelong* is "lasting throughout one's life."

7. (all the Christmas decorations); Brushing a horse's coat helps bring out the *sheen*.

8. dances on the stage, with and without partners; A *ballerina* is a female ballet dancer.

Reading Warm-up B, p. 187

Sample Answers

1. *La Bal au Moulin de la Galette*; Picasso produced *masterpieces* in several different styles.

2. (a popular outdoor café in Paris); *Backdrop* means "background or setting."

3. straw hats; A coffee table and a jewelry box are two things that might be *lacquered*.

4. (areas of shade); The second color painted on the wall *overlaps* the first.

5. effect of fleeting light; My grandfather has been an *inspiration* to me because he came to this country with nothing and worked hard to make a good life for his family.

6. (conversation); Another word for *intimate* is "close."

7. A woman dressed in blue; If I were going to pose for a *profile*, I would sit in such a way that the artist could see the side view of my face.

8. (the various subjects); If I were painting a picture of a moment of *intimacy* between a mother and a child, I would show the mother giving the child a bath.

Writing About the Big Question, p. 188

A. 1. reflect
2. understanding
3. adapt
4. history

B. Sample Answers

1. I saw a striking painting in a museum. I created a drawing of which I was very proud.

2. The painting I saw in a museum was modern and beautiful and challenged my **understanding** of the definition of "art." My **awareness** of different artistic styles was broadened, and I learned I liked less traditional artwork.

C. Sample Answer

Understanding how to interpret art is valuable because you gain insight into the perspectives of others. Artists can influence us by presenting a different vision of the world and the people and things in it. If we can learn to see things from a fresh perspective in art, we might see problems or challenges differently, too.

Literary Analysis: Analytic and Interpretive Essays, p. 189

Sample Answers

A. Authority: NONE

Reason: The author says that Degas wanted his paintings to look spontaneous and rushed; he supports this point with a detailed logical explanation of how Degas accomplished this feat. The author also says that Degas took inspiration from photographs and Japanese prints, offering proof in his description of *Carriage at the Races*.

Emotion: NONE. Although there are no examples, an argument could be made that the author is appealing to the reader's emotions by describing Degas's friendship with Paul Valpinçon and his fascination with baby Henri.

Values: The author contrasts the Eastern perception of Japanese prints as cheap souvenirs with the way Western artists valued these prints as art. The author also presents Degas's quest to make viewers feel that they are in the moment with him as a kind of shared value. He points out that Impressionism became so popular because many people share an appreciation for this spontaneous style.

B. Students should realize that this essay is both analytic and interpretive. The author presents factual descriptions and straightforward analysis of two of Degas's paintings. He brings his own ideas and values into his analysis when he evaluates Degas's style as "intimate, immediate, and realistic."

Reading: Distinguish Between Fact and Opinion to Evaluate Writers' Appeals, p. 190

Sample Answers

Facts: "The vertical beam the ballerina is touching extends to the top and bottom of the painting" and "Both Paul and the dog are gazing at the baby, who lies in the shade of the umbrella" (descriptions of the paintings); or "He produced about fifteen hundred drawings, prints, pastels, and oil paintings with ballet themes" and "He eventually became an enthusiastic photographer himself" (statements about Degas's accomplishments)

Opinions: Degas created the same fresh feeling with oil paints that could be achieved with pastels. Degas created a hasty, careless impression on purpose. Degas wanted his viewers to feel they were standing right beside him. One of Degas's greatest thrills was looking at his friend's father's paintings. Degas wanted *Carriage at the Races* to look like a photograph.

Support for Opinions: Mühlberger describes in detail how Degas made his oil paintings look like pastels. He states that Degas took a great deal of time to create paintings that look spontaneous. He describes how Impressionist artists tried to bring viewers into the moment through spontaneous-looking art. He also says that Degas was influenced by photographs and Japanese prints, giving proof through his description of how *Carriage at the Races* seems lopsided and cut off like a photograph.

Vocabulary Builder, p. 191

A. 1. No, a *lacquered* table will feel smooth because it is covered in a thick varnish.
2. Ideas are *immaterial* because they are not made of physical matter and cannot be touched.
3. She is thinking about the past, because she is remembering your first day of school.
4. No; a *silhouette* is only an outline drawing, filled in with one solid color, which does not provide much detail or color.
5. No; a *simulation* only has the appearance of something real, so no one was hurt.
6. No, a *spontaneous* event is one that happens all of a sudden without much or any planning.

B. 1. No, something *immense* is huge and not easily measured, so it would be too big to carry in a pocket.
2. No, something *immortal* is "without death," so its lifespan is infinite.
3. No, an *improbable* victory is one that was not expected.

Enrichment: Art and Photography, p. 192

Students' responses will vary depending upon the paintings and photographs they choose to analyze. Elements of paintings and photographs should be analyzed and compared.

"What Makes a Degas a Degas?"
by Richard Mühlberger
"The American Idea" by Theodore H. White

Integrated Language Skills: Grammar, p. 193

A. 1. Superlative
2. Comparative
3. Positive
4. Positive

B. Students' responses will vary. Check to be sure that positive adjectives are underlined once, comparative adjectives are underlined twice, and superlative adjectives are underlined three times. There should be at least six adjectives showing degrees of comparison in the paragraph.

Open-Book Test, p. 196

Short Answer

1. It is an appeal to authority—the authority of Degas's reputation as a painter.
   Difficulty: *Average* **Objective:** *Literary Analysis*
2. Possible answers:
   Fact: Subscribers to the Opéra bothered dancers backstage.
   Opinion: Degas's composition seems lopsided.
   A fact is absolutely true, while an opinion is just the way you think about something.

   Difficulty: *Average* **Objective:** *Reading*
3. Degas wanted to make his figures look more like charcoal drawings.
   Difficulty: *Average* **Objective:** *Interpretation*
4. Degas wanted viewers to feel that they were right there with the painter at the scene he was painting.
   Difficulty: *Average* **Objective:** *Reading*
5. Japanese prints cut off figures in a way that makes them more natural and immediate.
   Difficulty: *Average* **Objective:** *Literary Analysis*
6. The largest and darkest objects are in one corner.
   Difficulty: *Average* **Objective:** *Reading*
7. He explains that Degas wanted his paintings to seem more spontaneous, more like real life.
   Difficulty: *Average* **Objective:** *Literary Analysis*
8. Video games create the appearance of movement on a screen, not actual movement.
   Difficulty: *Challenging* **Objective:** *Vocabulary*
9. My action would be spontaneous because I did not plan it.
   Difficulty: *Easy* **Objective:** *Vocabulary*

10. Mühlberger sees Degas as an experimental artist because he tried to use oil paint in a new way.
Difficulty: *Challenging* **Objective:** *Interpretation*

Essay

11. Students should identify one of the paintings as most true to life and explain their choice. They should provide specific details from the painting, such as the use of color or how the painting is framed. They should integrate Mühlberger's arguments into their discussions.
Difficulty: *Easy* **Objective:** *Essay*

12. Students might identify techniques such as imitating pastels with oil paint, using a limited range of colors, making the painting look hastily done, cutting off the figures and forms, and placing subjects off-center. They should use these examples to support a clear argument about what makes a Degas a Degas.
Difficulty: *Average* **Objective:** *Essay*

13. Students should note that the essay is analytical because it breaks a topic into parts for explanation and analysis. It is interpretive because it forms judgments about the overall effect and value of Degas's paintings. Students should cite at least four specific examples from the selection to support their responses.
Difficulty: *Challenging* **Objective:** *Essay*

14. Several sources of information inspired Degas to paint in an original and unique way. For example, the look and feel of pastels contributed to his goal of capturing scenes with greater immediacy. The young art of photography inspired him to frame scenes in a more natural way. He also was influenced by Japanese prints, with their free-flowing, naturally framed style. All these sources of information clearly changed Degas as an artist.
Difficulty: *Average* **Objective:** *Essay*

Oral Response

15. Oral responses should be clear, well organized, and well supported by appropriate examples from the selection.
Difficulty: *Average* **Objective:** *Oral Interpretation*

Selection Test A, p. 199

Critical Reading

1. ANS: A   DIF: Easy   OBJ: Comprehension
2. ANS: C   DIF: Easy   OBJ: Comprehension
3. ANS: C   DIF: Easy   OBJ: Comprehension
4. ANS: D   DIF: Easy   OBJ: Reading Strategy
5. ANS: C   DIF: Easy   OBJ: Interpretation
6. ANS: D   DIF: Easy   OBJ: Interpretation
7. ANS: B   DIF: Easy   OBJ: Comprehension
8. ANS: D   DIF: Easy   OBJ: Interpretation
9. ANS: D   DIF: Easy   OBJ: Interpretation

10. ANS: B   DIF: Easy   OBJ: Reading Strategy
11. ANS: B   DIF: Easy   OBJ: Literary Analysis
12. ANS: B   DIF: Easy   OBJ: Literary Analysis

Vocabulary and Grammar

13. ANS: A   DIF: Easy   OBJ: Vocabulary
14. ANS: C   DIF: Easy   OBJ: Vocabulary
15. ANS: D   DIF: Easy   OBJ: Grammar

Essay

16. Students should identify techniques such as imitating pastels with the use of oil paints, using a limited range of colors, making the painting look hastily done, cutting off the edges of figures and forms, and placing the subject(s) of the painting off-center. They might describe details of *Dancers, Pink and Green* or *Carriage at the Races* to support their answers.
Difficulty: *Easy* **Objective:** *Essay*

17. Students should identify one of the paintings as their favorite and explain why they like it. They might choose *Dancers, Pink and Green* because they like the subject matter, the colors, the pastel-like effect, or the dancers' poses. They might choose *Carriage at the Races* because they like horses or babies; the muted colors; the fresh, open look of the scene; the way it is off-center; or the way the subject is cut off.
Difficulty: *Easy* **Objective:** *Essay*

18. Several types of knowledge helped Degas develop his style. For example, the look and feel of pastels contributed to his goal of capturing scenes with greater immediacy. The young art of photography inspired him to frame scenes in a more natural way. He also was influenced by Japanese prints, with their free-flowing, naturally framed style. All these sources of information clearly changed Degas as an artist.
Difficulty: *Average* **Objective:** *Essay*

Selection Test B, p. 202

Critical Reading

1. ANS: D   DIF: Average   OBJ: Interpretation
2. ANS: C   DIF: Average   OBJ: Comprehension
3. ANS: C   DIF: Average   OBJ: Comprehension
4. ANS: A   DIF: Average   OBJ: Interpretation
5. ANS: C   DIF: Challenging   OBJ: Interpretation
6. ANS: B   DIF: Average   OBJ: Interpretation
7. ANS: D   DIF: Average   OBJ: Reading Strategy
8. ANS: D   DIF: Challenging   OBJ: Reading Strategy
9. ANS: A   DIF: Challenging   OBJ: Reading Strategy
10. ANS: C   DIF: Challenging   OBJ: Literary Analysis
11. ANS: C   DIF: Average   OBJ: Literary Analysis
12. ANS: D   DIF: Average   OBJ: Literary Analysis

Vocabulary and Grammar

13. ANS: A	DIF: Average	OBJ: Vocabulary
14. ANS: A	DIF: Average	OBJ: Vocabulary
15. ANS: C	DIF: Average	OBJ: Grammar
16. ANS: C	DIF: Average	OBJ: Grammar

Essay

17. Students should identify techniques such as imitating pastels using oil paints, using a limited range of colors, making the painting look hastily done, cutting off the edges of figures and forms, and placing the subject(s) of the painting off-center. They might describe details of *Dancers, Pink and Green* or *Carriage at the Races* to support their answers.

    Difficulty: *Average*   **Objective:** *Essay*

18. Students should state that "What Makes a Degas a Degas?" is analytic because it breaks a topic into parts for explanation and analysis. Mühlberger chooses two of Degas's paintings to describe in detail for the audience so that readers can understand Degas's unique style and innovativeness. The interpretive parts of the essay include Mühlberger's implication that Degas made his paintings look hasty and incomplete on purpose. He goes on to imply that this makes Degas's work more valuable. Finally, he strongly suggests that Degas succeeded in achieving his lifelong quest of making viewers feel that they are beside the artist, looking at a scene.

    Difficulty: *Average*   **Objective:** *Essay*

19. Students might identify opinions such as Mühlberger's apparent belief that Degas successfully achieved a spontaneous effect with his paintings or his implication that Degas was particularly innovative and fresh in his approach to art. They might mention that he uses appeals to reason by providing many facts detailing Degas's techniques and inspiration. They might also argue that he used an emotional appeal by describing Degas's friendship with Valpinçon and the excitement young Degas felt looking at his friend's art collection. Appeals to shared values include the author's assumption that most art viewers would like to see scenes as if they were actually there and his assumption that most art viewers would be appreciative of new artistic techniques.

    Difficulty: *Challenging*   **Objective:** *Essay*

20. Several sources of information inspired Degas to paint in an original and unique way. For example, the look and feel of pastels contributed to his goal of capturing scenes with greater immediacy. The young art of photography inspired him to frame scenes in a more natural way. He also was influenced by Japanese prints, with their free-flowing, naturally framed style. All these sources of information clearly changed Degas as an artist.

    Difficulty: *Average*   **Objective:** *Essay*

from Desert Exile: The Uprooting of a Japanese-American Family by Yoshiko Uchida
from The Way to Rainy Mountain
by N. Scott Momaday

Vocabulary Warm-up Exercises, p. 206

A.
1. alliance
2. culture
3. competition
4. cautioning
5. assuage
6. rambling
7. confronted
8. disperse

B.
1. If I could put a *partition* anywhere in my home, it would be between the living room and dining room.
2. I have seen ducks and geese take part in a *migration*.
3. My favorite *depressing* books are *The End of the Affair* and *The Great Gatsby*.
4. No, if a song is *inherently* sad, it will stay sad regardless of the tempo.
5. I would expect people to act with great care toward something for which they feel *reverence*.
6. A large water tank makes a *conspicuous* landmark near my street.
7. As part of a *delegation* visiting a refugee camp, I would tour the camp and meet with administrators and committee members.
8. If I were *deprived* of every food item but one, I would choose the potato.

Reading Warm-up A, p. 207

Sample Answers
1. with the sparse furniture and awful food; *Confronted* means "having been faced with."
2. (boredom); *Assuage* means "to provide relief from something unpleasant."
3. (American); *Culture* is "the art, beliefs, behavior, ideas, and other expressions of a particular society."
4. Germany and Italy; An *alliance* is "a close agreement or connection between people or countries."
5. the boys in his barracks and those in the next barracks over; My sister and I were in an unspoken *competition* to get my parents' attention.
6. (fighting); *Cautioning* means "warning someone that something might be dangerous or difficult."
7. (long); A long and *rambling* story would move from one event to another without moving toward a real climax or resolution.
8. (the teams); They might *disperse* the teams and end the games to celebrate the end of the war.

Reading Warm-up B, p. 208

Sample Answers

1. <u>southeast</u>; Horses could help the *migration* go faster or farther.
2. (treaties); The Kiowas were *deprived* of their land by the United States government in the 1860s.
3. For a people used to traveling, there was something *essentially* hard about staying on a small piece of land.
4. (sad); I found the tragic epic *depressing*.
5. Buffalo were hunted and killed, possibly by the U.S. government, which made them much less *conspicuous*, or easy to find.
6. <u>the once-open land</u>; Fences or stakes could be used as *partitions* to divide up the reservation lands.
7. (leaders); A *delegation* is "a few people who represent a bigger group."
8. <u>for the sun, the moon, the stars, and the buffalo</u>; I feel *reverence* for unspoiled nature.

Writing About the Big Question, p. 209

A. 1. adapt
2. empathy
3. revise

B. Sample Answers

1. I was troubled when I first learned about the Holocaust in World War II. I was troubled when I learned that Japanese Americans were put in camps during World War II.
2. Learning about the Japanese-American internment camps made a big **influence** on me, because that situation occurred in the United States. I was surprised that our government would treat people that way, but **history** shows that it was an unsure time during the war when anything could happen.

C. Sample Answer

You should learn about important historical events because you can learn what not to do in the future. We can also learn from examples of great courage and dignity in the face of hardship and cruelty. It is important to be informed about history, so you can understand past societies but also your own.

Literary Analysis: Author's Purpose, p. 210

Sample Answers

1. to evoke the reader's sympathy; to emphasize how destitute the conditions in the internment camp were
2. to point out that other Americans were not being detained; to emphasize that the author's family had been cut off from their "normal" life
3. to illustrate how unstable the Uchidas' lives were; to suggest how little the Uchidas trusted the U.S. government
4. to recall his grandmother's early years; to pay tribute to the passing of a great tribe

5. to celebrate, honor, or reflect upon the land
6. to honor his grandmother; to mourn what has passed

Vocabulary Builder, p. 211

Sample Answers

A. 1. The heavy grocery bags were <u>awkward</u> to carry home.
2. This ointment should <u>lessen</u> the pain of the bee sting.
3. On Saturdays, I help my <u>frail</u> grandmother with her yard work.
4. <u>Wandering</u> peoples do not build permanent homes.
5. My knowledge of French is <u>weak</u>, but I do know that *merci* means "thank you."

B. 1. D; 2. A; 3. A; 4. B; 5. D; 6. C

Open-Book Test, p. 213

Short Answer

1. The author wants to show how unhealthy conditions were at the camp.
   Difficulty: *Easy* **Objective:** *Literary Analysis*
2. There is so little decent food that even something ordinary can seem like a treat to the inmates.
   Difficulty: *Easy* **Objective:** *Interpretation*
3. You would probably make the team because you would be highly skilled.
   Difficulty: *Easy* **Objective:** *Vocabulary*
4. Momaday's main purpose is to record the culture of his Kiowa ancestors.
   Difficulty: *Average* **Objective:** *Literary Analysis*
5. He wants to honor his grandmother and to connect his life with hers.
   Difficulty: *Challenging* **Objective:** *Literary Analysis*
6. I would not do well on the final exam because I would have only slight knowledge of algebra.
   Difficulty: *Average* **Objective:** *Vocabulary*
7. Both Uchida and Momaday think it is important to preserve and to communicate a written history of their people.
   Difficulty: *Challenging* **Objective:** *Interpretation*
8. Details for Uchida: wore Sunday clothes when being moved, lived in stalls, clever in finding necessities, played cards, wrote to friends and begged

   Details for Momaday: thought war was sacred, fine horsemen, nomadic, courageous and proud, sacrificed buffalo

   Both Uchida's and Momaday's people experience being separated or exiled.
   Difficulty: *Average* **Objective:** *Interpretation*
9. They are both strong, dignified, proud women who respect their cultural background.
   Difficulty: *Average* **Objective:** *Interpretation*

10. Uchida is more straightforward and factual, while Momaday takes a more emotional and poetic approach.
Difficulty: *Challenging* **Objective:** *Interpretation*

Essay

11. Students should note that Uchida's main purpose is to bear witness to the suffering of her family and other Japanese Americans who were uprooted from their homes and forced into camps during World War II. They should note that Momaday's main purpose is to pay tribute to his grandmother and to record the lost way of life and culture of his people, the Kiowa. Students should provide examples from each selection to back up their points.
Difficulty: *Easy* **Objective:** *Essay*

12. Students should note that *Desert Exile* tells about the forced removal of Japanese Americans from their homes during World War II. *The Way to Rainy Mountain* tells of two different uprootings—first, the author's ancestors' migration from western Montana centuries ago and, second, their forced relocation to a reservation. Students should identify Americans' distrust of the "enemy" during World War II and white people's desire for land ownership and cultural dominance as the reasons for the uprootings. Students should discuss Uchida's anger about her family's uprooting and Momaday's combination of respect toward the first uprooting and sadness about the second.
Difficulty: *Average* **Objective:** *Essay*

13. Students should write that *Desert Exile* is mainly about leaving home—the forced moving of the author and her family from their home and their forced relocation into an internment camp during World War II. Students should note that *The Way to Rainy Mountain* is mainly about the author's return to the home of his grandmother, which he visited often as a child. It is also a return to the culture of his Kiowa background. Students should discuss the emotions of anger, sadness, loss, and joy as parts of the selections' comings and goings.
Difficulty: *Challenging* **Objective:** *Essay*

14. Students should note that both selections record the mistreatment of major ethnic groups by the U.S. government: the Japanese during World War II, who were treated as potential enemies and relocated to camps; the Kiowa tribe, which was relocated to a reservation. Students might note that such incidents change their perception of the United States by helping them to realize that the country has not always lived up to its founding ideals of equality and justice for all. Based on this realization, they might go out of their way to treat all people with respect and take steps to preserve their own cultural history. Students should support their points with examples from the selections.
Difficulty: *Average* **Objective:** *Essay*

Oral Response

15. Oral responses should be clear, well organized, and well supported by appropriate examples from the selection(s).
Difficulty: *Average* **Objective:** *Oral Interpretation*

Selection Test A, p. 216

Critical Reading

1. ANS: B   DIF: Easy   OBJ: Comprehension
2. ANS: A   DIF: Easy   OBJ: Literary Analysis
3. ANS: D   DIF: Easy   OBJ: Comprehension
4. ANS: D   DIF: Easy   OBJ: Comprehension
5. ANS: C   DIF: Easy   OBJ: Interpretation
6. ANS: A   DIF: Easy   OBJ: Literary Analysis
7. ANS: B   DIF: Easy   OBJ: Comprehension
8. ANS: C   DIF: Easy   OBJ: Comprehension
9. ANS: D   DIF: Easy   OBJ: Interpretation
10. ANS: A   DIF: Easy   OBJ: Literary Analysis
11. ANS: C   DIF: Easy   OBJ: Literary Analysis
12. ANS: B   DIF: Easy   OBJ: Interpretation
13. ANS: D   DIF: Easy   OBJ: Interpretation

Vocabulary

14. ANS: A   DIF: Easy   OBJ: Vocabulary
15. ANS: C   DIF: Easy   OBJ: Vocabulary

Essay

16. Students should respond that in *Desert Exile,* the author and her family are forced to leave their home and go to an internment camp because during World War II, Japanese Americans were considered a threat to American society. Students should respond that in *The Way to Rainy Mountain,* the author returns to the home of his grandmother, which he visited often as a child, or to the "home" of his native Kiowan culture. He does so because his grandmother has recently died, and he wishes to remember her and honor her.
Difficulty: *Easy* **Objective:** *Essay*

17. Students should clearly identify a main purpose for each essay. Possible purposes for Momaday's essay include to inform readers about the history of the Kiowas, to honor the memory of his grandmother, or to reflect on his own history or culture. Possible purposes for Uchida's essay include to inform readers about the experience of some Japanese Americans during World War II, to bear witness to the injustices suffered by Japanese Americans during the war, or to attempt to come to terms with a painful past. Students should support their claims with examples from the selections.
Difficulty: *Easy* **Objective:** *Essay*

18. Students should note that both selections describe the poor treatment of the U.S. government toward major cultural groups: the Japanese during World War II and the Kiowa tribe. Students might note that such incidents change their understanding of the United States by helping them to realize that the country has not always provided fair treatment and equality for all people. Based on this knowledge, students might go out of their way to treat all people with respect. They might even take steps to learn about their own cultural background. Students should support their points with examples from the selections.
    Difficulty: *Average*   **Objective:** *Essay*

Selection Test B, p. 219

Critical Reading

1.	ANS: D	DIF: Average	OBJ: Comprehension
2.	ANS: B	DIF: Challenging	OBJ: Literary Analysis
3.	ANS: C	DIF: Challenging	OBJ: Interpretation
4.	ANS: A	DIF: Average	OBJ: Literary Analysis
5.	ANS: D	DIF: Average	OBJ: Interpretation
6.	ANS: D	DIF: Challenging	OBJ: Comprehension
7.	ANS: B	DIF: Average	OBJ: Interpretation
8.	ANS: A	DIF: Challenging	OBJ: Interpretation
9.	ANS: B	DIF: Challenging	OBJ: Literary Analysis
10.	ANS: A	DIF: Average	OBJ: Literary Analysis
11.	ANS: A	DIF: Average	OBJ: Literary Analysis
12.	ANS: B	DIF: Average	OBJ: Interpretation
13.	ANS: A	DIF: Average	OBJ: Interpretation
14.	ANS: C	DIF: Challenging	OBJ: Literary Analysis
15.	ANS: A	DIF: Average	OBJ: Interpretation

Vocabulary

16.	ANS: D	DIF: Average	OBJ: Vocabulary
17.	ANS: B	DIF: Average	OBJ: Vocabulary
18.	ANS: C	DIF: Average	OBJ: Vocabulary

Essay

19. Students should note that *Desert Exile* tells of the forced removal of Japanese Americans from their homes during World War II. *The Way to Rainy Mountain* tells of two different "uprootings"—first, the author's ancestors' migration from western Montana centuries ago and, second, their forced relocation to the "Staked Plains," or reservation. (Students may also mention the author's uprooting from his native Kiowa culture.) Students should identify Uchida's attitude toward her family's uprooting as offended or angry. They should identify Momaday's attitude toward the first uprooting as respectful and toward the second as resentful or mournful. Accept other reasonable responses.
    Difficulty: *Average*   **Objective:** *Essay*

20. Students may identify the authors' shared purposes as to inform readers about a piece of American history, to remember painful events in their family's past, or to heal old wounds. They may identify Momaday's unique purpose as to pay tribute to his grandmother or to the passing of a way of life. They may identify Uchida's purpose as exposing the grim realities of racial injustice. Accept other reasonable responses. Students should also include a logical assessment of the authors' relative successes.
    Difficulty: *Average*   **Objective:** *Essay*

21. Students should note that both selections record the mistreatment of major ethnic groups by the U.S. government: the Japanese during World War II, who were treated as potential enemies and relocated to camps, and the Kiowa tribe, which was relocated to a reservation. Students might note that such incidents change their perception of the United States by helping them to realize that the country has not always lived up to its founding ideals of equality and justice for all. Based on this realization, they might go out of their way to treat all people with respect and take steps to preserve their own cultural history. Students should support their points with examples from the selections.
    Difficulty: *Average*   **Objective:** *Essay*

Writing Workshop

Persuasive Essay: Integrating Grammar Skills, p. 223

A. 1. to dance; 2. with exuberance; 3. she also has had luck (also move *and*)
B. 1. My mom gardens to get exercise, to grow tasty food, and to create beauty.
    2. Her garden contains vegetables, shade trees, and flowering plants.
    In spring, she sows seeds, plants seedlings, and moves plants.

Vocabulary Workshop—1, p. 224

A. Sample Answers

1. **theme: 1** *n.* a unifying or dominant idea in a literary work
    The <u>theme</u> of the short story we just read was that facing one's fears can make one stronger.
    2 *n.* a short informal essay
    The teacher asked us to write a <u>theme</u> about the short story we read in class today.
2. **tone: 1** *v.* to strengthen and define muscles through exercise
    After weeks of following her exercise routine, Meg was thrilled to notice her improved muscle <u>tone</u>.
    2 *n.* a particular style or manner of speech or writing; an author's attitude or mood

The author's <u>tone</u> was humorous and light-hearted in the children's book I read to my little brother.

3. **address: 1** *n.* the location where a person or organization can be reached

    The publisher's <u>address</u> is listed on the company's Web site.

    2 *v.* to deal with or discuss

    If your teacher does not <u>address</u> the issue of the test review, raise your hand and ask about it.

B. Sample Answers

1. Context clue: does not have to read it

    There were <u>objects</u> scattered randomly around the child-care room.

2. Context clue: around

    A war to overthrow a government and establish a new one is a <u>revolution</u>.

3. Context clue: rough

    She was incredibly <u>rude</u> when she talked all the way through the speaker's presentation.

Vocabulary Workshop—2, p. 225

A. Sample Answers

1. **audience: 1** *n.* a group of spectators at a public event

    The <u>audience</u> applauded enthusiastically after the excellent performance of Shakespeare's *Hamlet*.

    2 *n.* a formal meeting with a high-ranking officer of a government or other organization

    She shook with nervousness before her <u>audience</u> with the queen.

2. **voice: 1** *n.* sounds uttered through the mouth

    Her <u>voice</u> was hoarse from coughing all night.

    2 *v.* to declare or proclaim something

    I will go to the next city council meeting to <u>voice</u> my support for bike paths in the city parks.

3. **composition 1** *n.* a written work; essay

    In his <u>composition</u>, Dan compared the two poems we read in class today.

    2 *n.* the makeup of something; the sum of what goes into making something

    The <u>composition</u> of this driveway is a combination of pebbles and dirt.

B. Sample Answers

1. Context clue: all that happened that day

    The still waters of the lake <u>reflect</u> the mountains and the sky like a mirror.

2. Context clue: things I care about most

    The author clearly <u>values</u> her family more than anything else in the world.

3. Context clue: clarity

    I get so nervous speaking in front of people that I must work very hard to clearly <u>articulate</u> my ideas during oral presentations.

Benchmark Test 6, p. 227

MULTIPLE CHOICE

1. ANS: B
2. ANS: D
3. ANS: C
4. ANS: C
5. ANS: A
6. ANS: B
7. ANS: B
8. ANS: D
9. ANS: A
10. ANS: D
11. ANS: B
12. ANS: C
13. ANS: A
14. ANS: A
15. ANS: B
16. ANS: C
17. ANS: D
18. ANS: B
19. ANS: C
20. ANS: B
21. ANS: D
22. ANS: C
23. ANS: B
24. ANS: C
25. ANS: A
26. ANS: D
27. ANS: A
28. ANS: C
29. ANS: D
30. ANS: B
31. ANS: A
32. ANS: C
33. ANS: A
34. ANS: B
35. ANS: A
36. ANS: A
37. ANS: C
38. ANS: A
39. ANS: A
40. ANS: B

ESSAY

41. Students should clearly state a position and use persuasive devices, formal language, and standard letter form.

42. Students should select an appropriate movie or performance to critique. They should provide examples to support their main critiques.

43. Students should adopt a position contrary to the one they actually hold. They should describe it clearly and support it with logic, facts, and appeals to emotion. Students should use one or more rhetorical devices, such as rhetorical questions or repetition.

Vocabulary in Context 3, p. 233

MULTIPLE CHOICE

1. ANS: A
2. ANS: C
3. ANS: A
4. ANS: D
5. ANS: A
6. ANS: D
7. ANS: B
8. ANS: D
9. ANS: C
10. ANS: A
11. ANS: B
12. ANS: B
13. ANS: A
14. ANS: C
15. ANS: D
16. ANS: C
17. ANS: D
18. ANS: B
19. ANS: C
20. ANS: B